THE
JUVENILE
COURT
SYSTEM

THE
JUVENILE
COURT
SYSTEM

SOCIAL ACTION AND LEGAL CHANGE

Edwin M. Lemert

ALDINETRANSACTION
A Division of Transaction Publishers
New Brunswick (U.S.A.) and London (U.K.)

First paperback edition 2010
Copyright © 1970 by Transaction Publishers, New Brunswick, New Jersey.

This book is printed on acid-free paper that meets the American National Standard for Permanence of Paper for Printed Library Materials.

Library of Congress Catalog Number: 2009041276
ISBN: 978-0-202-36340-0
Printed in the United States of America

Library of Congress Cataloging-in-Publication Data

Lemert, Edwin McCarthy, 1912-
   The juvenile court system : social action and legal change / Edwin M.
   Lemert.
        p. cm.
   Originally published: 1970.
   Includes bibliographical references and index.
   ISBN 978-0-202-36340-0
      1. Juvenile justice, Administration of--California--History. 2. Juvenile
   courts--California. I. Title.

KFC1195.L46 2009
345.794'08--dc22

                                                                    2009041276

Contents

Preface

This study was inspired by the conviction that "a story needed to be told"—namely, that of the controversial events or small-scale revolution that led to revision of California's juvenile court law in 1961. The tense struggles among opposing groups and factions, clashes between colorful personalities, and the unprecedented strategic bypassing of "normal" legislative usages under the generalship of an astute lawyer-lobbyist seemed too prizeworthy to be allowed to slip into history unchronicled by social science. Fortunate timing made funds available to the Center for the Study of Law and Society from the Office of Juvenile Delinquency and Youth Development of the Department of Health, Education, and Welfare. And I was given maximum freedom, without which this kind of investigation would have been difficult.

The evolving requirements of the study very shortly surpassed mere historical reporting, presenting a challenge to analyze critical issues of contemporary justice as they affected minors and parents. It became clear that contemplated changes by law in the ideology and structure of the California juvenile courts posed basic questions about the viability of human integrity in the face and context of bureaucratized court procedures. Whether children were entitled to a measure of civil rights, whether a court could combine paternalistic procedure, rehabilitation enterprises, and organizational expediency with fairness and justice to the child became for the first time subject to official inquiry, professional debate, and legislative scrutiny. If juvenile justice was to be made a dominant value, the thorny question of how law revision could best secure its prerequisites in the structure and procedure of the juvenile court had to be answered.

Overarching these humanistic and instrumental questions was a larger, sociological query as to how change of such magnitude could take place after decades of dilapidated growth and stagnation in the existing juvenile court law. Some sort of socio-legal theory, as well as provisional interpretation, was imperative if the materials were to be made subject to orderly and more profound analysis. The burden of such a theory is taken up in Chapter One, which sets forth a conception of paradigms, normal evolution, and revolution in law. Subsequent chapters in turn apply the theory to the data, reserving special attention in Chapter Five for considering resistance to legal change and the processes by which it gives way to consolidation of revolution and initiation of the adaptive process of normal law. Finally, there is discussion of substantive aspects of juvenile justice as it comprehends human affect and meaning, touching on what some would regard as existential elements of justice.

No hard methodology was followed in this research. Data came from numerous field interviews, documents, archives, letter files, and committee and commission reports. Several studies "in depth" were made of selected juvenile courts, and toward the end a questionnaire was circulated to all chief probation officers in the state, of which 98 per cent responded.

I am deeply appreciative of the time and assistance given me by officials of the California Youth Authority, legislators, judges, hard-working probation officers, and by Jack Pettis and Cy Shain. For his cogent criticisms as well as warm personal encouragement, I give special thanks to Sheldon Messinger.

If there is an apposite moral to be had from the study, it is that "revolution from within" is still possible. The establishment is not beyond succor.

1
Introduction

What follows is an account and analysis of social action designed
to reform procedures in the juvenile courts of California. In
general, it deals with the social action that led to legislative reform, truculent resistance to the action, and the consequences of
these. My twofold task is to describe and account for what
amounted to a small-scale revolution in the laws regulating the
juvenile courts of the state, and to inquire into the consequences
this revolution had for practices in the courts and related
agencies of law enforcement. At the same time, this study has a
bearing on a theory of legal change. Accordingly, it is addressed
to three questions: (*a*) a general query as to how law, particularly procedural law, develops on a long-term basis; (*b*) more
specifically, under what conditions and by what processes revolutionary changes in law occur; and (*c*) to what extent social
change can be directed or controlled by means of legislative
enactments.

LEGAL CHANGE

The sociologist seeking to discover regularities in the process
of legal change gets caught between the heavily theoretical bent
of modern sociology and the critical, pragmatic themes present
in much American legal philosophy and writing on the history
of law. A close focus on historical factors by earlier writers tended

to fix the idea that no generic theory of law is possible, and that "principles" at best are applicable only to discrete bodies of the law.[1] Similarly, early sociological jurisprudence and "legal realism" were not highly productive of theory, but rather ran heavily to negative criticism, even nihilism. Sociologists currently inquiring into the law run the risk of being overly concerned with its immediate problems or merely applying their methodology to studies in the well-trodden area of the judicial process.[2]

The abortive efforts in years past to develop a science of law and the confused state of legal theory today may well be the result of excessive preoccupation with case law and the search for principles that guarantee absolute certainty in predicting the outcomes of cases.[3] Hope for a broader theory of law also has been deferred by the older idea that legislative change is catastrophic, or at best a spurious intervention into an otherwise pragmatic process of legal growth. Thus codification of law has been more the subject of polemics than of research. Finally, the fast-welling growth of administrative law in the present century and the difficulty of integrating it with case law of the courts has clouded the horizons of those searching for recurrent uniformities in legal development.

An underlying problem may have been that researchers thus far have failed to address themselves fully to problems peculiar to interrelationships among judicial, administrative, and legislative processes. Furthermore, there has been a lack of recognition of the importance of distinguishing between procedural law and substantive law, with too much emphasis on the latter. It is very likely that a generic sociological theory of law, to be profitable,

1. See W. S. Holdsworth, *Some Lessons from Our Legal History* (New York: Macmillan, 1928), p. 110.

2. See Harry Jones, "A View from the Bridge," *Law and Society*, special supplement to *Social Problems* (summer 1955), especially 44ff; also Jerome Skolnick, "The Sociology of Law in America," *ibid.*, pp. 34–9.

3. For example: Frederick Pollock, "The Science of Case Law," in *Essays in Jurisprudence and Ethics* (London: Macmillan, 1882), Chap. IX. Llewellyn, in seeking to correct the nihilism of early legal realism, insisted that the behavior of judges was not adventitious, and the need was to look for patterns and tendencies in case series, rather than for conformity to rules and principles. However, he, like others, concentrated on cases. (Karl Llewellyn, *The Common Law Tradition* [Boston: Little-Brown], 1960).

will have to be oriented to the study of procedures, and the formal and informal organization of administrative agencies and legislatures, as well as courts, rather than to substantive principles of law.[4]

PROCEDURAL REFORM

Procedure as a general topic of interest, of course, has not been neglected by legal historians and philosophers; concern with procedure has antecedents in primitive law, Roman law, and medieval law. Endeavors to reform legal procedure have a lengthy history in England and other civil-law countries, and numerous legal changes in nineteenth-century America justify calling it a century of procedural reform, notable for widespread legislative codification of court rules as well as of substantive law.[5] The twentieth century likewise has witnessed important reforms in legal procedure, the most impressive being those of Federal Rules of Civil Procedure, brought about by joint action of the U.S. Congress and the U.S. Supreme Court. These reforms in turn stimulated a number of states, including California, to follow the lead of the federal courts in simplifying their procedures.[6] Finally, beginning with the 1950's, there has been a rapid series of far-reaching and controversial appellate decisions in federal and state courts explicating rights of the accused in adult criminal proceedings.[7]

4. This is closely akin to Llewellyn's view that research should start with "remedies," conceived in a modern sense of behavior. Karl Llewellyn, "A Realistic Jurisprudence: The Next Step," in *Essays on Jurisprudence From the Columbia Law Review* (New York: Columbia University Press, 1963), pp. 149–83.

5. Edwin W. Field, *Recent and Future Law Reforms* (London, Pamphlet in University of California Berkeley Library 1843); Max Rheinstein (ed.), *Max Weber on Law in Economy and Society*, (Cambridge: Harvard University Press, 1954).

6. Peter Freund, "The Essentials of Modern Reform in the Litigative Process," *Annals of the American Academy of Political and Social Science*, Vol. 287 (May 1953); Arthur T. Vanderbilt, *The Challenge of Law Reform* (Princeton: Princeton University Press, 1955), Chaps. I, III.

7. Edward Barret, "Police Practices and the Law," *California Law Review* 50 (1962), 11–55.

While nineteenth-century legal reform movements appear to have sprung from humanitarian motives, or perhaps from the quest for a more universal form of justice, those of the twentieth century have been fathered by administrative concerns, technological and organizational complexities, and sheer population growth. The large absolute increase in law matters reaching the courts, intruding from many precincts of society, plus the multiplication of courts and judges, pose pressing questions as to how the judiciary should be organized, what policies it should follow, and what its relationship to the large-scale organization of the "administrative state" should be. The administration of a mounting body of public law, and the actions of numerous quasi-judicial administrative agencies regulating the lives of corporations and associations, as well as licensing individuals to practice professions and occupations, have tremendously magnified the importance of legal procedure in modern society.

LEGAL REVOLUTION

A great deal of legal development is or has been evolutionary, in the sense of being a gradual, cumulative growth of rules, one building on another. Most pronounced in specific case decisions of the judicial process, this growth can nevertheless be observed in legislative amendments and codifications of existing laws, as well as in the daily decisions of administrative agents of government. To some extent even regulatory commissions and boards become bound by precedents of prior decisions and evolve systems of law.[8]

If, however, organic growth is a feature of legal development, so is revolution, taking form in discrete changes, discontinuities, or "new departures" in legal ideas and practices. This was clearly recognized by Holdsworth in his comments on legal theories:

8. For an example, see Philippe Nonet's study, "Administrative Justice: A Sociological Study of the California Industrial Accident Commission," Ph.D. dissertation, Center for Study of Law and Society, University of California, Berkeley, 1966.

Some theories have not been ephemeral. They have provided an illuminating generalization of new facts, which has been generally accepted, and they have therefore shaped public opinion in the new age and made them accepted commonplaces which . . . are powerful agents in moulding a constitution. . . . They have opened up new points of view to which old rules and principles must be adapted.[9]

Frequently cited examples of revolutionary law are those that stirred reforms of the eighteenth and nineteenth centuries in England—above all, Jeremy Bentham's principle of utility.[10] Others to which revolutionary impact has been credited are the concepts of sovereignty, of incorporate persons and incorporate groups.

Revolutionary reforms in law, procedural reforms especially, that occurred in the nineteenth century in both England and the United States were mainly legislative. They were accomplished only in the face of extensive and powerful resistance from practitioners of the law, namely lawyers and judges, a fact all the more impressive when one considers their peripheral origin, being fomented by a few persons either marginally committed to the legal system or outside it completely.[11] Equally impressive was the dramatic publicity and public opinion marshaled to initiate legislation of these reforms, as seen in the activities of English and Scotch law societies at the time, and in Charles Dickens' legal caricatures.[12]

The ubiquity and stubbornness of resistance to radical legal change suggests that, as a system or systems of law mature, con-

9. *Some Lessons from Our Early History*, p. 111.

10. *Ibid.*, p. 192; see also Jeremy Bentham, *A Fragment on Government* (London, 1776) ; also his *Principles of Morals and Legislation* (New York: Hafner, 1948) .

11. Vanderbilt, *loc. cit.*; Field, *loc. cit.*, 25f; David D. Field, "Law Reform in the United States and Its Influence Abroad," *American Law Review* (1891) , pp. 518, 521; Caleb P. Patterson, *The Administration of Justice in Great Britain* (Austin: University of Texas Press, 1936) , Chap. IV. Arthur E. Sutherland, "The Machinery of Procedural Reform," *Michigan Law Review* 22 (1922) , 295.

12. *Bleakhouse* (London: Bradbury and Evans, 1853) ; William Holdsworth, *Charles Dickens as a Legal Historian* (New Haven: Yale University Press, 1928) ; Robert Neely, *The Lawyers of Dickens and Their Clerks* (Boston: The Christopher Publishing House, 1938) .

ditions are created that make anything beyond minor adaptive alterations in the systems unacceptable to those who are identified with them. This becomes manifestly clear when attention is extended beyond the law as a system of concepts to its concomitant practices and associated organization.

> So it is with reform in law. All the forces of tradition, of established habit, and in many cases of personal interest are united against reform, and the inertia of the busy men accustomed to existing methods and often too old to learn new ones—of men who are content to say "Let well enough alone" without inquiring too closely whether it is "well" or not. . . .[13]

The conservatism of lawyers and judges confronted with proposed changes inheres in the reification of systems of rules by which courts operate. This in turn is reinforced by the existence of a highly specialized legal profession with an outlook made homogeneous by a common reporting system, the reduction of law to accepted textbook sources, and methods of legal education and teaching that transform concepts into precepts.[14]

LEGAL REVOLUTION AND SCIENTIFIC REVOLUTION

Assuming that there are broad similarities between law and science, it is possible that in the absence of any well-worked-out theory of legal change, a theory of scientific revolutions may be useful for determining the processes by which legal revolution comes about, as well as for organizing and interpreting the special data of this study.

Kuhn has argued cogently that the key to scientific revolutions

13. Moorfield Storey, *The Reform of Legal Procedure* (New Haven: Yale University Press, 1921), p. 16.

14. *Some Lessons from Our Legal History*, p. 16; Sutherland, "The Machinery of Procedural Reform," *loc. cit.*; Lord Chorley, "Procedural Reform in England," *David Dudley Field Centenary Essays*, ed. Alison Reppy (New York: School of Law, New York University, 1949), 99f; Henry Fowler, "A Psychological Approach to Procedural Reform," *Yale Law Journal*, Vol. 43 (1954).

is the appearance of new paradigms, which offer categorically different perspectives on facts and which make possible or cause a change of "world view" among scientists.[15] Paradigm innovation must be contrasted with *normal science,* which is essentially a form of puzzle-solving unattentive to facts without relevance to existing or accepted paradigms. Normal science, as the term suggests, has a moral or value base; it is a system demarcating classes of relevant facts worth study, a specially devised technology and material apparatus, together with empirical experiments designed to articulate a paradigm. As such, it carries multifarious commitments of a community of scientists to textbook ideas, methodology, research organization, colleagues, and rules and lines of activity. Paradigms thus are constitutive of the structure of science.

> They . . . prove to be constitutive of the research activity . . . in learning a paradigm the scientist acquires theory, methods, standards together, usually in an inextricable mixture. Therefore, when paradigms change, there are usually significant shifts in criteria determining the legitimacy both of problems and proposed solutions.[16]

According to Kuhn, new paradigms appear because of anomalies, which are facts left unexplained by extant paradigms. As these increase in number, doubts about old paradigms or awareness of their deficiencies spread, and a crisis arises. New paradigms promise to explain or reconcile the anomalies as well as the facts articulated by the old paradigms. Novel paradigms most often are created by youthful scientists, primarily because they are less committed by prior practice to the traditional rules of normal science; they are freer to conceive new images of the world, new sets of rules for problem-solving, and to sympathetically entertain new classes of facts. By the same reasoning, resistance to new paradigms is strongest among older scientists, who have long-standing practical commitments to the established ways of perceiving their worlds of study.

15. Thomas S. Kuhn, *The Structure of Scientific Revolutions* (Chicago: University of Chicago Press, 1962) .
16. *Ibid.,* p. 108.

PERILS OF PARADIGMS

Transposing theoretical models from one discipline to another carries a temptation to try to account for too much, or to ignore important differences between subject matter or between classes of facts that may be relevant in one field but not in the other. Nevertheless, a distinction between *normal law* as a cumulative enterprise, and legal revolution as the transition to new legal principles, offers a provocative way of formulating hitherto known but unorganized facts about legal change. The notion of anomalies as facts or cases ill-fitting traditional principles of law, which augment to a crisis prerequisite for the generation of new legal concepts, is equally attractive for the purposes of this study. Locating the sources of resistance to change in the functioning claims of going systems, as well as in ideological loyalties, seems applicable to legal, as well as scientific, revolutions.

At this point, however, there is some divergence, since legal revolutions are consummated more slowly than scientific ones, owing to differences in the testing processes of different fields. For example:

> One can test the value of medicine in its practical effects on selected cases. The result of a few experiments closes debate. The effect of change in the law, or in legal procedure, cannot be tested as quickly, and hence must long remain a subject for discussion with subsequent delay.[17]

Another notable difference between legal and scientific revolutions lies in the obscuring effects of legal fictions on radical transformations in law. Words and phrases may be so interpreted or classes of facts so defined that a whole new pattern of law is furthered under the guise of precedent or *stare decisis*. Jerome Hall, for example, has well described how large and significant changes in informal procedures for mitigating criminal justice

17. Storey, *The Reform of Legal Procedure.*

in nineteenth-century England were sanctioned and concealed through the application of administrative fictions.[18] However, it is intriguing here to recall Kuhn's assertion that scientific revolutions tend to be made invisible by a kind of falsification of scientific history through revisions of textbooks, which lend specious continuity to otherwise fundamental departures from traditional science.[19]

If there is a major weakness in Kuhn's analysis, it is his tendency to see the scientific world as made up primarily of interacting individuals, ignoring, for example, the obvious tremendous effects of the organized support and direction of science by government, corporations, universities, and foundations. Similarly, he fails to touch on the sectarian tendency of scientists, and the formation of "schools of scientific thought." [20]

In any event, it is plain that legal reform, especially that effected by legislation, frequently if not typically takes place through the interaction of groups. Hence, even if the general attributes of the revolutionary process in science described by Kuhn are tenable, they must be modified to allow for the importance of groups in the dynamics of legal reform. Groups are of central importance because they affect processes of evaluation and decision-making, as well as the form and course that resistance to reform takes. In societies in which individuals must seek fulfillment of their values through organized groups to which they give allegiance, a process of evaluation, as contrasted to simple value satisfaction, occurs. This means that values or aims tangential and even contrary to many individually held values must be supported when group decisions are made.[21]

18. *Theft, Law and Society,* rev. ed. (Indianapolis: Bobbs-Merrill, 1952), Chap. IV.

19. *The Structure of Scientific Revolutions,* Chap. XI.

20. Leslie White, *The Social Organization of Ethnological Theory* (Houston: Rice University Studies, 1966) , p. 52.

21. See W. F. Cottrell, "Men Cry Peace," in *Research for Peace* (Oslo Institute in Social Research, 1954) , pp. 112–25; also Earl Latham, *The Group Basis of Politics* (Ithaca, N.Y.: Cornell University Press, 1952) .

SOCIAL ACTION AND PLURALISM

Social action differs from scientific activity in that it is much
more concerned with direct action and ends sought than it is
with facts, hypotheses, and the relevance of facts to hypotheses.
Reform movements of the past often were directed toward
changing people, which is to say, changing a whole pattern of
values to which they putatively subscribed. Social action in
modern-day Western society is less a movement to annihilate
existing values and create widespread acceptance of new values
than is is a form of planned intervention in an ongoing process
to *influence the order in which values of different groups are to
be satisfied. The objective is to modify sequences of overt action
through influencing decisions at points of power, rather than to
change the values of groups and individuals participating in the
decisions.* Conversion to the abstract or moral rightness of programs is less important than change in action patterns in particular situations.

This is not to say that unorganized, irrational, expressive
social movements born of individual "strain" and "deprivation"
have disappeared or lost importance.[22] Nor can it be denied
that there are social movements and counter movements best
defined and analyzed as "symbolic crusades," dedicated to protecting or advancing whole "styles of life." [23] Nevertheless, the
functional pluralism of modern society, and the diversification
and complexity of value aggregations and individual value hierarchies, necessarily lead to a means orientation in social action.
To survive or succeed, social action quickly takes organized
form, utilizes professional staff, relies on research methods and
findings, and operates within time and budgetary limitations. At
the same time, there is a necessary subordination of expressive,
moral, symbolic functions to calculational, strategic, and bargain-

22. For this type of analysis see Neil J. Smelzer, *Collective Behavior* (New
York: Free Press, 1963) , p. 8.
23. Joseph Gusfield, *Symbolic Crusade: Status Politics and the American
Temperance Movement* (Urbana: University of Illinois Press, 1963) .

ing elements inherent in much if not most modern organizational interactions.[24]

Election of a pluralistic model for the analysis of social action in the present instance is advised, with recognition that some sociologists would favor "class," "status group," personality structure, or situated behavior models. Noted, too, is that pluralism has been subjected to criticism. A theoretical difficulty has been the specification of conditions under which interaction counterbalances the values of competing groups without carrying society down the path of confusion, decay, or self-destruction. Overemphasis on the mere facts of organization and the articulation of interests may underplay the importance of explicit and implicit rules that apart from such interests regulate group interaction. Furthermore, social action or organization of interests may be exclusively in terms of such rules. That social action can through law alter the rules and thereby alter the pattern of value satisfaction between groups and individuals is one of the happy possibilities of pluralism.[25]

LEGISLATIVE CHANGE AND SOCIAL CHANGE

American sociologists in some respects have traveled a full circle in their speculations about the efficacy of legal change as a means of directing the course of social change. In the early days of sociology, a conviction that social reforms could and should be brought about through legislation was widely held. "Attractive legislation," for example, was one of the chief means advocated by Lester F. Ward to achieve his vision of social telesis.[26]

24. The distinction between means-oriented social action and irrational action was first made in a little-noted report some years ago. See J. Stewart Burgess, "The Study of Modern Social Movements as a Means for Clarifying the Process of Social Action," *Social Forces* 22, (1943–44), 269–75.

25. For discussions of pluralism see: David Truman, *The Governmental Process* (New York: Knopf, 1951) ; H. M. Magid, *English Political Pluralism* (New York: Columbia University Press, 1941) ; Leicester Webb, *Legal Personality and Political Pluralism* (Melbourne: Melbourne University Press, 1958) , esp. 178–97.

26. *Applied Sociology* (Boston: Atheneum Press, 1896) , pp. 337–39.

Others also believed that a "science of legislation" was possible.[27] However, in time the more conservative views of William G. Sumner came to prevail on this subject.[28] The monumental example of the failure of national Prohibition, and the rediscovery of the primary group in research on military and industrial organizations, strengthened the sociologists' conviction that informal, rather than formal, controls were decisive in shaping behavior. More recently, major trends and events have compelled sociologists to re-examine long-held conclusions about law and social change, and to consider again the possibilities of social reform through law.

As organizations and associations increase in size and power, it becomes less probable that patterns of action can be successfully changed or directed through interaction in locally based institutions. At the same time, it is more likely that groups in action will turn to the state as an agency of intervention to defend their own values or to promote values of groups that are favorable correlates of their own. Thus social action more frequently than in the past takes place in a context of power relations and coercive controls that are monopolies of the state. Legislation as well as litigation has become an important means by which groups seek to legitimize their claims and encapsulate

27. Ernst Freund, *Legislative Regulation* (New York: Commonwealth Fund, 1932); Ernst Freund, "Prolegomena to a Science of Legislation," *Illinois Law Review* 13 (1918) , 264–292; Robert Sorensen, "Sociology's Potential Contribution to Legislative Policy Determination," *American Socio. Review* 16 (1951), 239–43.

28. *Folkways* (Boston: Ginn, 1907) , p. 87. More recently it has been argued that Sumner was not as pessimistic about social reform by law as he is generally believed to have been. Harry Ball, and George and Ikeda Keyoshi, "Law and Social Change: Sumner Reconsidered," *American Journal of Sociology* LXII (1962) , 537–40. Writers sharing a conservative view on reform through legislation, but with qualifications are: Frank Parson, *Legal Doctrines and Social Progress* (New York: Viking, 1911) ; L. L. Bernard, *Social Control* (New York: Macmillan, 1939) , Chap. XX. Albert Dicey, *Law and Public Opinion in England* (London: Macmillan, 1952) ; Theodore Roosevelt, *American Ideals* (New York: Putnam 1897); Roscoe Pound, "The Limits of Effective Legal Action," *22nd Annual Report of the Pennsylvania Bar Association* (1916), pp. 221–39; R. M. MacIver and Charles Page, *Society: An Introductory Analysis* (New York: Rinehart, 1949) , pp. 175–81; R. La Piere, *A Theory of Social Control* (New York: McGraw-Hill, 1954) , pp. 316–22.

their values in a favorable position in social structure. Whether in fact they succeed, or to what extent, or what untoward consequences may follow is at best an open question.

Some social scientists who became involved in legal action to obtain greater educational opportunity for American Negroes in the early 1950's argued from weak and uneven evidence that social change can be achieved through legal action if the law is unequivocally pronounced and consistently enforced.[29] Others have a more qualified view that law change may not directly produce desired social changes but nevertheless can initiate them.[30] In contrast to these positions, Honigman, an anthropologist, concluded from his study of the problem in a non-Western society that attempts to guarantee value dominance by projecting conflicting interests into the political arena or area of public law does not necessarily lead to conflict resolution, and that the result may be a continuation of conflict in different form.[31] Finally, there are more dismal research conclusions that legislation or judicial orders may have consequences opposite to changes intended, or may precipitate conditions less desirable than those existing prior to change.[32]

It is significant that much of the recent research and speculative writing on the subject of inducing social change through law has formulated the problems within a context of pluralism. Unfortunately, there is no agreement on how pluralism operates; several writers have made it a condition of successful social

29. "The Effects of Segregation and Consequences of Desegregation," Appendix to Appellant's Brief at pp. 13–14, Brown v. Board of Education, 347 U.S. 483 (1954) ; Kenneth Clark, "Desegregation: An Appraisal of the Evidence," *Journal of Social Issues* 9 (1953) , 2–76.

30. Arnold Rose, "The Use of Law to Induce Social Change," *Transactions of the Third World Congress of Sociology* VI (1956) , 52–63.

31. John J. Honigman, "Value Conflict and Legislation," *Social Problems* 7 (1959) , 34–9.

32. See, for example, Harold and Florence Goldblatt, "The Effective Social Reach of the Fair Housing Practices Law," *Social Problems* 9 (1962), 365–70; Don Hager, "Housing Discrimination, Social Conflict and the Law," *Social Problems* 8 (1960), 80–7; for discussion of studies showing unanticipated and questionable consequences of changes in court procedure, see Maurice Rosenburg, "Court Congestion: Status, Causes, and Proposed Remedies," in *The Courts, the Public and the Law Explosion,* ed. Harry Jones (New York: Prentice-Hall, 1965) , pp. 46–59.

change by means of legal action,[33] while another has stressed the inconclusiveness of legal action in pluralistic situations.[34] Further research, however, requires emphasis on the pluralistic basis of goals as well as of resistance.

PLURALISM AND THE GOALS OF SOCIAL ACTION

Social action also can be viewed from its point of impact, and if impact is defined as that which follows intervention into an ongoing process, then it generally describes the perspective of this study. Some impact research by sociologists has taken the shape of "evaluation studies," designed to estimate or measure changes in attitudes or behavior in relation to the aims of newly instituted programs or policies. The practical difficulties of organizing and carrying out this kind of research are considerable and have received comment.[35] Here only two things need to be said about them: (1) the goals of programs being evaluated often are obscure or they change during the course of evaluation; (2) many of the programs have originated and are pursued in an atmosphere of conflict and controversy.

These observations suggest that programs of action arising from situations characterized by value dissensus may have consequences different from those in which there is consensus, for the reason that the chosen goals have generic differences. In such instances clarity of goals cannot simply be assumed; their nature must be ascertained in some effective or "real" sense, as through investigation of the group interaction that produced the goals.

For purposes of research the social scientist must identify with the goals of social action, but in so doing, he must be able to locate the basis of these goals in the diverse values of particular

33. Arnold Rose, *op. cit.*; Warren Breed, "Group Structure and Resistance to Desegregation in the Deep South," *Social Problems* 10 (1962) , 85–93.

34. Honigman, *op. cit.*

35. Howard Freeman, "Conceptual Approaches to Assessing Impacts of Large Scale Intervention Programs," *Proceedings of the American Statistical Association Social Statistics Section* (1964) ; 192–98. Robert Morris (ed.) , "Centrally Planned Change: Prospects and Concepts," *National Association of Social Workers* (1964) ; Ernest M. Jones, "Impact Research and Sociology of Law: Some Tentative Proposals," *Wisconsin Law Review* (spring 1966) , pp. 1–9.

groups. Through inquiry into past interaction, he can best determine how these values are distributed in social structures or
positioned with reference to power or access to power. This
allows him not only to explain how the legal action occurred
but also to say things about the means likely to be available for
implementation of legislated goals, and the likelihood of their
amendment or even ultimate repeal. The mere fact that goals
of action become law does not *ipso facto* guarantee full, uniform,
or consistent recourse to the power of the state for their support.
Powers of the state wend their way back in intricate ways to the
powers of groups.

A significant point seldom heeded in efforts to sharply separate
social action and its effects is that interaction changes the pattern or action of individuals or populations subject to law prior
to its enactment or change.[36] Group conflict often crystallizes
values in the form of enduring issues; group cleavages are created, and new forms of defensive organization may appear, along
with intransigence and interpersonal hostilities. Taken together,
these forms of opposition often get forged into a part of the
larger phenomena of resistance to social action.

RESISTANCE TO SOCIAL ACTION

The argument pursued here is that social action in value-conflict
situations, when "successful," alters the position of certain values
by upgrading them in a public pattern of action, meaning that
henceforth they will be satisfied before others in a variety of
group and individual contexts. Whether this occurs, whether
"target"-value orders remain unchanged, or whether unsought
values are upgraded and change the pattern of action to one of
resistance must be discovered through research.

Resistance, of course, is not necessari'y fatal to social action.
However, a science of social action, if applicable, must facilitate

36. Stewart Macaulay, "Changing a Continuing Relationship Between a Large
Corporation and Those Who Deal With It"; "Automobile Manufacturers, Their
Dealers and the Legal System," *Wisconsin Law Review*, (summer and fall, 1965) ,
pp. 483–575; 740–858.

predictions of the probable occurrence, extent, and form of resistance. Thus are those planning the strategy of intervention equipped to face further crucial questions as to the available power and means of overcoming resistance, and estimate whether attendant losses offset goal gains. Knowledge of the latter in turn permits the social scientist to make more comprehensive assessments of the worth of the goals themselves. It also strikes directly at the heart of a more fundamental question, namely, the merits and demerits of legal action in contrast to other forms of social action to achieve the same goals.

THE BASES OF RESISTANCE

There is scant sociological knowledge about the phenomena of resistance to induced social change; discussions of the subject must be found in scattered contexts in other fields. In jurisprudence the issue gets phrased as one of enforceability of law, and traditionally, American legal scholars have paid it little attention.[37] Public administrators and those who write about them have been more sensitive to problems of resistance, but seem to limit their concern to the question of authority. Applied anthropologists tend to see resistance mainly in terms of patterned values and attitudes.[38] In those few instances in which sociologists have considered resistance to change, it has been likewise from the viewpoint of attitudes.[39] Attitudinal studies or

37. Roscoe Pound, "The Limits of Effective Legal Action," p. 230; Karl Llewellyn, "A Realistic Jurisprudence: The Next Steps," in *Essays on Jurisprudence From the Columbia Law Review,* (New York: Columbia University Press, 1963) , pp. 148–83.

38. See George Foster, *Traditional Cultures and the Impact of Technological Change* (New York: Harper, 1962) .

39. Reinhard Bendix, "Compliance Behavior and Individual Personality," *American Journal of Sociology* 58 (1952), 292–302; L. D. Eron and R. S. Redmount, "The Effect of Legal Education on Attitudes," *Journal of Legal Education* 9 (1957) , 431–43; Richard Schwartz, "The Effectiveness of Legal Controls," manuscript, Northwestern University; Richard La Piere, *op. cit.,* p. 369; W. F. Cottrell, *Energy and Society* (New York: McGraw-Hill, 1955) , pp. 271–75. Sumner is perhaps the only older sociologist who outlined and discussed a set of concepts for estimating "probable support" or resistance to proposed legislation. See Harry Ball and George and Ikeda Keyoshi, *op. cit.,* 538 ff.

personality-structure studies admittedly are helpful in determining the intensity with which values are held and in making estimates of the degree of "moral indignation" likely to be provoked by social action. Their effectiveness is limited, however, because many people pay only lip service to values and norms, and because it is difficult to reproduce in questionnaires or interview schedules the situational and ecological realities of individual choice-making. More important is the fact that in pluralistic societies persons who are subjects of legal change respond to issues as they perceive them in relation to their own value hierarchies, rather than to the public intent of social action. These issues get created or defined at points of interactions where the demands for change are made.

While issues can be ephemeral or spurious, nevertheless an evolutionary-revolutionary perspective on legal change requires that issues that prevail, recur, and accumulate be deemed to have identifiable connections with *interests* of individuals and groups. Interests are specialized values, or *claims* that persons or groups have on others or on material things for services, time, attention, use, and enjoyment. Interests connote immediacy and valuing of something as a means to an end. People thus may assign value to a procedure because it is instrumental in satisfying diverse interests. A deputy sheriff may value a legal procedure because it is a means to increase his salary through fees; a prosecutor because it enables him to successfully prosecute cases; a judge because it saves time and helps keep his docket clear.

Issues are definable as value conflicts in which interests are present in varying degrees and are articulated with varying amounts of clarity. The underlying processes of valuation in which interests are aggregated and polarized into issues are not always or necessarily accurate or rational; individuals and groups may misjudge their interests, or time may be required to sort out and order their interests in a prospectively changing situation. Some people are defensively oriented, which causes them to perceive threats to their interests that are minimal or even nonexistent. Finally, some, such as children, only vaguely understand their interests, or are incapable of knowing them, leaving the task of their expression to others.

Rights may be thought of as interests sanctioned in varying degrees and ways by the coercive power of the state, or interests consensually recognized, so that they are unquestioned parts of an established pattern of action. One of the outstanding characteristics of the administrative or welfare state is the extent to which it positively or politically articulates interests of classes of its population and seeks through legislation, adjudication, and administration to raise them to the level of rights.[40]

THE NATURE OF ISSUES

No ready-made scheme for classifying issues is at hand. However, they can be sorted out in a very rough way according to the *kinds* of values at stake, the *costs* of any change in their order, and the perceived *legitimacy* of the change. Several distinctions in kinds of values are useful in predicting the rise of issues and resistance. One is between implicit and explicit values, and here it can be said that issues are more likely to arise when threatened values are well defined (converted into interests?) in relation to other values than when they are only vaguely held. The familiar differences between sacred and secular values obviously suggests the greater probability of resistance when the former are under attack. Finally, a line can be drawn between substantive and procedural values. While procedures commonly are thought of as means to the fulfillment of values, it is also true that they become values in themselves under certain circumstances. Norms

40. The distinction between values and interests may be gratuitous, indicating no more than difference between ends-values and means-values. However, the term "interest" will be used largely because of its common usage in the literature of law and politics.

Legal realism appears to reject ends-means analysis in favor of purely behavioral analysis. See Jerome Frank, *Law and the Modern Mind* (New York: Anchor Books, 1963) ; also his *Courts on Trial* (New York: Atheneum, 1963) .

However, Llewellyn, who is ordinarily regarded as a legal realist, makes it clear that such concepts as rules, rights, and interests, and presumably ends-means schemes, are tenable if they are inferred from overt action, rather than subjectively intuited as being discoverable "in the mind of the judge." Karl Llewellyn, "A Realistic Jurisprudence," *loc. cit.;* this is pretty much W. F. Cottrell's general point of view on social action, which I have attempted to follow here. See his "Men Cry Peace," *loc. cit.*

of organizational procedure may be informal as well as formal, and in some cases they are regarded as unwritten but well-understood "rules of the game." While some changes can be accommodated within existing rules of procedure, others cannot. Change in the basic rules of interaction or the threat of such often arouses resistance because they represent sacred values, taken as self-evidently right and unquestionable.

"Rules of the game" tend to result from past accommodations of individuals and groups in terms of status and power. They are reinforced in the daily interaction of concerned parties and are likely to be instrumental means to ends other than those sought by social action. Changing rules of the game may or may not threaten directly these other values, but it does make their continued satisfaction doubtful and thus puts them in issue. Those subject to change may see their choice as changing or not changing the "system," rather than acquiescing in changes in part of the system to preserve the rest.[41]

In other situations resistance is compounded from the aggregation of values neither exclusively sacred nor of an "either-or" nature critical to the preservation of a system. In these settings resistance may take form in bargaining or transactional behavior: individuals and group representatives make choices on a give-and-take basis, sacrificing something of lesser value to gain or protect something of higher value. In this process it is often the *costs* of means of following proposed lines of action, apart from values *per se*, which become deciding factors in resistance. Generally these costs are anticipated in terms of time, money, effort, and psychic stress necessary to implement a contemplated action.

The impact of social action in highly differentiated society tends to be segmental and unevenly distributed; hence costs do not fall equally on affected groups and individuals. For this reason the issues they raise often reduce to questions of who will have to bear the burden of the proposed changes, rather than of the substantive worth of the changes. In sorting out issues, people view changes in the light of their probable effects upon

41. W. F. Cottrell, *Energy and Society*, p. 273.

means already allocated to satisfying other values. Changes may be resisted if they call for greater expenditures of time, money, or energy to maintain these commitments. Thus a board of supervisors in a county with a low tax base may oppose a law creating local mental health clinics on a contributing basis, not because it opposes help for mentally disturbed people, but because it is already committed to a heavy program of road-building from which it can't retreat. In another county the board may resist or be indifferent because it already has cheaper or even superior means to the same end through the use of facilities of a nearby outpatient clinic. It is from a kind of sociography of costs particularizing which groups and individuals are asked to make value or cost sacrifices that predictions of resistance can most reliably be made.

When the costs of change fall more heavily on some groups than others, those affected may come to resist through a sense of injustice, believing that the demands of the program or law are unfair, or that they are being denied "equal protection of the laws." There are situations, however, in which resistance must be traced to other than substantive values or more tangible cost factors. This kind of resistance has an incomprehensible quality in that the proposed action may have no adverse effects or may even carry benefits for the recalcitrants. Indeed, in some instances the latter appear to be unaware of the particular kinds of demands being made upon them. Here resistance can be comprehended only in terms of the perceived legitimacy of the legal action.

Legitimacy derives from the notion, especially strong in Anglo-Saxon legal institutions, that an action is valid only if it proceeds from the consent of those subject to it. Judgments like these are commonly made from the way policy is formed, laws enacted, or court decisions reached. They are also formed from ideas defining those precincts of human life that the law or the state may or may not invade, or from ideas as to what penalties may be applied. Finally, resistance may be ideologically founded when changes are brought about by groups regarded as "not having the right," or by those deemed unqualified to make the related decisions for change.

UNANTICIPATED CONSEQUENCES OF CHANGE

Theoretically, resistance can be interpreted broadly to mean apathy, superficial compliance, and diversionary action amounting to sabotage or subversion, as well as open defiance and opposition or organized conflict. In addition to these immediate consequences of social action, others may be far less foreseeable because they are second- or third-order results. Thus social action changes law, which in turn sets other changes into motion, and so on, in a chain of actions or interactions. The end products may include new and unwanted forms of human action.

Where procedural rules reflect some sort of balance of values reached through past interactions, as seems to be true in systems of justice within law courts, or in a stabilized administrative organization, it is not always possible to say that changes sought by laws or new rules will end at prescribed points. A whole new pattern, paradigm, or order of value satisfaction may eventually appear.

ISSUES, ANOMALIES, AND CRISES

If legal issues by and large are traceable to conflicts of values and interests, then it follows that law may be adaptive or maladaptive, depending on whether it safeguards values, interests, or rights. When the law fails to provide procedures, remedies, or positive orders for this purpose, it falls short of meeting human demands and is maladaptive. This is felt most keenly when other means of safeguarding interests are unavailable or are too costly to use. The individual cases in which recognizable interests through petition or trial are left unsatisfied or are frustrated are anomalies. If there are enough anomalies, they become fertile ground for the rise of issues, depending on the nature of social communication. When issues accumulate and draw in a wide spectrum of diversified interests, a crisis in law exists.

Common to legal crises is the more generic issue of the fairness or justice of law or procedure. The ubiquitous concern with justice and fairness can be ascribed to universal values inherent in natural law, but it may be more realistic to regard them as acquired through childhood socialization in primary groups, particularly in play and games. It is here that "rules of the game" are learned, together with pragmatic respect for the fundamental presuppositions of human interaction.[42] Adult experience reinforces this learning and engenders the idea that without rules and procedures, fairness and justice in social life is unlikely. But, at the same time, adults also learn that particular procedures and rules are problematical in their efficacy.

The common law of England is apotheosized as the source of the doctrine of supremacy of law, or justice through law, but in operation it left something to be desired, as where the award of damages was an insufficient remedy, or where a suit against a powerful adversary was difficult to win. The revolutionary concept of equity and the creation of separate equity courts came from anomalies like these. Over several centuries, however, equity procedure became so tangled and costly that it too became anomalous law. Crisis again generated a radical new concept of utilitarian law, to be implemented by means of legislative reforms in court organization and procedure. Anomalies of both law and equity came to light as societies turned to mass production and distribution of goods by corporations, and as it became necessary to protect the interests of classes of workers, consumers, clients, and unemployables. With mass production came the great legal development of the twentieth century—rule-making by regulatory agencies, and administrative justice. Some have called this a return to "executive justice," whose evils the rule

42. For discussions of this problem: Edmund N. Cahn, *The Sense of Injustice* (New York: New York University Press, 1949); David Matza, *Delinquency and Drift* (New York: John Wiley, 1964), Chap. IV; Edmund Bergler and Joost Meerloo, *Justice and Injustice* (New York: Grune and Stratton, 1963); Allen Barton and Saul Mandlovitz, "The Experience of Injustice as a Research Problem," *Journal of Legal Education* 13 (1960), 24–9. Garfinkel's demonstrations of effects of deliberately deviating from presumed rules of routine activities and games are instructive here. He seems to be arguing that such rules should be studied by a kind of Gestalt sociology, as implied by the title of one of his core articles. Harold Garfinkel, "The Routine Grounds of Everyday Activities," *Social Problems* 11 (1964), 225–50.

of law was designed to prevent; but it is also recognized that its rapid growth must be laid to maladaptation of traditional legal machinery.

> The present popularity of executive justice . . . is attributed to defects in our legal system, to an inadequacy of our legal tradition to the demands of a new idea of justice. The problem of adjusting the law, shaped by the individualism of the past three centuries . . . in the United States is aggravated by . . . a bad adjustment between law and administration.[43]

In the early part of the twentieth century, the American judiciary was content to relinquish broad areas of work to commissions, boards, and administrators. In recent decades there has been strong feeling that administrative justice in the modern age may recapitulate many of the ancient evils identified with courts of all-powerful monarchs, namely arbitrariness, prejudice, political control, and denial of simple elements of procedural fairness. The extent to which this is true may be debated, but the anomalous existence of dual systems for adjudicating conflicts of interests in our society cannot. A supervening issue is whether conflicts of interests meeting jurisdictional criteria for hearing in regular courts will be adjudicated under law, while those adjudicated by administrative means are independent of law or at best tenuously subservient to it. The issue reflects the need, not only for courts to reorganize and simplify procedure toward the greater administration of justice, but for regulatory agencies and administrators to evolve procedures or an "ethos of adjudication" that give the rule of law a higher position in the order of values they satisfy.[44] Whether "the twain shall never meet," or whether a creative synthesis is possible in the midlands of law and administration, is one of the central concerns this study seeks in part to clarify.

43. Roscoe Pound, "Justice According to Law," *loc. cit.*, p. 255.
44. The phrase is Pound's. Roscoe Pound, "The Rule of Law and the Modern Welfare State," *Vanderbilt Law Review* 1 (1953) , 31; Harry W. Jones, "The Rule of Law and the Welfare State," in *Essays in Jurisprudence From the Columbia Law Review*, pp. 410–13.

JUVENILE JUSTICE

Generally, executive justice has moved along a one-way street, with administrators assuming or being clothed with judicial prerogatives. This has been most obvious in regulatory activities and welfare administration, but executive justice also has invaded the criminal law, detectable in powers of probation commissions, parole boards, and boards of corrections, grand examples being the Adult Authority and the Youth Authority of California. Only incidentally and exceptionally have courts metamorphized into something like administrative agencies. Traffic courts and other informally specialized courts, such as those handling drunkenness cases, or perhaps divorce and small-claims courts, have taken on many of the qualities of administrative agencies. Their distinctive features are the large numbers of cases handled, the swiftness with which they are dispatched, and the implicit presumptions of guilt or liability. The quality of the justice they administer, however, remains questionable.

The juvenile court, in contrast to the above developments, stands almost alone as a deliberate effort to innovate a special form of executive justice within the existing framework of American court systems. Its creation has been termed the "great social invention of the nineteenth century," and a revolutionary idea in defining and handling problems of children.[45] But the origins of the juvenile court in the United States are less well described as legal reform than as a revolt against legal procedure for coping with juvenile problems affecting the community. The origins are found in the convergence of certain social movements aimed at removing children from criminal court jurisdiction and effecting their more humane treatment by agents of the state. Overriding goals were the protection of children from exploitation and the corrupting influences of urban environments, and the provision of welfare assistance. These were to be

45. Roscoe Pound, "The Juvenile Court and the Law," *National Probation and Parole Association Yearbook, 1944* (New York, 1945), pp. 1–22; Alfred Kahn, *A Court for Children* (New York: Columbia University Press, 1953), Chap. X.

achieved through informal proceedings and individualized treatment. Seen in this light, the juvenile court was antiprocedural or, at the very least, aprocedural. Procedures were to be dictated by fatherly concern of a judge, humanitarian philosophy and clinical considerations.

The diverse origins of the juvenile court in many jurisdictions, coupled with the tendency of early partisans to describe the court in ideal terms, make generalizations about the legal rationale for its intended organization and procedure difficult. Some advocates held that the juvenile court descended from the English Chancery and that it utilized equity proceedings under the doctrine of *parens patriae*, which in literal terms means that the state through the court acts in the capacity of a substitute father. This interpretation, however, is better regarded as a rationalization than as a realistic description of practices as they actually came into play in the court.[46] The court became different things in different places, and even today, varies with the type of cases or problems coming before it.

The absence of a legally definitive procedure in the early juvenile courts cannot be attributed entirely to desires of its advocates to vest it with an atmosphere of informality. There was little guidance or procedural directives in statutes establishing the courts in various states, because legislators saw them primarily as child-welfare agencies.[47] Other kinds of factors militated against the evolution of generic legal procedure within the courts themselves. Among these: (1) The line of continuity between traditional courts of law and the juvenile court proved to be very tenuous, owing to the use of lay judges and the low level of commitment and interest among legally trained judges assigned to it. (2) Relatively few appeals were taken from juvenile court decisions, and when they were, higher court decisions sustained wide limits of discretion for the lower court; hence an important source of clarification necessary for the crescive

46. Paul Tappan, "Juridical and Administrative Approaches to Children with Problems," in *Justice for the Child*, ed. Margaret Rosenheim (New York: Free Press, 1962), Chap. VII.

47. F. J. Davis, "The Iowa Juvenile Court Judge," *Journal of Criminal Law, Criminology, and Political Science* 42 (1951–52), 338–50.

growth of law was absent. (3) Early probation officers and welfare workers connected with the court were nonprofessional and had little conception of procedure or its importance. (4) Clients of the court tended to be powerless people, often ethnic minorities, little equipped to make articulate demands on the court. (5) Legal counsel was seldom present to initiate adversary or other action that might have generated continuity with criminal or other legal procedure.

The failure of juvenile courts as a whole to evolve a generic legal procedure does not mean that distributively they failed to develop procedures of their own. In the earlier history of these courts, procedures evolved rather freely from the interaction of participating individuals and groups with a direct interest in the proceedings, among whom, depending on the community, were police, judges, probation officers, welfare workers, church workers, and law enforcement people. This interaction for the most part was localized and mainly reflected the interests and order of values prevailing in the local community.[48] Interpersonal relations had much direct and indirect effect on procedures, and the court characteristically was identified with the personality of the judge. One of his unique problems was to preserve the autonomy of the court in the midst of strong pressures continually exerted on it.

LATER EVOLUTION OF THE JUVENILE COURT

The evolution of organization and procedures of juvenile courts for more than half a century was so uneven and diversified as to defy common characterization. Development was slow, almost glacial, and fulfillment fell far short of the ideal. It required twenty-five years, until 1925, before a majority of states had

48. The best available documentation on the early history of a particular juvenile court probably is in Ben Lindsey and Rube Burrough, *The Dangerous Life* (London: Harold Shalor, 1931) ; considerable historical data on the diverse origins of early juvenile courts can be found in Hastings Hart, *Preventive Treatment of Neglected Children* (New York: Russell Sage Foundation, 1910) , especially Chaps. XII, XVII, and XXIII.

fallen in line behind Illinois in passing juvenile court legislation. A study in 1920 disclosed that only 16 percent of juvenile courts then in existence (2034) had achieved the bare minimum of requirements to justify the name.[49] Rural areas lagged far behind the urban, so much so that many had purely nominal juvenile courts. The critical missing elements were adequate probation service, use of social information in adjudication and dispositions, methods of detention other than jail, and informed judges educated to the purposes of the court.[50]

The spirit of positivism that flowered during the hectic Depression years of the 1930's, the upgrading of social work, psychiatry, and psychology, plus the professionalization of probation officers, inaugurated the "age of treatment" in the juvenile court, causing its image as an arena of fatherly intercession into children's lives to fade—a diminution at times thrown into sharp relief by conflict between judge and social worker. With the accelerated urbanization of American society following World War II, many juvenile courts were transformed by voluminous case loads and specialization into bureaucratic organizations. Complex organization of the court, rotating judges, community pressures, and the development of "policies" by probation departments made it less and less possible to say who was protecting the special interests of the child. No longer could it be assumed that the interests of the judge or the probation officers were identifiable with the child's. Confusion mounted over the purposes of the court.

CHANGING VIEWS OF THE JUVENILE COURT

A certain amount of public dissatisfaction with the juvenile court institution has been more or less endemic in American society, evidenced by early attacks on its constitutionality and by the continuing struggles to upgrade its standards of treatment. As time wore on, the great enthusiasms heralding the birth and

49. Evelina Belden, *Courts in the United States Hearing Children's Cases*, U.S. Children's Bureau, Publication No. 65 (1920).
50. *Ibid.*

early years of the court began to dampen. What had been called the "great social invention of the nineteenth century" lost some of its sacred aura as the occasional lone voice of a dissenting judge or frustrated lawyer began to be joined by others. It began to be perceived that the high expectations for the court were not fulfilled; proof that it had helped to prevent crime or lessen recidivism was difficult to discover. By 1950, dour sociological critics had begun to wonder if the juvenile court did not actually contribute to crime or inaugurate delinquent careers by the imposition of the stigma of wardship, by unwise detention and the incarceration of youth in institutions more likely to corrupt than reform.

The first strong blows at the later-day juvenile court were struck by the sociologist-lawyer Paul Tappan, who was well armed with first-hand knowledge of New York youth courts, as well as being fully acquainted with relevant literature. It is both revealing and significant that an unpracticed lawyer, with a sociological background should be the one to attack the juvenile court for its denial of due process of law to youth taken under its jurisdiction. This accusation gained force as an integral part of sociological criticism, which exposed the gross confusion of purposes in the juvenile court together with the fallacy of assuming welfare functions for which it was unfitted.[51]

Tappan's charges had a solid empirical basis in his research on the court for wayward girls in New York City. He demonstrated clearly how the loose administrative application of legal classifications to girls in this court led to their effective stigmatization in the network of metropolitan welfare agencies, thus explicating what George H. Mead once called the "modern elaborate organization of taboo." In a larger way Tappan sharply illuminated the dubious consequences of the largess of court power to treat the "whole child," when it operated through group-made policy decisions in a milieu of functionally organized child-welfare services.[52]

---

51. Paul Tappan, "Treatment without Trial," *Social Forces* 24 (1946), 306–12.
52. Paul Tappan, *Delinquent Girls in Court* (New York: Columbia University Press, 1947).

Tappan's strong interest in reform and his contentious presentation of materials caused his work to fall short of a full theoretical analysis of the juvenile court. In the same way, much of the criticism subsequently levied against the juvenile court was couched in legal or ideological terms. Questions about the structure of the juvenile court were little discussed in the context of the changing nature of the larger society. A completely neglected aspect of the problem was the changes taking place in social categories of youth, and their implications for the great powers exercised by juvenile courts and related correctional agencies.

IN LOCO PARENTIS

In a less obvious way the changing perspectives on the juvenile court were portents of challenges to the rising level of authority imposed on youth in American society. This was implicit in the history of the juvenile court, which coincided closely with the shift of the socialization process away from the family. The necessity for prolonged education, compulsory education laws, and the growth of an identifying "teen-age" culture differentiated a category of *youth* from *children,* both of whom, however, remained under the legally undifferentiated categories of "juvenile" and "minor." [53] In essence the juvenile court, along with schools, police, and correctional agencies, extended control for a longer and longer period of time over "children," and expanded control in more and more areas outside the home, all under the aegis of paternalism.

While the juvenile court became part of the nexus of pyramiding controls serving positive intervention to raise and maintain social and technological standards, the legal illusion preserved was that the court intervened only on evidence of family failure. Also kept alive was the illusion that the juvenile court acted as

53. For a discussion of changing statuses of youth, see Hans Sebald, *Adolescence* (New York: Appleton-Century-Crofts, 1968) , pp. 38–9, 95–118.

a family surrogate, and had primary-group characteristics, despite its having become functional and associational. An added incongruity was the perpetuation of a family model for the court to exert controls over youth at ages (fourteen to twenty-one) where the family never had been influential.

2

The First Revolution and Normal Law

The evolution of laws relating to the dependency, neglect, and criminal acts of minors and their practical uses in California were shaped by its relatively late and stormy emergence as a state, its rapid and heterogeneous growth, and the stubborn resistance maintained in local communities against new concepts and values coming with an urban way of life. The laws reflected many false starts, retreats, and new beginnings, often setting requirements at odds with one another or failing to provide adequate means for seeing them into effect. This owed partly to the legislators' inability to foresee and allow for consequences of the new laws, and partly to the difficulties of securing support for new state activities, which multiplied expenditure of tax monies and invaded areas of social life hitherto regarded as inviolate.

While no one ideology or assemblage of values governed the practical uses of the laws by police, judges, court, and welfare people dealing with children, nevertheless the efforts at *changing* these practices by legislation do disclose distinctive patterns of values. These patterns may be categorized according to historical periods in the evolution of state organizations responsible for the direction and supervision of agencies with control over children and parents. First was the pre-juvenile-court era, which terminated in the creation of the juvenile court law itself. Thereafter followed successive periods of administrative supervision (or attempted supervision) of the juvenile court law by three state departments—Charities and Corrections, Welfare, and the California Youth Authority. Each of these departments held to its own conception of the law, to an underlying philosophy, and to characteristic methods for gaining practical compliance or conformity with its goals.

THE PRE-JUVENILE COURT ERA

As is well known, early California, especially in the north, passed through a period of public disorders resulting from an absence of law and the influx of people drawn from many parts of the nation and world by the lure of its gold fields. The frenetic environment in these gold-mining towns and especially in the boisterous seaport entry of San Francisco was hardly conducive to a stable family life and the raising of children. A backwash of social ferment was also felt in California towns that lost much of their adult male population to the mines, leaving no one to maintain public order and control crime.

One of the outgrowths of the disorganized and unorganized state of community life in the north was the establishment in 1858 of the San Francisco Industrial School to provide for children under eighteen "leading an idle or immoral life." [1] The

law allowed commitment of children to this school on application by three citizens to a police judge or court of sessions.[2] In settling on an industrial school, primarily educational but also placing children in foster homes, authors of the legislation acted in harmony with the more advanced thinking in other states, where disillusionment with reform schools had begun.

In 1860 the legislature, sensitive to criticism about the way minors were being handled in the prisons of the state, took a step backward and authorized a state reform school. The school was

---

1. Valeska Bary and Frances Cahn, *Welfare Activities of Federal, State and Local Governments in California, 1850–1934*, Bureau of Public Administration, University of California (Berkeley: University of California Press, 1936) , p. 46. The popular terms for such children were "hoodlums" and "street Arabs."
2. *Ibid.*, p. 47.

short-lived, however, for San Franciscans were unwilling to send their youth there, and no funds were made available to transport boys from other parts of the state.[3] Thus prisons continued to be used as places of confinement for youthful criminals.

The pattern of sending more serious juvenile offenders to prison appears to have been well established from California's statehood. From 1850 to 1860 over three hundred youths under twenty served time in state prisons.[4] In the year 1886 there were 184 prison inmates below age twenty-one.[5] At the same time, as elsewhere in the nation, local authorities often held juveniles in the same jails with adult criminals. In time, the San Francisco Industrial School increasingly became correctional, but for a variety of reasons it was unable to carry more than a small share of the state's juvenile criminal commitments. The change made this school completely unsuitable for less serious juvenile offenders.

General public dissatisfaction with the plight of homeless, destitute, and delinquent children caused a legislative committee in 1881 to urge action to "gather up, shield, and protect" an estimated 50,000 children "unreached by the regular schools."[6] A later commission, in 1884, pursued this line with concrete recommendations for a state reform school at Whittier and an industrial school at Preston. As first provided by law, judges could send minors convicted of crimes to either institution; in addition, destitute or incorrigible children could be sent to the Whittier school on complaint by a parent or guardian.[7]

Meantime, swells of the child-welfare movement first organized in the East reached California, producing a West Coast version of the movement in the Boys and Girls Aid Society in 1874. In addition to providing or arranging for the care of neglected, dependent, and delinquent children in its home in San Fran-

3. *Idem.*, p. 49.
4. W. C. Frankhauser, *A Financial History of California*, University of California, Publications in Economics (Berkeley: University of California Press, 1913), p. 390.
5. Report of California State Penological Commission, Sacramento, 1887, p. 10.
6. Report of Assembly Committee on Prisons of California, Sacramento, 1881.
7. Report of California State Penological Commission, p. 38.

cisco, the society worked informally to achieve fuller observance of the compulsory education law of 1874. The society also agitated for new legislation, first succeeding with a juvenile probation act in 1883, then with another in 1887, making it unlawful to confine children under sixteen in jails. The first probation law allowed police or courts to place juveniles on probation under the supervision of nonsectarian agencies organized for this purpose.[8]

Early legislation on child welfare in California grew in part out of a humanitarian concern with the need for alternatives to imprisonment for criminal minors, but it also expressed a core of Puritan, Calvinist values that stressed the importance of education as a means for developing self-discipline and inculcating morality. These values were made quite explicit in the legislative directives to California reform schools, which were instituted for the "confinement, discipline, education, employment and reformation of juvenile offenders." [9] In the case of the Preston school, disciplinary values were further emphasized by a military-type organization and authority.

While the prime values of child-placement agencies seem far removed from those of individuals and groups favoring reform school education, nevertheless generically similar Puritan concepts of child-rearing show in their concern with the "rescue" of children from dissolute parents and in their justification of state intervention to place children in families or trades in order to see them educated, trained in productive work, and "disciplined under law." [10]

By the end of the nineteenth century, disillusionment with reform schools that didn't reform was widespread. Furthermore, the routine and wholesale removal of children from their homes and local environments and their placement in distant areas began to be questioned. Often children were sought mainly to obtain cheap labor, without regard for their education and welfare;

8. Bary and Cahn, *op. cit.*, p. 37.

9. *California Statutes* (1889) , Chap. 103, Sec. 1; Chap. 108, Sec. 1.

10. Military-type discipline and a threefold classification of inmates symbolized by dress and differential privileges were in effect in the home operated for boys. See annual reports, Boys and Girls Aid Society, San Francisco, 1900–02.

and those apprenticed in trades had scant protection from exploitation. Sectarian and other values frequently took precedence over the welfare of the child. It was for these and related reasons that many individuals and associations working for child welfare in the latter part of the nineteenth century began to believe that child labor and compulsory education laws had to be achieved above all. The ultimate establishment of the juvenile court was partly the result of group action seeking an effective means or agency for enforcing laws that, while expressing welfare and humanitarian goals, lacked specific applicability.

The laws enacted in California for the control and care of dependent, neglected, and delinquent children up through 1900 at best were primitive and incomplete, particularly in regard to their administrative means of enforcement. Thus, although education had been made compulsory, there were no provisions for attendance officers; probation could be granted to juveniles, but there was no state agency or agent responsible for its supervision. Confusion existed for some years over the age limits for children being sent to Preston and Whittier schools. Segregation of delinquent and dependent children at Whittier was incomplete, and girl as well as boy offenders were committed there. Legal requirements for admissions and financial payments frequently were amended and changed, and some evidence suggests that the way in which payments were made tended to increase commitments to penitentiaries, directly contrary to the purposes for which the reformatories were instituted.[11]

Although social reform was very much in the air in California at the end of the nineteenth century, the legislature was peopled largely with conservatives, who were little disposed to enlargement of welfare functions of the state, particularly if they meant tax increases. Their *laissez faire* attitudes were supported, or perhaps exploited, by powerful corporate interests, especially railroads, which dominated the legislature until 1910. In the first decade of the new century this power was broken, and new forces

11. Preston School of Industry, Third Biennial Report of the Board of Trustees, 1897–98, p. 5; see also William Hendricks, "California's Juvenile Courts," M.A. thesis, U.C.L.A., 1955, p. 6.

stirred as moral reformers began to turn to political means to advance their ends.[12]

Meantime, the populations of San Francisco and Los Angeles grew apace, and children came to be more and more of a problem to the police in these cities, particularly with the increase in immigration.[13] In the absence of a system of probation and satisfactory facilities for placing children, judges and court officers had the formal legal alternatives of reform school, prison, or jail to deal with those coming before them. As occurred in eighteenth-century England when the penalty often greatly outweighed offense,[14] the courts turned to fictions and pious subterfuge, particularly in cases of petty offenses; district attorneys refused to file complaints after arrest, or the judge dismissed the complaint after it was filed. In other instances the court went through the motions of a trial but postponed disposition by ordering indefinite continuances. One such demonstration of spurious juvenile justice was recalled by a Los Angeles judge:

> If the attorney for the defendant and the attorney for the people, committing magistrate, and the Superior Judge, whose duty it was to deal with the case, had followed the mode and procedure outlined by law, the children would have been sent to Whittier or Ione for their minority, which would have been 12 years for the youngest child. . . . As a matter of fact, the boys were made to answer, were brought up to Superior Court for arraignment, stood in line while admonished by the Superior Judge, who had been advised of the situation, and then the case was indefinitely postponed and the children allowed to go during good behavior.[15]

Needless to say, although some delinquent youth were chastened by these procedures, not so others. Judicial rebukes often

12. See Franklin Hichborn, *Story of the Session of the California Legislature of 1915* (San Francisco: James H. Barry, 1916) , Chap. 18.

13. Thomas S. McKibbon, "The Origin and Development of the Los Angeles County Juvenile Court," M.A. thesis, U.C.L.A., 1932, p. 17.

14. See Jerome Hall, *Theft, Law, and Society* (Indianapolis: Bobbs-Merrill, 1935), Chap. IV.

15. Thomas S. McKibbon, *op. cit.*, p. 15. The idea that the law historically has resulted in flagrantly cruel punishment of children has been challenged as propaganda of those involved in the juvenile court movement. See Tony Platt, "Juvenile Justice," M.S., Center for Study of Law and Society, University of California, Berkeley, 1965.

tended to become meaningless, especially for repeaters. The problem of policing juveniles ushered in with the rise of city life in California was little touched by these methods. Yet, in the absence of family and community controls, police had little choice other than to arrest, jail, and charge children. It was these more visible aspects of juvenile justice—public arrests, transportation to jail in paddy wagons, open hearings in court along with criminals, misdemeanants, and prostitutes, as well as prison sentences—that so aroused the ire and fire of humanitarian organizations in San Francisco and Los Angeles at the turn of the century.

BIRTH OF THE JUVENILE COURT LAW

Whether California would have enacted a juvenile court law when it did if Illinois had not already done so is debatable. It might be said that conditions were favorable at the time, but the evidence of diffusion, borrowing, and following the lead of other states is unmistakable.[16]

Women and women's organizations more or less spearheaded the drive in California, as they had in Illinois. One leader of the movement in Los Angeles had been familiar with the campaign for a juvenile court in Chicago, and another had actually participated there. The California Club of San Francisco, which took the lead in getting the bill first introduced, was directly patterned after a comparable women's organization in Chicago. Settlement-house workers were equally active in campaigning for a court in both states.[17] The California law, of course, followed the Chicago, rather than the Colorado, model.

16. Actually, as early as 1859, E. R. Highton recommended to California Governor Weller a plan similar to the Swedish welfare boards. It provided for a board of censors under state jurisdiction with power to commit "boys and girls on the road to ruin" to a children's aid society. However, owing to "inchoate conditions," the plan was "unacknowledged." Report of E. R. Highton to H. E. George Stoneman on State Prison Reform, San Francisco, 1884, p. 14.

17. Dorethea Moore, "The Work of the Women's Clubs in California," *American Academy of Political and Social Sciences* 28 (1906), 257–60; Thomas S. McKibbon, pp. 15–19.

The first attempt to pass the law failed, blocked by cost-conscious elements in the legislature. In a second effort in 1903 the State Federation of Women's Clubs enlisted support from the Commonwealth Club, Associated Charities, and the Boys and Girls Aid Society, then returned to do battle for the juvenile court bill. Indefatigable females throughout the state distributed copies of the proposed law, arranged conferences, issued press releases, and lobbied on a personal basis. Persuasion of legislators was elaborated in graphic terms with 175 illustrative case documents. But even with this impressive host of support, passage of the law was secured only through a legislative compromise whereby public funds could not be used to pay probation officers.[18]

In 1905 the original law was greatly expanded and formally titled the McCartney Juvenile Court Law. In addition to specifying fifteen bases for acquiring jurisdiction over minors, the new law provided for detention homes, probation committees, salaries for probation officers in all counties, penalties for contributing to delinquency, written probation reports, procedures for commitments to Whittier and Preston, and established a definite locus for the court in the superior court of each county.

But the new law was not to settle easily into the statute books for some years to come. In 1904 the board of Charities and Corrections had taken the juvenile court under its wing and recommended its extension from the pioneer counties (San Francisco, Los Angeles, and Alameda) to all counties of the state. To this end investigations were initiated and conferences sponsored that inspired the more geographically inclusive, as well as more fully specified, law of 1909. While the board in its report of 1910 took much satisfaction from the achievement of the "best laws yet enacted," nevertheless clouds had appeared on the socio-legal

18. William D. Hendricks, "California's Juvenile Courts," Master's thesis, University of California, Los Angeles, 1955, p. 9. Specifying unpaid probation officers as a condition of passage of the first juvenile court law also was a device of legislators in other states, such as Illinois and Pennsylvania. See also Hastings Hart, *Preventive Treatment of Neglected Children* (New York: Russell Sage Foundation, 1910), pp. 210–12.

horizon. The report noted: "There are a few counties which have not yet risen to the possibilities of this law." [19]

Either this was a bland understatement of facts or the board people were blind to the state of affairs in San Francisco, where by 1910 dissatisfaction with the effects of the law was unmistakable. Particularly disturbing were legal problems having to do with dependent children.

> Rescue and protection of dependent children in some places is now more difficult, more expensive, more uncertain, and less permanent than under the old annoying and clumsy guardianship proceedings in the Probate Court.[20]

Much of the difficulty in San Francisco centered on the mushrooming practice of invoking juvenile court procedures to reform "unfit parents," to more or less compel them to be moral, or to avoid divorce. Children in large numbers were held under temporary commitments, with the unhappy result that costs to the court multiplied ten times in an eight-year period. The situation was further muddied by disagreements over hearing procedures for dependent and deliquent children, and also by the issue of whether parents should be held more accountable by law.[21] Further fuel for conflict lay in the administration of the Mothers' and Widows' Pension, used to supplement state aid. All applicants were required to be processed by the juvenile court, and if there was some doubt about their moral status, they were placed under the court's supervision. It was also necessary for children whose fathers had been sentenced to prison or committed as insane to receive assistance through the juvenile court. In many instances relatives of children refused to appear before

19. State Board of Charities and Corrections, Fourth Biennial Report, Sacramento, 1908–10. Actually some dissatisfaction was expressed over working of the law as it stood in 1905; a spokesman for the board at least implied some difficulty: "I think that with a little co-operation on the part of the police, judges, and Judge of the Superior Court in construing it, would make the law amply elastic to cover the needs of all people." Second Biennial Report, 1906, pp. 125–26.

20. *Transactions of the Commonwealth Club of California*, Vol. V, No. 4 (San Francisco, 1910), p. 214.

21. *Ibid.*, p. 215.

the court for these reasons and because of its image as a delinquency depot.[22]

As pressures were exerted and more counties sought to capture the form or spirit of the juvenile court law, problems grew apace. Despite intervening amendments, by 1914 discontent with the law had grown to critical proportions. Yet positive solutions to the difficulties were slow to appear. The board of Charities and Corrections described the situation and recommended:

> that the Juvenile Court Law be modified that it will be more workable from an administrative point of view and better adapted to the needs of the children of this state. There is quite general dissatisfaction with the present act on the part of judges, probation officers and all people concerned in juvenile court work. However, the recommendations for its modifications have not yet been crystallized . . . various parties . . . are working on a revision and a conference has been called. It is hoped that there will be definite recommendations at this time. [23]

Amendments to the law in 1913 did little to pacify the disputants. Indeed, there is a hint of skulduggery in the legislature in a brief reference to the irregular process by which one of two competing bills found its way to the governor's desk for signature.[24] While sources on the period are thin, there is reason to believe that the underlying conflict may have been between moral-reform-oriented groups on one hand, and judges and probation officers on the other. The court officers were reluctant to have their hands tied by highly specific legal directives for the removal of children from the custody of their parents. The depth of their feeling is revealed in a judge's comment on a Commonwealth Club resolution to hold parents more accountable by juvenile and superior courts.

22. State Board of Control, Children's Agent Report, Sacramento, 1914, p. 14.
23. Sixth Biennial Report, 1914, p. 19.
24. *Transactions of the Commonwealth Club of California*, Vol. X, No. 2 (Sacramento, 1915), pp. 98, 99. The disputed law in effect disqualified judges from sitting in juvenile court after three years. See "New Juvenile Act Ties Court's Hands," the San Francisco *Examiner*, September 6, 1913, p. 4; also the San Francisco *Call*, June 1913, p. 3.

I sincerely trust no attempt will be made to prescribe the exact processes that the court should follow in these cases. The legislature should lay down the essentials which are to govern. That ground has generally been covered . . . beyond that the legislature should not circumscribe the exercise of judicial authority in these cases.[25]

Cast in a mediating role, the board of Charities and Corrections arranged a series of conferences, north and south, seeking to bring order into the bedlam of voices and find some common meeting-ground for the clashing views on court jurisdiction and procedure. The conferences seem to have succeeded in their aims:

> Misunderstandings were explained and differences harmonized so that the bill presented to the legislature [1915] passed with very little modification (and) met as nearly as was humanly possible the needs and desires of all juvenile court workers.[26]

The legislation of 1915 completed the heavy-labored birth of California's first juvenile court law, which then prevailed until 1961. Whether the legislation in fact resolved differences or whether the conflict died away for other reasons cannot be determined. Perhaps the struggles had a therapeutic effect by allowing accommodations to be made in which a *modus vivendi* with the law was crystallized. Perhaps formal acceptance stemmed from a more relaxed attitude toward the law, based on the discovery that parts of it could be or would be ignored without penalty. In any event, the law of 1915 left wide areas open for differences of interpretation and the growth of divergent practices.

DIVERGENT EVOLUTION

In the first decade of the century that saw the juvenile court brought into being, California was like a vast hinterland with a

25. *Transactions of the Commonwealth Club of California*, Vol. V, 1910, p. 248.
26. Seventh Biennial Report, 1916, p. 12ff.

scattered population of low density, concentrated in and around
the two large urban centers at San Francisco and Los Angeles.
Forty-nine of the state's fifty-eight counties had less than 50,000
people. Arrayed in sharp contrast to these were Los Angeles, with
504,000 people, San Francisco, with 416,000, and Alameda, with
264,000. Between these extremes, there were only six counties that
could boast of populations between 50,000 and 100,000. Social life
was still very much peculiar to locality; urban-rural differences
were very marked, as were the social and cultural contrasts between San Francisco and Los Angeles. No two counties were alike
in size, geographic accessibility, economic base, or cultural tradition.

Problems of child welfare were by no means lacking in the
hinterland areas of the state, but they had a special quality of
their own. Their nature and relation to the contingencies of an
extractive economy were poignantly described by a state children's agent:

> A vast deal of the state is still untouched by railroads . . . yet much of
> the most significant and important life of the state is carried on in
> remote communities. By the very nature of the occupation which
> they offer, their problem of orphaned children is frequently high.
> The lumber camp, the mine, the dredger, have all offered up a toll
> of families deprived of husband and father. The dry ranch . . . and
> little mountain farm . . . have afforded meager substance . . . out of
> question when the man is gone and a broken woman is left alone
> with a brood of little people. Deserted mining towns still have a
> residuum of small prospectors [and] when such a man dies he leaves
> a family stranded.[27]

One gets the impression that child problems in these areas
were more likely to be defined in terms of dependency and
neglect, rather than delinquency. As in San Francisco, those
administering state aid to children in remote counties were concerned lest it encourage immorality in homes, and there were
times when agents refused aid, causing children to be sent to the
juvenile court. However, the issue of immorality of mothers was

27. Children's Agent Report, p. 8.

muted by the absence of relief organizations for investigation, and by considerable tolerance among county supervisors, as well as an anti-bureaucratic attitude that was specifically critical of "overvisiting" recipients of state aid.

Development of juvenile courts was most rapid in the three large counties, where they took form and meaning from the special child-welfare problems dramatically demonstrated in cities. A considerable portion of these were generated by large populations of children, one or both of whose parents were foreign-born.[28] In part, childhood problems of the day inhered in the adverse conditions of city life, in part they were created by societal definitions stemming from higher standards of health, housing, school attendance, and parental supervision. Furthermore, the urban areas had numerous organized groups actively supporting or promoting advances in child care and protection, and unlike their rural counterparts, they had more organized services and funds available for those purposes. In a sense they could afford to have such problems.

Aside from the generalized urban-rural contrasts, differences in the development of juvenile courts in California counties are difficult to reduce to any common tendency. Divergent evolution took many forms, but the more important differentiation appeared in the form and use made of probation, in conceptions of detention, and in functions assigned or assumed by probation committees. By 1908, fourteen counties had probation officers giving attention to juveniles. Twelve years later, all but three sparsely populated counties had such officers; however, only thirty-one of these were serving full time. Part-time workers received ten to seventy dollars a month. Further evidence of a frugal hand in the provision of probation service is indicated by the fact that in fifteen counties the officers wore more than

28. As recent as 1934, 41 per cent of youths admitted to the Whittier school were foreign-born, or native-born of foreign or mixed parentage. J. H. Williams, "Early History of the California Bureau of Juvenile Research," *Journal of Juvenile Research*, XVIII (1934), 199; for data on these special problems see Pauline Young, *Pilgrims of Russian Town*, (Chicago: University of Chicago Press, 1932), pp. 195–220.

one official hat, i.e., served in other county offices at the same time.[29]

As late as 1929, three counties still had not hired probation officers, whereas in other counties they were full-time employees. This becomes less impressive, however, when one considers that only a small minority could claim professional training. Even by 1928 almost two-thirds of the Los Angeles County probation officers had other than social-work training or experience, including such occupations as barber, elevator operator, meter inspector, cleaning and pressing operator, and U.S. Marine.[30]

Little consistency could be discovered among counties in the location and use of detention facilities during the first decades of , juvenile court history. Many counties used detention homes as orphanages. In 1920 an inquiry by the board of Charities and Corrections disclosed that sixteen counties had detention homes, six relied on privately subsidized homes, nine placed children in rooms in the county hospital, one customarily sent children to a detention home in another county, and twenty-two were in the process of building detention homes.[31] In those counties where jails and hospitals made do as places of detention, segregation from older criminals and undesirable adults was not or could not be realized.

Confusion over the functions of probation committees has been endemic in California from early times up to the present. The first probation committee evolved from the action groups that agitated to establish a juvenile court in Los Angeles. These groups later emerged as a committee to raise funds for the salaries of the first probation officers.[32] Subsequently this committee turned into an advisory board, and ultimately came to administer the juvenile hall. The law of 1915 envisioned that committees like these would investigate organizations through which children were to be placed, visit wards of the court, and recommend appointments of probation officers. Actually, many

29. Ninth Biennial Report, 1920, p. 119.
30. W. Turney Fox, "Fiftieth Anniversary of the Juvenile Court in California," *California Youth Authority Quarterly* 6 (1953), 6.
31. Ninth Biennial Report, p. 119.
32. McKibbon, *op. cit.*, pp. 23–4.

supporters of the movement for a juvenile court, including some judges, had expected much of the court's work to be assigned to probation committees. Although the law fell short of this expectation, some judges proceeded to delegate a considerable share of the court's responsibilities to the committees anyway.

> Unfortunately the act gives but little power to the committee beyond the nominating of a probation officer, and the visiting of certain charitable institutions. It has but little force . . . In Santa Clara county, however, the Judge of the Juvenile Court has given the probation committee some of the powers of the Juvenile Court, and the committee has taken hold of the cases that have come under its observation in a manner that has given great results.[33]

In contrast, some counties never appointed probation committees. Where they were organized, their activities had little to give them a common stamp. Some committees reported cases in need; some dealt with cases of truancy; some searched for placement homes; and some obtained clothing and other items for court wards. Still others, such as the Santa Clara committee, undertook hearings and made dispositions, members in effect becoming court workers. In counties where children were placed through an agency, there was little need of a committee to investigate, while courts in counties making placements in different parts of the state could scarcely expect the task of investigation to be carried out by a lay committee.[34] By 1921 the provisions of the law for probation committees were recognized as vague and ill-conceived directives.

> Reports of probation committees and conferences with many members of these committees indicate that their activities and interpretation of their responsibilities as defined by law varies widely in different counties . . . they feel their duties are too vaguely defined by law and . . . in rural communities they are asking for a definite program.[35]

33. M. H. Hyland, "Juvenile Court Methods of Santa Clara County," *Preston School Outlook*, VII (1909), 3–11.
34. "Juvenile Court Work in California" (anon.), *Preston School Outlook*, VII (1909), 3–11.
35. Ninth Biennial Report, p. 117.

Round-table conferences held in Los Angeles and San Francisco in February 1921 on "Functions of Juvenile Probation Committees in Smaller Counties" did nothing to clarify the law. The fruitless sessions only added to a general sense of futility among Charities and Corrections board people, who were seeking to bring practices in line with the law. Their report for that year concluded:

> Every county in California is a law unto itself in social matters and there is a wide diversity in understanding and administering county problems affecting dependents and delinquents.[36]

THE QUEST FOR UNIFORMITY THROUGH ADMINISTRATIVE CONTROL

In 1929 the supervision of both adult and juvenile probation, to the extent the law allowed, was assigned to the new Department of Welfare, marking a new phase in efforts to bring consistency to juvenile court procedures in California's far-flung counties. Prior to this time the board of Charities and Corrections had worked to establish state controls over child placement and adoption. The first laws passed on these matters in 1903 lacked clarity, and were not fully corrected until 1913, at which time the licensing of placement agencies and boarding homes became powers of the board.[37] In actual practice, however, the system of licensing evolved in an asymmetrical fashion, combining state inspection, inspection by licensed agencies, and inspection delegated to local health authorities.[38]

Placements of children from juvenile court occupied a special, privileged position, for the law of 1903 did not require a judge to place children in licensed homes. Nor did this become mandatory until 1929. However, placement remained, and even today

---

36. *Ibid.*, p. 119; for a later view on the spurious nature of probation committees, see Vaughn D. Bornet, *California Social Welfare* (New York: Prentice-Hall, 1956) , pp. 102–04.
37. Cahn and Bary, *op. cit.*, 25ff.
38. *Ibid.*, p. 31.

remains, an area where the scarcity of available homes favors administrative expediency over compliance with statute. Noncompliance with the law also feeds from conflicting values and judgments as to what is an acceptable home. Sporadic cold war goes on between court workers and social welfare administrators, in which pressures of the situation and locally formed opinions clash with state-imposed standards.

METHODS OF CONTROL

Both the board of Charities and Corrections and its successor, the Department of Welfare, leaned heavily on individual contacts, and local and state conferences and institutes, in their search for a common foundation of practice among those administering the juvenile court law. Behind these methods lay a conviction that discussion would lead to a working consensus, which would cause judges and probation officers to modify day-to-day operations in line with objectives outlined in the law. Only once does the harsh note of coercion sound in a board report, in 1926, when a sharp rise in the number of children being held in jail prompted a general warning: "The Board will seek to enforce the law." [39]

Under the administration of juvenile probation by the Department of Welfare, attempts at control through conferences and published reports were continued. Communication with probation officers was further amplified through the monthly publication of *Probation News*. This proved to be little more than a bulletin whose news items and comments were pervaded by the values and ideology espoused in the rising field of social work. At the same time, the *News* struck a much more legalistic note than was true in the older Charities and Corrections board reports. The attention of probation officers was regularly directed to appellate court decisions and Attorney General opinions bearing on the juvenile court, and occasionally the items

39. Report of State Board of Charities and Corrections (1922–26), Sacramento, 1926, p. 161.

took sharp, didactic form, more or less instructing workers on procedures required by law.

A kind of editorial prodding to conform with juvenile court statutes was inserted in most copies of the *News* under the caption "Lest We Forget." These reminders, a little like housekeeping maxims, probed a number of critical areas where local practice fell short of statutory requirements:

(1) continuing detention of children in jails;

(2) detention without a court order;

(3) necessity of investigation, written reports, and presence of the probation officer in court when findings and dispositions were made;

(4) requirement of closed hearings;

(5) segregation of minors from "persons of evil influence";

(6) recording and reporting of reimbursements to the county by parents for costs of maintaining wards;

(7) submission of annual reports.

The more direct and positive policy toward standards for juvenile court work and probation began to be asserted by the Department of Welfare almost from the first. The director of the department articulated their position in an address before members of the National Probation Association in 1929:

> The object of the State's participation is to give delinquents and potential delinquents an opportunity to be kept out of the criminal class . . . regardless of the remoteness of the communities in which they live, or the lack of social understanding of local authorities.[40]

Despite these strong words, no legal action ever was taken by the department against errant probation officers. Perhaps the reason was that although probation officers had been held by legal opinion to be county officers, in reality they were agents of the court; to attack them would be to attack the local judge.[41] During the 1930's, department policy drifted away from the idea that local probation officers could be educated to a "better understanding

40. Cited in "Proposed State Probation Systems," *Transactions of the Commonwealth Club of California*, XXX, No. 8, Part 2 (San Francisco, 1936) , p. 309.

41. See Nichol v. Koster, 157 Cal. 416 (1910); Gibson v. Civil Service Commission of Los Angeles, 27 Cal. App. 396 (1915) .

of what their job is." A plan for a state system of probation, founded on an earlier endorsement of the idea by the California Probation Officers Association, took hold, and agitation was begun to convert it into law in 1936. The plan (or plans, for there were two) included the attractive offer of badly needed financial help to counties from the state treasury. However, as might have been anticipated, this movement ended in failure, foundering on the issue as to whether probation workers should be state officers or agents of the county court. An ominous section in one of the proposals would have made officers who failed to comply with applicable rules of the probation commission guilty of a misdemeanor. Opposition from smaller and nonurban counties was too much to overcome; the legislation did not materialize. The commentary of the State Supervisor of Probation, who favored the milder of the two plans, is rueful testimony to the political strength of counties and to the localism that finally blocked acceptance of either proposal:

> If the doctrine of State's Rights has been sacred in the South, the doctrine of county rights is more sacred here.[42]

RISE OF THE SUPERAGENCY FOR YOUTH

The struggle to make juvenile court procedures more uniform and consistent with law in large part was submerged by the sweeping socio-economic changes of the depression years of the 1930's and by the nation's entry into World War II. The wholesale assumption of many local welfare services by the federal and state governments, along with changes in economic organizations, moved American society rapidly toward the form of an administrative state, whose growth was speeded by the postwar rise of militarism, American style. Among the many lusty offspring of the administrative state in California was the California Youth Authority, brought forth by legislative action in 1941.

The main purpose of the C.Y.A., as it came to be called, was social protection—"to protect society by substituting training and

42. "Proposed State Probation Systems," *loc. cit.*, p. 318.

treatment for retributive punishment of young persons found guilty of public offenses." [43]

While the legislation was vague as to the specific means by which this protection was to be accomplished, it generally proposed that criminal courts commit youthful offenders under twenty-three (later lowered to twenty-one), to an administrative authority with fulsome delegated powers, rather than dispatching them directly to prison. In contrast to this direct mandate to adult courts, juvenile courts were given discretionary power to commit cases to the C.Y.A. Broad support for the over-all correctional innovation came from a growing appreciation that rate-wise the crime problem was primarily a problem of youth and young adults, a fact no less true in California than in the nation. In addition, many counties were concerned over the heavy increases in referrals to juvenile courts, made critical by a shortage of local detention and clinical facilities. More generally, it was recognized that the state had lagged far behind in its penology programs, in the construction of correctional facilities, and in the recruitment and training of correctional workers.

Instituting the C.Y.A. was a major move toward administrative justice, for the court was relieved of much of the authority to commit young offenders to state institutions. Members of the board of the C.Y.A. could consider cases without strictures of legal procedure—set sentences or "terms," as well as order institutional and other forms of treatment. The delegated powers were unquestionably broad, and opened the door for policy considerations to affect directly the disposition of cases. That the creation of such powers would have a strong impact on the juvenile courts was less apparent at first than it was later, and even then, it was more a matter of growth and circumstance than it was of a plan.

Inspiration for the C.Y.A. stemmed from the Model Act, incorporating recommendations by the American Law Institute, published in 1937.[44] However, the California legislature de-

43. Report on California Laws Relating to Youthful Offenders (C.Y.A.) , Sacramento, 1965, p. 75.
44. Youth Correction Authority Act, American Law Institute, 1940.

parted from the Model in several important ways, two of which had direct bearing on the juvenile courts, as noted. Instead of making commitments mandatory above a specified age, California lawmakers decided they should be optional, leaving it a matter of joint jurisdiction between juvenile courts and the C.Y.A. Consequently, judges could commit youths to the C.Y.A. and then, if they so wished, order them discharged. On its side, the C.Y.A. could accept or refuse cases, and also after acceptance, if deemed appropriate, send youths back to their communities. The second variance from the Model Act was to keep probation within the local courts, the juvenile court included, rather than to convert it into a state-controlled system.

The qualified use of the Model Act indicates that the legislature trod much more carefully in the area of juvenile court jurisdiction than of the adult courts, for commitment to the C.Y.A. was not and did not become mandatory, although the right of a juvenile court judge to revoke a commitment once made was later eliminated. The court's local autonomy also was reaffirmed by explicitly worded statutes:

> Nothing in this chapter [Act] shall be deemed to interfere with or limit the jurisdiction of the juvenile court.[45]

Or again:

> Nothing in this section [1737] shall limit or restrict the jurisdiction and powers of the juvenile court under sections 775 and 779 [power to committal orders] of this code.[46]

THE C.Y.A. SEEKS CONTROL

The C.Y.A. Act and its subsequent amendments, while deliberately staying the hand of the state in juvenile court matters, nevertheless assigned certain limited powers of control to the C.Y.A. director. These consisted of the authority to require re-

---

45. *California Statutes* (1941) , Chap. 937, Art. 1704, p. 2523.
46. *Op. cit.* (1963) , Chap. 443, Art. 1737.

ports from the courts, to inspect juvenile halls and county camps benefiting from the C.Y.A. or state subsidies, to set standards for juvenile detention, and to formulate standards for probation work. Significantly, however, these powers were never employed, at least not coercively. Instead they were subordinated to a policy of co-operation that more or less became the official ideology of the C.Y.A. In effect, if not intent, these powers became a foundation for co-optative methods through which the organization sought to achieve its goals, methods that evolved primarily from work done by the Division of Field Services.

While co-operation was specifically encouraged by the C.Y.A. statutes, its widespread application was a virtue fathered by necessity. Shortly after the launching of the C.Y.A. as a going concern, the public learned of serious problems at the Whittier State School for Boys. Numerous runaways from the institution and two dramatic suicides, capped by seven different superintendents in one year, made it painfully clear that something had to be done about this long-time trouble spot and others in the state's nexus of reform schools. After considerable public agitation, including an Assembly Interim Committee investigation, Governor Warren in 1942 asked the C.Y.A. to take on the administration of the three youth correctional schools (Whittier, Preston, Ventura).[47]

In retrospect, it appears that this single action did more than any other to complicate, or even make impossible, the realization of the C.Y.A.'s goal of individualizing the treatment of youth. The reasons lie outside the scope of this study, but suffice it to say that the need to support and administer existing institutions, as well as construct new ones, soon established budgetary priority for the Division of Institutions, and came to occupy the largest share of time, energies, and attention of administrators and staff. Recruitment practices, in-training programs, and job assignments tended to preserve a custodial pat-

---

47. Karl Holton, "Youth Correction Authority in Action: the California Experience," *Law and Contemporary Problems* 9 (1942), 653–66; Albert Deutsch, *Our Rejected Children* (Boston: Little Brown, 1952), pp. 108ff; John R. Ellingston, *Protecting Our Children from Criminal Careers* (New York: Prentice-Hall, 1948), p. 62ff.

tern of action within the Division of Institutions, despite the
C.Y.A.'s informal dedication and official allegiance to the purposes of individualized treatment.[48]

The C.Y.A. sought its objectives with both formal and informal means, including carefully organized conferences and
committees. In formulating standards for juvenile halls and for
probation work, the C.Y.A. director appointed committees of
judges, probation officers, juvenile hall superintendents, and
others to decide on criteria, rules, and preferred procedures;
these recommendations were then compiled in reports and later
published in brochures, which were distributed to juvenile court
workers throughout the state.[49] Problems that arose from the
overlapping jurisdiction of the C.Y.A. and the juvenile courts
were met in a similar fashion. For example, in 1955, judges were
brought together to discuss the long delays (30 to 120 days in
some counties) between court commitments and C.Y.A. accept-
ances of the youths. As a result of the meetings, many judges
began to grant probation in cases that previously would have
been sent to the C.Y.A. The conferences succeeded so well that
the C.Y.A. was soon embarrassed to find itself with empty beds,
and was compelled to modify its policy.[50]

CONTROLS FROM WITHIN—THE CALIFORNIA
PROBATION, PAROLE, AND CORRECTIONAL
OFFICERS ASSOCIATION

Another indirect but nonetheless formal method for swaying
the course of action in juvenile courts lay in the partial co-
optation of the California Probation, Parole, and Correctional
Officers Association (C.P.P.C.A.), particularly through its leadership, which has come mainly from chief probation officers. The
relationship between this association and the C.Y.A. has been

48. Robert Lee Smith, "Youth and Correction: An Institutional of the California Youth Authority," M.A. thesis, University of California, Berkeley, 1955.
49. Heman Stark, "Standards for Juvenile Halls," *Federal Probation* XXIV
(1960), 35–41.
50. Robert L. Smith, *op. cit.*, p. 64.

undeniably close and interdependent. First, a large number of C.Y.A. workers have been recruited from among probation officers, and second, the C.Y.A. is regarded by many of them as one of their main channels for professional advancement. Another explanation for the intimate organizational tie is the obvious common interests shared by local juvenile court personnel with C.Y.A. parole and field workers, and the considerable direct communication they have with each other. Promotion of C.Y.A. values also is achieved through training institutes held for probation officers and determining the content of programs and discussions of the association members at state-wide meetings. C.Y.A. staff people may exert their influence in a more formal way as well, securing the adoption of official resolutions or committee reports at these meetings.

The C.P.P.C.A., of course, has not been merely a front organization for the C.Y.A., because influences are mutual, and, as shown, the co-operative policy of the latter has been carefully maintained. Probation officers seldom if ever complain that C.Y.A. officials dominate their association, but they have on occasion ruefully observed that its voice tends to be that of probation officers from the larger counties of the state, who are closely bound in various ways to the C.Y.A. Furthermore, regional chapters of the association have held meetings at which the C.Y.A. has often been notably absent. Finally, a reclusive contingent of probation officers, like absent members of the English House of Lords in its later days, have never attended meetings of the association.

The participation of probation officers in affairs of the association turns very much on large-county, small-county differences. Probation officers in larger counties, where there are several or rotating judges, are much more independent, hence freer to co-operate with the C.Y.A. Those in smaller counties often have been beholden to a single judge or long tenure, as well as to county supervisors, who frequently have a personal or proprietary attitude toward the probation department. A probation officer bearing home word of the latest practices advocated at association meetings may meet with less than enthusiasm on their part. This is one reason why the C.Y.A. has attempted to obtain changes through convening conferences of judges from time to time. However, as will be seen, judges do not always lend themselves as well to co-optation as probation officers.

INFORMAL CONTROLS—THE SERVICE APPROACH

C.Y.A. field workers come into direct contact with juvenile courts in connection with commitments of youth, parole supervision, recommitments, and inspection of juvenile halls and county camps. The parole officer has no formal status in the court, but he does have some informal power to shape decisions made there, chiefly as a local interpreter of the probable disposition of a youth after he has been committed. Some judges have been willing to send their charges to the C.Y.A. only on the assurance that they will be handled in a certain way. Other judges and probation officers have adhered to a "we-take-care-of-our-own" attitude, or have looked on the C.Y.A. as a last resort. Moreover, certain judges and police have regarded the C.Y.A.'s facilities simply as means for removing a persistent trouble-maker from the community, and strongly resist his return. Difficulties pile up for the parole officer whenever a youth is paroled directly from the Reception Center after a short stay, in effect being granted probation previously denied him in the juvenile court. This, of course, may reflect unfavorably on the wisdom of the judge or the probation officer, and may stir up antipathy among the local police. Thus the C.Y.A. parole officer has frequently been a passive, rather than active, influence on the juvenile court, particularly when he attempted to speak for the board before cases had reached it. When this practice came to be recognized in its full implications, C.Y.A. administrators took steps to end it.[51]

The policy of co-operation with youth agencies in local areas, as well as the mediating role of the C.Y.A. necessarily assumed by field people, has meant that relatively little effort has been made to urge local judges and probation officers to comply with

51. *Ibid.*, p. 76; see also Paul J. McKusick, "The Youth Authority Will . . . ," *California Youth Authority Bulletin* 2 (1949), 24.

the juvenile court law as such. Instead, the emphasis has been on discovering oblique ways to raise standards through the widest and fullest possible acceptance of C.Y.A. "programs." Some of these have been sought in plans requiring new legislation, others in schemes devised and promoted with means immediately available to the C.Y.A. State subsidization, unsuccessfully pushed by the Department of Welfare in earlier years, eventually was achieved under C.Y.A. auspices by converting it into an optional, matched-funds plan, and confining its uses to the construction of county camps and juvenile halls.[52] This form of subsidy has been effective in larger counties having richer sources of taxation, or where several counties have had enough common interests or the geographic unity to permit a jointly operated camp.

It would be wrong to leave the impression that C.Y.A. people have been unconcerned with laws and legislation that might bring uniformity to juvenile court procedures. However, the pressing need for a budget to support the C.Y.A.'s Division of Institutions has meant that where the choice has had to be made between upgrading juvenile court operation through new legislation and maintaining dominant organizational interests, the latter has prevailed. The subservience of field workers to local community opinion argued for caution in urging change in juvenile court procedure by coercive legal means. It may also explain why the C.Y.A. has made itself felt in legislation impinging upon the juvenile court primarily through other organizations, such as the C.P.P.C.A., the Governor's Advisory Committee on Youth, and special commissions of the legislature.

SURVEYS AND RECOMMENDATIONS

A final noteworthy technique by which the C.Y.A. sought to give new directions to juvenile court work grew out of early surveys conducted by the organization's Field Services Division. These studies became an integral part of delinquency preven-

52. Report on Standards for Juvenile Halls (C.Y.A.), 1958; Report on California Laws Relating to Youthful Offenders (C.Y.A.), 1963, pp. 44–47.

tion and probation consultation services, and, in keeping with the policy theme of co-operation, were initiated on invitation from county supervisors, judges, probation officers, and juvenile justice commissions. The first surveys tended to be broad inquiries into a wide gamut of activities of local agencies: law enforcement, traffic courts, juvenile court, probation, schools, and recreation. Subsequently, however, the surveys changed into more specialized evaluations or assessments, particularly with regard to probation services.

Ordinarily, the C.Y.A. was brought in for a survey when local agencies had a particular purpose in mind, such as increasing the number or salary of probation officers. While these goals readily fit in with the C.Y.A.'s conception of service, the opportunity to use the surveys to detect court or probation procedures inferior to C.Y.A. standards, and to recommend specific changes, was readily exploited. Recommendations at first tended to be couched in the didactic manner of items in the old *Probation News*. Later surveys became much more professional in tone, not unlike management-consultation reports.

The *C.Y.A. Quarterly*, which in a sense is the collateral descendant of the *Probation News*, has provided a media to bring current ideas to the attention of probation officers, judges, and court workers. Even though a house organ, the *Quarterly* draws contributions from many people in the judicial and correctional fields, as well as from others only indirectly concerned with the juvenile courts. Articles may be solicited with a general purpose in mind, but only on occasion are they written to advance special C.Y.A. views. The C.Y.A. also from time to time publishes reports, guides, and information brochures—among them, *Rights and Liabilities of Minors* and *Juvenile Court Petitions*—as well as the biennial *California Laws Relating to Youthful Offenders*.[53] These and other publications are distributed in the service tradition, but undoubtedly also with the hope that less compliant judges and probation officers will read them and change their ways.

53. Warren E. Thornton, Report on Rights and Liabilities of Minors (C.Y.A.), 1964; Thomas A. McGee, Report on Juvenile Court Petitions (C.Y.A.), 1966.

It is difficult to say just how much and in what ways facts brought to light by the C.Y.A. surveys have affected its policies, decisions, and action with reference to the juvenile court law. It is, however, significant that the Field Services administrator in charge of the first surveys, Heman Stark, later became director of the C.Y.A. itself. What can be said with certainty is that the surveys for the first time made available specific information on how juvenile courts, probation departments, and local law enforcement affected youth in a large number of counties.[54] This information was accumulated and filed with a state organization charged with a large measure of responsibility for youth problems in the state. Furthermore, this organization, the C.Y.A., exercised a great deal of political, if not legal, power, and increasingly came to be seen by legislators as one of the main channels of communication with juvenile courts of the state. In effect, an organizational mechanism now existed that greatly raised the social visibility of juvenile court practices throughout the state.

54. By 1948, surveys had been conducted in thirty-two counties and five cities. Reports on Program and Progress (C.Y.A.), 1948, p. 115.

3
The Transformation of Informal Justice

The advent of the C.Y.A. took on historic importance for juvenile justice in California primarily from its function as a clearinghouse and center for the accumulation and organization of opinion about the diverse juvenile courts of the state. Otherwise, its policies and programs, as well as the more remote influences from the U.S. Children's Bureau and the National Probation and Parole Association, were no more than marginal or peripheral forces in the later evolution of these courts. Juvenile court growth remained essentially local in nature. Much, if not most, of the development of these courts during the 1940's and 1950's resulted from day-to-day decision-making, informal interaction, and accommodations that took place within local communities and county areas. The aggregate record of these crescive growths came to light in the previously mentioned C.Y.A. surveys, probation services studies, a survey conducted by the *Stanford Law Review,* and several special commission studies by the legislature. The most comprehensive survey was made by the juvenile justice commission, whose recommendations led to the revision of the law in 1961.

THE PERSISTENCE OF INFORMAL JUSTICE

The surveys alluded to above offer striking proof that the great diversity of juvenile court procedures so characteristic of California counties in early decades did not diminish with passing time and, if anything, grew apace. They also illustrate the many ways in which juvenile justice continued to be administered informally by law enforcement people, such as sheriffs' deputies, police, prosecuting attorneys, and minor court justices, as well as by probation officers and judges. At the same time, these studies reflect the radical changes taking place in the social contexts of informal justice, in some cases appearing as contrasts between juvenile justice in "old" and "new" communities, in others as contrasts between old and new practices within the same community.

Informal justice as it pertained to juveniles in the earlier history of California tended to express the *gemeinschaft* qualities, of the local community, its social isolation, centripetal social interaction, and the dispersed authority of its law enforcement officers. While time and change have eroded much of these away, residues persist and still mold police practices in many localities. In some sense they even become a nostalgic ideal for the policing of juveniles in modern settings. According to a C.Y.A. police consultant:

> In many a small community the police are still able to develop considerable personal relationships with and understanding of youth problems; the chief of police, sheriff, or other officers handle each youth who has committed a law violation individually, usually with considerable knowledge of the child's background, his parents and the community. Not so in the large community. Specialized juvenile units staffed with officers interested in and specially trained to handle youth have been developed. These specialized units are endeavoring to supplant the old-time policeman and his community understanding, and to maintain the traditional attitude of police towards helping juveniles.[1]

As late as 1945, preference for the informal handling of juvenile offenders was not only commonly recognized in some counties; it was even a matter of some pride:

1. John P. Kenney, "The Police and Youth," *California Youth Authority* 2 (1949), 14.

In this county (Glenn) it is possible to handle many juvenile matters informally without always strictly following the laws of [probation] department procedure.

A number of factors explain why law agents and court workers in California counties with small, relatively stable populations, often dominated by ranchers and agriculturalists, have leaned heavily toward informality in dealing with juvenile problems. Such officials not infrequently are part of a web of reciprocal social and economic relationships that may involve parents, relatives, and friends of youths coming to their attention. The fact that "word gets around" and that law agents have to "live with" or face these people daily inclines them to handle youth gingerly or to be sincerely concerned with keeping the youth and his family from embarrassment and avoidable difficulty. Furthermore, in some areas the detached residence of sheriffs' deputies more or less requires that they be judges as well as policemen. The sheriff himself, as an elective official, is usually more interested in serving people and keeping peace between them than in making arrests. There are also indications that cultural differences dispose police and probation officers in ranch and agricultural counties to greater tolerance for youthful deviance along certain lines than is true for urban areas. Paradoxically, there is also a tendency for people in these communities to be more punitive than their urban counterparts when they do take formal action, or when certain kinds of offenses are committed.[2]

When communities in smaller counties do resort to formal procedures with punitive objectives, there is a kind of generic informality underlying the action. By this is meant that frequently the action arises from community-wide moral indignation, or from crises in which important individuals, families, or agricultural associations have an interest. In these instances the

2. In northern or mountain counties, residents tend to overlook drinking, fighting, and sexual experimentation by boys. On the other hand, if they damage expensive ranch equipment or shoot or steal cattle, the reaction is apt to be a strong one. This plus the lack of probation services may explain why in early years juvenile first offenders from these counties were sometimes sent to reform school. Preston School of Industry, Twelfth Biennial Report, Ione, 1916, p. 41.

juvenile hearing seems to serve as a purposeful dramatization of conflicting local values that would be difficult to resolve in other ways. In one county it was common practice to call the prosecuting attorney in as a symbolic act. The probation officer explained that this was done because of "the formal air it gives to filing the petition," and because "It's a good thing to have the prosecuting attorney present in cases where parents of the juvenile engage an attorney."

It is difficult to say surely how many California counties are or have been generally disposed to informal procedures with juvenile offenders, or just how they are differentiated from other counties. However, one study concludes that some counties do differ significantly from others on this score, and also that a preference for informal procedures is negatively associated with rates of commitments to the C.Y.A.[3]

INFORMAL JUSTICE BECOMES ADMINISTRATIVE JUSTICE

Informal justice may be a function of small community size, relative isolation, and the fact that people who are in direct, continuous interaction must compromise, bargain, and mutually respect each other's claims and pretensions to status. However, it is equally true that informality is an attribute of administrative justice operating from a more impersonal organized base.[4] This became more and more obvious in the course of juvenile justice in California after 1940. It might even be said that informality was inherent in the rapid growth and socio-economic change within the state. The nature of the changing "functional necessities" can be stated only speculatively, and they properly call for a separate study. However, it is fairly plain that the new demands were closely associated with population growth within

3. Joachim P. Seckel and Stuart Adams, "A Study of Six California Counties with Atypical Juvenile Court Commitment Rates," Research Report No. 17 (C.Y.A.), Sacramento, 1960.
4. For this hypothesis, see Peter Woll, *Administrative Law, the Informal Process* (Berkeley: University of California Press, 1963).

the state, which multiplied the number of youth coming into contact with the police and juvenile courts. The in-migrant nature of much of this population probably swelled disproportionately the number of first offenders entering the police-court network.[5] In addition, there was a great increase in the ownership and use of automobiles and a lowering of the minimum age for drivers' licenses, which contributed heavily to the flow of juvenile traffic offenders into the court. Many of these offenders were from middle-class, rather than lower-class, families. A final possible ingredient of change may have been the rapid attenuation of the family as a supervisory agency over children, possibly greater in California than elsewhere.

Changes having a more direct and discernible impact on the basis of juvenile justice must be sought in the structure and operation of law enforcement agencies themselves. The most significant of these changes was the rapid growth of police departments throughout the state, owing to technological as well as population growth. The jurisdictions of urban police departments were expanded to include new areas as more places became incorporated. At the same time, police agencies were undergoing specialization and departmentalization. Sheriffs' departments likewise underwent changes; they became more departmentalized, and resident deputies gave way to those patrolling by cruiser car and telephone, much in the fashion of urban police. State police also expanded into new areas and activities. An important consequence of this expansion has been the spreading influence of the organizational traditions of the police, who, in contrast to sheriffs' men and constabularies, have historically been more subordinate, more subject to discipline, and less discretionary in their patterns of action. Police have been more answerable to centralized control, and in recent times often expected to carry out a bureaucratically determined department policy.[6]

5. Seckel and Adams, *op. cit.* p. 11.

6. It has been stated that incorporation of areas has often been the result of local desires for better police protection than sheriffs' departments can supply. Gordon Misner, "Recent Developments in the Metropolitan Law Enforcement," *Journal of Criminal Law and Criminology* 50 (1959–60) , 505.

POLICE VALUES AND POLICE POLICY

While the police are sometimes pictured as ruthless tyrants
rounding up defenseless children for arrest, the C.Y.A. community studies prove otherwise. They reveal that small-town
police, sheriffs' deputies, California highway patrolmen—even
metropolitan police—fully value the need to "give youth a break"
or "let him have a second chance." Perhaps even more than
social workers, police have appreciated the undesirable consequences of arrest, fingerprinting, and giving youngsters a "record." Furthermore, it is obvious that arresting young children
is hardly a feat that adds to a policeman's status, either in the
community or within his department.

As police departments become more bureaucratized, they tend
to clarify and order their values, and the individual policeman
must give his allegiance to this value order regardless of his
particular values or inclinations. Special bureaus within the
department necessarily become subordinated to other bureaus
or the whole. Ordinarily, where they exist, juvenile bureaus are
closely connected with detective bureaus, and may be effectually
subservient to their needs. The prevailing organization values
of urban police as a whole can be summed up as repression of
crime, maintaining of public order, and recovery of stolen property. In situations where values of child welfare and protection
conflict with police values, there is little question as to the order
in which they will be satisfied. In repressing crime, the urban
policeman frequently becomes something of an on-the-spot policy-
maker, but for reasons different from the deputy sheriff's in a rural
area. He does so because the large number of laws makes it impossible for him to arrest all violators. Hence he makes choices in
terms of what he thinks will best diminish crime in his area or
preserve order, within the limits of time and resources available.[7]
In the case of children his choices are complicated, because he is
expected to co-operate and support as best he can the values of the

7. Bruce Smith, "The Policeman's Art," in *Police Systems in the United
States,* rev. ed. (New York: Harper, 1960), pp. 16–26.

juvenile court and welfare agencies. The choice is more difficult when juvenile offenders fall within the fifteen- to seventeen-year age group, or when their acts touch sensitive public issues, such as gang violence. From this point of view, the creation of juvenile bureaus in police departments is an attempt to solve the policeman's dilemmas through specialization and administrative ordering of decision-making. A significant consequence is that the errant juvenile is much more likely to be "processed" in an organizational sense than is true in rural areas. The tendency to proceed by arrest and processing of juvenile offenders undoubtedly was stronger in cities and counties where police departments were becoming bureaucratized and their members professionalized. The Los Angeles Police Department was a conspicuous example of these trends after World War II. Establishing a separate juvenile bureau was more important than acquiring specialized police officers on the local force. This structure set decision-making apart informally as well as formally, diminishing interaction between juvenile officers and the rest of the force. Professional standards also lowered the likelihood that police would have any locality, friendship, or kinship ties with local populations.[8]

Whatever the major trends in the policing of juveniles in California, the procedures or discretionary lines of action avail-

8. Studies have indicated that professionalization of juvenile officers and establishment of juvenile bureaus are more advanced in Western states than in Eastern and New England states. Also, police departments in western cities have been less affected by strictures of old-style political machines based on reciprocities with ethnic or immigrant groups and are more oriented toward impersonal demands of middle-class suburban populations. See James Wilson, "The Police and the Delinquency in Two Cities," in *Controlling Delinquents*, ed. Stanton Wheeler (New York: John Wiley, 1968), pp. 9–30; George W. O'Connor and Nelson A. Watson, *Juvenile Delinquency and Youth Crime* (Washington, D.C.: International Association of Police Chiefs, 1964), pp. 78–9. Other literature on police and juveniles: Carl Werthman and Irving Piliavin, "Gang Members and the Police," in *The Police*, ed. David Bordua (New York: John Wiley, 1967), pp. 56–98; Irving Piliavin and Scott Briar, "Police Encounters with Juveniles," *American Journal of Sociology* LXX (1965), 209–11; Nathan Goldman, *The Differential Selection of Juvenile Offenders for Court Appearances* (Washington, D.C.: National Council on Crime and Delinquency, 1963); Aaron Cicourel, *The Social Organization of Juvenile Justice* (New York: John Wiley, 1968), Chaps. IV–VI.

able to the officers around 1945 were multiform. The possibilities were the following:

(1) Reprimand the youth, notify his or her parents, and dismiss the case in less serious or in first offenses. "Friendly supervision" in some cases.

(2) File a petition, particularly in cases of truancy and incorrigibility.

(3) Refer the juvenile to the prosecuting attorney, who could dismiss the case, adjust it informally, refer it to the probation officer, or issue a complaint preliminary to prosecution.

(4) Arrest the juvenile and bring him before a justice court or lower court, where he might be dismissed with a lecture, fined, sent to jail, or formally certified to the juvenile court, where filing a petition was mandatory.

The alternatives described here embrace the range of choice when California counties are considered as a whole. The extent of their use in different counties and their selection by various law persons were determined by the ends pursued by particular police departments, by the means available for reaching those ends, and finally by the cost of the means. Means were limited by county size, time and distance required for travel, numbers of juvenile cases needing attention, accessibility of probation officers and their attitudes toward police responsibilities, and, finally, the willingness of justice courts to assume responsibility for juvenile cases.

An important factor in transforming informal police handling of youthful wrongdoers has been the large size of many California counties and the geographic remoteness of many communities. Given these, an increase in the numbers of juvenile offenders resulted in discretionary informality on "policy" grounds, in which organizational values rather than "old-time policeman" values predominated.

The size of the county has resulted in a difference of policy by the juvenile court towards offenders in Riverside and those in outlying districts . . . with offenders living in outlying districts, the policy is to reduce the numbers of filings in juvenile court to a minimum. This means that local Peace Officers and Justices of the Peace exercise considerable discretion in dealing with juvenile offenders . . . local officers are reluctant to take action that will necessitate appearance in Riverside when some way can be found to dispose of the case without making the long trip to the county seat.[9]

POLICE PROBATION

When referrals of delinquent youth to a probation department were ruled out because of time-distance factors and heavy case loads of overworked probation officers, or because of strong local feeling that the community "should take care of its own," the police in a number of California areas turned to crude probation methods of their own, which came to be known as "informal supervision" or "handling within the department." In some towns this meant that the police chief talked with the youth and his parents, then released him. Here and there the police chief was assisted by a local juvenile council, to which he could refer such cases. Otherwise, youthful arrestees, with parental agreement, reported to the police at specified intervals with the understanding that formal action would be withheld.

The application of police supervision has varied considerably both between and within counties. Data collected by the juvenile justice commission in 1958–59 showed that approximately 30 per cent of police and sheriffs' departments serving populations of 25,000 or more reported the use of informal supervision of juveniles. The median number supervised was 25, with a range of 10 to 50.[10] Another survey, in 1957, listed twenty-three counties in which disposition was informal, mainly coastal counties, northern "cow counties," and several large agricultural counties to the south: Imperial, San Bernardino, and River-

9. Report on Delinquency and Youth Services in Riverside County (C.Y.A.), 1946. Signs that this statement may have been a justification for a kind of expediential informality are inferred from the increase in detention cases by 100 per cent from 1940 to 1944. In the same period, mileage reported by probation officers went up two-thirds.

10. I. J. Shain and Walter R. Burkhart, Report of the Governor's Special Study Commission on Juvenile Justice (Part II), Sacramento, 1960, p. 102.

side.[11] Communities within the same county varied a good deal in the proportion of juveniles handled by departmental supervision, as shown in Table 3.1.

Table 3.1. Police Disposition of Juvenile Arrests, Orange County, 1945[12]

Disposition	Town		
	Santa Ana	Fullerton	Anaheim
Advised and released	192	9	25
Voluntary supervision	105	6	35
Petitions	74	34	37
Total	371	49	97

Police probation in California seems to have originated between 1925 and 1930, generally coinciding with the establishment of juvenile bureaus in police and sheriffs' departments.[13] Some towns experimented with police supervision, then discontinued it, and there has been a decline in its attractiveness as an alternative disposition to release or referral. A peculiar disadvantage of police probation, apart from its divergence from salient police purposes, which may have accounted for its fluctuating use in the past and its controversial nature, arises from case failures or recidivism. Youth unresponsive to police supervision who turn into repeaters make for an awkward situation; on referral to the juvenile court, they are legally no more than first offenders. It is difficult for the probation officer to justify a harsh recommendation, especially if no adequate record of the youth's offenses is available. In some counties extensive reliance on police probation led the probation officer to file petitions routinely on all referrals. Hence it might be said that in such situations extensive informal justice led to more formality at a different stage in the processing of juveniles.

11. "The California Juvenile Court," *Stanford Law Review* 10 (1958), 471–524.

12. Report on Planning for Youth in Orange County (C.Y.A.), 1947, p. 55.

13. E. W. Biscaluz, "Responsibilities of a Sheriff for a Juvenile Delinquency Control Program," California Law Enforcement Officers Conference on Delinquency Control, Department of Justice, Sacramento, 1944, p. 15.

PROCEDURAL BYPASSES—CERTIFICATION

A number of reasons have been given to explain why the police in California have more or less pre-empted the right or power to administer justice to juveniles. For the most part, however, these apply to dispositions on the lenient side, dismissals, or informal surveillance. What line of action has been favored by the police in cases requiring more stringent or definitive action? Undoubtedly the choice of more professionalized probation officers and court workers has been referral, with the expectation that a petition would be filed. Customarily, however, in some counties police brought juvenile offenders before justices of the peace and local municipal courts. There they were lectured, put on probation, or even fined. They could also be certified to the juvenile court from these courts.

The police practice of turning offending juveniles into the lower courts was an adaptation to the growth in county populations after 1940, reflected in the heavier workloads of both police and probation officers, as well as in the crowded court calendars. Probably it was the only immediate means by which juvenile traffic offenses, which increased faster than population, could have been dealt with. So long as it was these and minor law violations in question, judges and probation officers, as well as the police, could justify the procedure to themselves and others. Legislation in 1945 more or less legalized the existing state of affairs in many areas by allowing juvenile court judges to appoint minor court judges, justices of the peace, and recorders as referees. A C.Y.A. inquiry in 1950 disclosed that fourteen of fifty reporting counties had appointed a total of ninety-one justices to serve as referees. Many of these tended to be mountain or cow counties. However, three counties—Fresno, Siskiyou, and Mendocino—accounted for fifty-four of the ninety-one referees.[14]

14. James York, "Justice of the Peace—Study Made of Referee Use," *California Youth Authority Quarterly* 3 (1950), 22–5; by 1958, lower court judges were being used as referees in twenty-eight counties, about half exclusively for traffic offenses. Report of Governor's Special Study Commission on Juvenile Justice, p. 28.

But population growth, work-load increases, and time-distance factors only partially explain why the police in a number of California counties brought juveniles into lower courts rather than to the juvenile court. In many areas, for example, the police sought to limit the discretion of probation officers in disposing of cases sent to them, particularly where youth were continuing sources of trouble in the community. Arresting these offenders led lower courts to certify them to the juvenile court, where filing a petition was mandatory. Older juveniles or those considered by the police to be unfit for juvenile court were sent to regular superior courts, where certification back to the juvenile court was unlikely if no one questioned the youth's age.[15]

A 1957 survey listed twenty-four counties that employed certification. Five of these bordered the coast, nine were heavily agricultural, and the largest number, ten, were mountain "cow counties." With the exception of Sacramento County, no county having a large urban center used certification. The method was used primarily for serious crimes; only in a few counties was it a routine practice.[16] In many less urbanized counties of California, differing conceptions of the minimum age of responsibility and a stronger punitive attitude for serious juvenile offenses, as well as administrative expediencies, lay behind the preference for certification. Differences of attitude were further emphasized by the usual reply from urban jurisdictions on the question of its use: "Never!"

INFORMAL PROBATION

If the police have administered justice informally in many areas of California, it has been equally true for probation officers. To some extent, informal probation is a function that inheres in

15. Failure to determine the age of youth appearing in superior courts may have been related to an older, long-standing practice whereby judges distinguished between "judicial age" and actual age so as to send older youth to the reform school at Preston rather than to prison, much to the discomfiture of its superintendent. Preston School of Industry, Thirteenth Biennial Report, Ione, 1918, p. 21.

16. "The California Juvenile Court," loc. cit.

the probation officer's power to file or not file a petition. In all likelihood, it evolved out of the practice of granting continuances and the willingness of many judges with juvenile court assignments in the past to delegate much of their authority in that area to the probation officer in order to be free for other court work they deemed more important. Informal probation in some degree can be considered a reciprocal of police practice in areas where sheriffs' deputies or the police have chosen to pass on the duty of decision-making in doubtful cases. Otherwise, it can be assumed that the same factors encouraging police probation also have operated to sustain the older custom of informal probation.[17]

Table 3.2. Average Percentage of Referrals of Boys to California Juvenile Courts Handled by Informal Probation, 1956 through 1960 [a]

Counties Classed by Population[b]	Average Per Cent Given Probation	Range
(A) over 500,000	7.4	0.8–20.0
(B) 200,000–499,000	10.8	4.1–16.7
(C) 100,000–199,000	23.1	7.7–33.2
(D) 50,000– 99,000	18.4	.0–51.7
(E) 10,000– 49,000	22.0	4.1–40.2

[a] Tabulated from *Delinquency and Probation in California*, prepared for the C.Y.A. by the Bureau of Criminal Statistics, Sacramento.
[b] Populations as of 1958.

Evidence that informal probation has been an adaptation to significant ecological, social, and cultural differences between counties lies in the nature of the association between the extent of its use and the population of the county, an association that persisted up through 1960, the eve of the revision of the juvenile court law.

Data summarized by Table 3.2 show that less populous coun-

17. In the past in other states it has been held to be desirable, probably because of the belief that volunteer agents, who assisted in early probation work, should have a large measure of responsibility for juvenile offenders. Hastings Hart (preventive Treatment of Neglected Children), pp. 271–75.

ties, especially those under 200,000, were more likely than heavily populated counties to rely on informal probation. Further, the range of variations for counties of each class from year to year proves to be inversely related to county size. Not shown but equally impressive were fluctuations in its use from year to year in some of the smaller counties. Some showed a steady drop in informal dispositions, some a linear increase, and others irregular changes. The lower and more consistent percentages in larger counties account for the steady rate for the entire state, which hung around 9 to 10 per cent for the five-year period.

Generally, the more bureaucratized probation departments in larger urban counties have employed informal probation sparingly, and it is interesting that the rate of use in Santa Clara County, which entered the 500,000 population class in 1958, dropped rapidly from a high of 32.9 per cent in 1956 to 9.4 per cent in 1960. The greater variability in twenty-eight smaller counties of less than 100,000 residents can be laid to seven counties that have had characteristically low rates of use. Three of these—Merced, Humboldt, and Mendocino—used informal probation rarely or not at all during the five-year period. Hence much weight must be given to the personal views and individual decisions of probation officers and judges if one is to understand how smaller counties deal with their youth problems. The conceptions judges have of their roles in the juvenile court often have been a critical factor in the choice of informal over formal procedures.

INFORMAL JUDICIAL ACTION

If my thesis is correct—that the California juvenile court evolved from informal justice based on humanitarianism and primary group values to a kind of informal justice dictated by ecological factors, administrative considerations, and specialized group interaction—then further evidence of this evolution should appear in early and later forms of judicial action. This is probably easiest to see in the uses made of court hearings and in the quality of judicial dispositions. Unequivocal indication of a free and informal attitude on the part of judges toward court hearings comes from data showing their reliance on pre-hearing conferences. In a probation survey published in 1957, two thirds of thirty-six responding judges stated that they held such hearings, in which ordinarily the only person present was the probation officer. Parents were present in about one third of the cases, and less frequently such persons as the arresting officer, the defense attorney, and school officials. Thus it seems that juvenile justice of the court in the past was not only frequently informal but also *ex parte* and *in camera*.

However, there are signs of a bimodal pattern in the frequency with which judges held pre-hearing conferences. Thus nine of twenty-five judges in the sample had these meetings in 100 per cent of their cases, whereas ten reported such hearings in just 5 per cent or less of their cases. This was consistent with a similar divergence in the judges' conceptions of their roles in regularly scheduled court hearings; about half saw their duties primarily as talking with and counseling the parents and the child, while the other half placed in first order the getting of facts and the questioning of the principals and witnesses. Other hearing functions emphasized by many of the judges were: justifying the court's action to the child, selling the disposition plan to the parents, and impressing the child with the seriousness of his conduct. The least frequently mentioned role-task was ruling on evidence a.1d objections.[18]

On the basis of these data and impressions gathered from interviews with judges and probation officers, it may be postulated that a small number, perhaps a quarter, of juvenile court judges in California before 1961 identified fully with their roles and assumed major responsibility for most or all of the cases flowing through their courts. Quite conceivably they accepted literally the guardianship, *parens patriae* concept for their roles. In contrast, there was probably a comparable number of judges who were either unreceptive to the juvenile court philosophy or bound by a legalistic outlook, which led them to make the hear-

18. Special Study Commission on Correctional Facilities and Services, Report on Probation in California, Sacramento, 1957, p. 52.

ing itself the means for determining the facts of the case and
the time and place for making findings and dispositions. In between these two distinctive groups may have been those judges
who tried to strike some compromise or balance between the
polarized roles of the juvenile judge.

Another measure of judicial informality in juvenile procedure,
harking back to an older, pre-juvenile court custom, was the
granting of continuances. In effect this was a means whereby the
judge himself granted informal probation or gave his sanction
to such action by the probation officer. One study in 1958 reported
that judges in forty-six counties ordered continuances. During
that year, 2,000 of 35,000 boys on probation in the state were
serving under continuances. Most courts handled fewer than
twenty-five per cent of their cases in this way, and it is valid to
say that those in small, rather than large, counties employed it
most frequently.[19] Another study revealed that of courts in
fourteen counties using continuances as "treatment," only three
served substantial urban populations.[20] It is probable that continuances in large urban counties have tended to be used much
as they are in criminal or civil courts—to allow further facts to
be obtained, or to arrange for counsel or witnesses who could
not otherwise be present. In small jurisdictions there may have
been the greater tendency to make continuances a form of disposition itself. Finally, it is possible that for the "middle" group
of judges, who were neither completely paternalistic nor legalistic in their orientation, the continuance may have been a solution for their dilemmas in difficult-to-decide cases.

Further indication that summary dispatch took precedence
over rules in judicial procedures for juveniles lay in the disin-
clination of judges to hold detention hearings, required by law
after 1945. In 1958 at most no more than twenty-two judges conducted hearings prior to detaining youth. Even where these
hearings took place, the probation officer often was the only
other person present. While an absence of pre-detention hear-

19. Report of Governor's Special Study Commission on Juvenile Justice,
pp. 47, 48.
20. "The California Juvenile Court," *loc. cit.*

ings was not peculiar to less populous counties, differences of this kind were present. Thus about half the judges holding hearings sat in counties with heavy populations, as opposed to less than a quarter in smaller counties. In a number of loosely operating juvenile courts, nothing more was required to detain a youth than for the probation officer to place forms before the judge to be signed. In one or two counties, judges likely to be absent even signed blank forms in advance for potential use.[21]

In retrospect, it seems probable that judges in small counties who gave their allegiance to *parens patriae* enacted their roles as benevolent-stern authority figures—in one judge's words, "like a father who takes immediate action when his son is in trouble, without undue concern for legalities." [22] Still other judges in small counties, who were little interested in juvenile work or who, because of their legalistic style of adjudicating, felt uncomfortable with their juvenile court roles, were content to delegate responsibility for dispositions to a probation officer, intervening only in the serious cases, or perhaps in those where important persons or powerful interests in the community were involved. Both kinds of judicial role conceptions contributed to maximum informality or extra-legality in carrying out the work of the juvenile court.

The changes with which juvenile judges and the juvenile courts had to contend, especially after 1940, were the heavier calendars, the rising expectations of diagnostic and treatment services, and the administrative rationalization of the larger court system of the state. In urban centers the problems that arose were met by bureaucratization of juvenile courts and probation departments, plus professionalization of personnel. Full-time juvenile court judges were appointed on a rotation basis, and referees added to cope with the heavier intake of cases.

21. Report of Governor's Special Study Commission on Juvenile Justice, p. 78.

22. The judge making this statement also had little confidence in study reports on youth coming before him, claiming that he could "learn more about the case in five minutes of questioning the boy and his parents than I can from reading a thick report with statements from social workers and psychiatrists."

Probation departments became more independent, and roles and
procedures in and out of court tended to become more sharply
defined. In many ways the judge in the large urban court became much like a welfare administrator disposing of business in
routinized case conferences. The volume of cases in large courts
and the short time allowable for hearings meant that decisions
there more and more frequently were made in a real sense by
probation officers, at the same time heavily conditioned by the
internal problems and probation policies.

In small counties with one or two judges,[23] who were usually
handicapped by a shortage of qualified probation officers, the
juvenile court simply had to make do with what resources were
at hand. As controls by the state Judicial Council made judges
more accountable for their time, and when necessary, reassigned
them temporarily in other jurisdictions, judges had to either
work harder or neglect part of their work. Given competing
claims on their time, many judges undoubtedly gave the lion's
share to civil, adult criminal, probate, and other cases, and
placed juvenile cases on a low priority, particularly nonserious
cases. If I am correct in reconstructing the probabilities, it was
inevitable that more responsibility fell on probation officers,
juvenile hall personnel, camp superintendents, police and sheriffs' deputies, and justices of the peace. Proof that this was hap-
pening is to be seen in the various improvised methods devised
to take care of the swelling mass of juvenile traffic offenses in
many counties after 1940.

At this point the evolution of juvenile justice in California
can be summarized as a divergent growth that gave rise to a
variety of extra-legal practices reflecting substantial changes, not
only in the juvenile courts, but equally or more in the organization and work of law enforcement agencies responsible for the
bulk of its referrals. In some ways this evolution resembled the
origin of equity in civil law; it was also like the anomalous
circumventions, subterfuges, and "pious perjuries" that eighteenth-century juries in England devised to mitigate the harsh-

23. As of 1953 there were still thirty-one one-judge counties in the state.
Assembly Interim Committee on Judiciary, Progress Report to Legislature,
Regular Session, Sacramento, 1953, p. 196.

ness of penalties in criminal trials.[24] But these similarities are superficial at best, for the broad areas of sanctioned discretion for the juvenile courts to do their work originated as a statutory charter, and the subsequent adaptations were quite different in origin. In effect these courts were given powers to intervene in and regulate the lives of children and parents. At first these powers were often, perhaps characteristically, oriented to particularistic human needs, but subsequently they became instruments of organizational policies, or expressions of administrative and ecological necessities. Hence Tappan's view that juvenile courts are more akin in spirit and method to contemporary administrative tribunals than to courts seems to be valid for the California case.[25] But even here there is divergence, for the juvenile courts as a whole developed less procedural uniformity in regard to notice and hearings than was true of adjudication in administrative agencies.

One line of thought proposes that the evolution of administrative justice in the United States has been away from the common law toward an essentially informal procedure, with the added idea that inquisitorial procedures antithetical to common-law forms more or less inhere in administrative justice.[26] An opposite line of thought is to be found in the well-documented study by Nonet, of the California Accident Commission, which shows how an administrative agency starting from a broadly chartered welfare base nonetheless evolved a body of well-defined rules of law.[27] The wide separation of these views indicates the need for careful empirical studies to discover the conditions under which particular administrative agencies do or do not propagate rules and procedures sufficiently distinctive and uniform to designate as law. Among questions to be settled are the

24. Jerome Hall, *Theft, Law, and Society* 2nd ed. (Indianapolis: Bobbs-Merrill, 1952), Chap. IV.

25. Paul Tappan, *Juvenile Delinquency* (New York: McGraw-Hill, 1949), p. 169.

26. Peter Woll, *Administrative Law—The Informal Process* (Berkeley: University of California Press, 1963), p. 29ff.

27. Phillippe Nonet, *Administrative Justice: A Sociological Study of the California Accident Commission* (Berkeley: Center for the Study of Law and Society, 1966).

conditions under which judicial review may influence the growth of administrative law. From Monet's study, it appears that judicial review was indeed instrumental in helping to clarify and secure a specific set of rights for injured workers.[28] On the other hand, it is extremely doubtful that the appellate process shaped, altered, or redirected the growth of juvenile justice in California in any significant way.

JUDICIAL REVIEW

The position of the juvenile courts within the larger court system of the state, and statutory provision for appeals, presume judicial constraint and some degree of responsiveness of juvenile judges to opinions handed down from appellate courts. But the specialized nature of the juvenile court, both in its conception and conditions of operation, as well as in its clientele, made these presumptive controls nominal or tenuous. California's experience up through 1960 would not justify a stark conclusion that appellate rulings had no effect, but over-all they did comparatively little to institute more standardized means to the varied ends sought by juvenile courts in the state. Nor did they impede the growth of administrative discretion or the loose delegation of decision-making. At times, especially in the early days of the juvenile court, appellate decisions explicitly sanctioned a broad interpretation of the juvenile court law, as well as "irregularities" or "lack of niceties in procedure." [29]

One reason why appeals played a small part in the evolution of juvenile court procedure was their relatively small number; from 1906 to 1960 the total was about 115, with an average of about two per year. Selected decades reveal 24 appellate cases between 1910 and 1919; a drop to 17 between 1920 and 1929; a further drop to 11 between 1930 and 1939. In the 1940's the number rose slightly to 15, followed by a sharp increase to 38 in the decade immediately preceding the revision of the law. In

28. *Ibid.*, pp. 362–72.
29. E.g. *in re* Woeff 183' Cal. 602 (1920); V. B. Marr v. Superior Court of Siskiyou County, 114 C.A. 2d 527 (1952).

general, the periods of more frequent appeals have coincided with the two revolutionary phases of the juvenile court's history: its early formative years, and those preliminary to the revision of 1961. These clusterings would seem to support a connection between accumulating anomalies and legal change, particularly the large number of cases taken on appeal between 1950 and 1960.

Another possible reason why California appellate rulings made only a feeble contribution to a more articulated structuring of the juvenile court can be found in the appeal process itself. About two fifths of all the appeal actions were through writs, such as *habeas corpus*, prohibition, *mandamus*, and *certorari*. In many of these cases the appellate judges took the position that where remedy by appeal from a judgment existed, the writ could not be used to review the evidence upon which the judgment was based.[30] This probably reflected delays on the part of parents and minors in taking advantage of their right to appeal within the allotted time interval. Hence the need to use a "collateral attack" on the jurisdiction of the court by a writ. Actually, the right to appeal, although established early by law, was compromised by the fact that records often were too sparse for appeal judges to make informed decisions; hence they had to rely on "inferences."

Judgments were reversed on appeal, or writs issued, in approximately thirty-two cases during the fifty-seven years of juvenile court history before 1961. Unfortunately, not many of these cases raised issues directly relevant to the organization and working of the courts. For example, fifteen of the reversals were allowed because of lack of findings, but several of these were concerned with custody in cases of abandonment, in which courts have always insisted on high standards of proof. In about six of the reversals, questions of due process of law were directly or obliquely confronted—such as the right to appeal, the right of cross-examination, the right to counsel, the right to refuse to answer self-incriminating questions, and the right to hearing for possible certification from criminal to juvenile court. In only

30. E.g. People v. George Brecida Lavandera, 108 C.A. 2d 431 (1951–55).

two cases did appeal judges intervene to modify disposition orders of judges below.

The tenor of appeal decisions where judgments were upheld was largely a validation or restatement of the purpose of the court as a welfare institution in which proceedings were civil, not criminal. Reversals in some cases could be interpreted as censures of individual judges, but seldom if ever did they imply criticism of the policy of the juvenile courts themselves. Early decisions were "in bank," and dissenting opinions, eight in all, did not come until the 1950's. While they signaled increasing judicial uncertainties about fundamental aspects of the juvenile court, by this time the movement to alter the court by legislative revision was already under way.

Whatever the appellate courts had done by 1960, they had not shown any appreciation that modern conditions might have outmoded the old philosophy and meager legal rationale for the juvenile court. The well-worn theme that proceedings in juvenile courts were not criminal prevailed. In only one case, in 1952, did the higher court take an exceptional view, namely that the traditional rationale for the juvenile court law "for all practical purposes is a legal fiction. . . . Courts cannot and will not shut their eyes and ears to everyday contemporary happenings." [31] Four years later, in a dissenting opinion, one judge echoed this uneasiness: "In the final analysis the juvenile court is a judicial institution." [32] And finally, in 1957, an appellate court was sufficiently disturbed by a Los Angeles case to state: "From the record . . . it is hard to say . . . whether or not we have some sort of assembly line administration of the juvenile court law." [33]

But these were little more than straws in the wind, at most belated recognition of possible defects in the institutional pattern of the juvenile court. A purview of the appeal process leaves it doubtful that any ideal purpose of clarifying and integrating various parts of the juvenile court law had been met. The difficulty also may have been due to the inherent qualities of

31. *In re* Lupe Contreras, 109 C.A. 2d 787 (1956).
32. People v. Dotson, 46 C.A. 2d 899 (1956).
33. *In re* John Alexander, 152 C.A. 2d 458 (1957).

the appellate process, which is essentially reactive. Hall stated that the reach of legal innovation by appeals was restricted by the necessity of achieving desired ends through the redefinition of a body of formal rules.[34] A more likely idea is that the values and perceptions held by California appellate judges ill-disposed them to see the problems of the juvenile court in terms of basic policy and institutional design. Rather, problems of the court were seen as personal, to be solved by censure of the occasional high-handed or ill-chosen judge.

LEGISLATION—THE WRITTEN LAW

Whether there is a dialectical connection between judicial interpretation of law, administrative law, and legislated or written law is a debatable question. Hall, using Maine's ideas as a departure point, described the development of Anglo-American criminal law in terms of lag and adaptation, involving the interplay of all three processes. According to his summary, the narrowness of case-law reinterpretations by judges leads to administrative adaptations in dispensing justice not sanctioned in the written law—figuratively, a kind of criminal equity. In time the legislature takes heed of what is being done and enacts new statutes to direct these practices along the path of explicit law, whereupon "a new cycle sets in." [35]

Hall properly gave importance to public opinion as a stimulus to legislative adaptions of law, but did not attempt to analyze the legislative process itself other than to call attention to the "method of specific, narrow legislation [which] was typical and traditional." [36] The method he refers to is change by amendment, a process no less characteristic of legislation today than in the period of which he wrote. Its chief effect, if not purpose, is to ratify or authorize existing practices and claims, to give them the sanction of the state.

The later history of the juvenile court law in California, or

34. *Theft, Law, and Society*, p. 149.
35. *Ibid.*
36. *Ibid.*, pp. 137, 140.

indeed of its entire history from 1915 to 1960, took this form, being largely a history of piecemeal amendments. Statutory alterations originated from the discrete actions of large probation departments, C.Y.A. people, members of the C.P.P.C.A., law enforcement associations, judges, prosecuting attorneys, individual legislators, and interim committees or special commissions of the legislature. The number of bills introduced to reword, add, or subtract from extant rules of the juvenile court has always been high in relation to those actually brought out of committee and passed. Generally speaking, bills that passed reflected problems experienced in particular counties, or difficulties some agency was having with portions of the existing law, or uneasiness about omissions of the law on matters currently perplexing court workers. Amendments often were designed as exceptions or exemptions to allow a county or class of counties to follow desired procedures, or, in other cases, to legalize those already in effect. This pattern of adaptive amendments emerged very early in law changes that allowed larger counties to pay probation officers. It was further illustrated by the legislation of 1933, authorizing courts in third-class counties to appoint referees, and in 1945 amendments allowing juvenile judges to designate minor judges, justices of the peace, and recorders as referees.

Legislative action to change the juvenile court law during the period from 1915 to 1961 is best described as a process of uneven accretion of statutes and amendments that recapitulated the problems and divergent needs of different counties. The resultant law, or assemblage of laws, in many respects was archaic, duplicative, inconsistent, and insufficient to sanction many of the practices that had evolved around the juvenile court. Legislative action had neither systematized nor clarified the law; nor could it be said that the law corresponded to a body of values, policy, or underlying understandings that justified speaking of its legislative intent. In many provisions it was like a garment made of patches on patches.[37]

37. The pre-1961 California juvenile court law listed a number of anachronisms as grounds for assuming jurisdiction by the juvenile court: "gathering alms," begging, peddling, wandering, singing or playing instruments and entertaining in public places, visiting public billiard rooms, saloons,

Rather than trying to comprehend the California juvenile court law on the eve of revision as reflecting a particular philosophy or set of ideal values, it is far better to see it as the result of conflict between group values, and their accommodations and compromises as worked out in the arena of the legislature—a form of "compromise law." The general cleavage of values, which became articulated in legislative commission reports and which confronted legislative committees, broke down into views of those who wanted to make the law more punitive, those who wanted to broaden its protective and treatment functions, and those, such as lawyers and judges, concerned that traditional legal rights of juveniles and parents be preserved or even enhanced. In the background of these views, and often of salient importance in disposing of proposed changes, were reservations expressed by practitioners of the law—probation officers, correctional officers, police, and administrators cognizant of limitations of personnel, time, and budgets affecting day-by-day working of the law. Insofar as juvenile court judges were cast in administrative roles, they too expressed these instrumental values. Completely absent from interim committee reports or legislative amendments was any appreciation of the extent to which this pre-emptive administration of justice had in fact become the axis around which the juvenile court revolved.

ABORTIVE REVOLUTION

Obviously, legislation does not automatically provide effective remedies for deficiencies of judicial review and administrative overgrowth in the law. Insofar as legislation is reactive and spe-

---

"being in any house of assignation," and venereal infections. The law also made such things as intemperance, moral depravity, adultery, and divorce by parents presumptive evidence for taking jurisdiction. Jurisdictional criteria were repeated in several different places without cross-references. All of this illuminates the process of planless accretion at work. Thus, between 1941 and 1959 there were fifty-three provisions added to the law, 149 changes by amendment, but only twenty provisions were repealed. Source: Report on California Laws Relating to Youthful Offenders (C.Y.A.), Sacramento, 1959, Chap. II.

cifically adaptive, it suffers from the same weakness as judicial reinterpretation; it does not and cannot transcend the original set of ideas on which it rests. In the case of the California juvenile court law, amendments either were restricted by the old paradigm of a *parens patriae*, noncriminal court or they were empirical adaptations of means to diverse ends, vaguely rationalized on old grounds or without discernible ideological referents at all.

Revolutionary legislation, in contrast to that which is normal or empirically adaptive, takes root in an opinion process, which, beginning with crisis, becomes focused, controlled, and geared to the realities of power. Just such opinion could be seen between 1945 and 1950 in the aggregate activities and reports of legislative interim committees. But it would be an exaggeration to say that these committees showed a unity of purpose; rather, their concerns were protean, dealing with causes and prevention of crime and delinquency, or with corrections, detention, and jails.[38] Their recommendations tended to become synthetic compilations, which only incidentally touched issues germane to the structure of the juvenile court.

In 1949 a maximum effort was made to revise the juvenile court law by a Special Study Commission on Juvenile Justice. The numerous recommendations of the commission moved across a wide spectrum of matters, from the juvenile court itself to public welfare, schools, community organization, and research. Included was a hard core of proposals to firm up procedures in the court, among them: provision of a legal basis for police to take juveniles into custody; legal validation of informal probation; notice to parents; a time limit for filing petitions after detaining a child; and a requirement that findings be made in cases where youths over sixteen were certified from adult to juvenile courts. Other recommendations dealt with bail for minors, writs of *habeas corpus*, the recording of felonies follow-

38. See Report of Assembly Interim Committee on Crime Prevention and Correction, Sacramento, January 1947, pp. 71–127; Supplementary Report of Assembly Interim Committee on Detention Homes and County and City Jails, Sacramento, March 1948, pp. 661–83; Final Report of Assembly Interim Committee on Crime and Corrections, Sacramento, July 1949, pp. 5604–19.

ing commitment of youths to the C.Y.A., and the citing of parents to show cause why juvenile court complaints should not issue against them.[39] Yet few of these or the other proposals of the commission survived to become law.

Those familiar with events during the life of the 1949 juvenile justice commission generally have written off its efforts as abortive or outright failures. Failure was ascribed to the tense political situation prevailing that year, resulting from sensational exposés of organized gambling and vice in the state, and also to the inexperience and ineptitude of commission members dealing with legislators. One of the salient difficulties, however, was the magnitude of the commission's proposal to convert the juvenile court into a family court, with district rather than county jurisdiction. The idea stirred strong resistance, particularly among judges and the incumbent governor, Earl Warren, who thought the plan would lead to fragmentation of the courts. This view was shared by the chief justice of the California Supreme Court, Phil S. Gibson, then strategically situated as head of the judicial council charged with administration of the court system of the state.

In more general terms, the 1949 commission failed to become a vehicle for revolutionary change because its work neither derived from nor generated a unified set of ideas. True, the various procedural recommendations of the commission in toto amounted to a narrowing of the discretionary powers of the juvenile court toward a due-process model; but the proposals for a family court and a youth court were antithetical moves to enlarge the juvenile court's jurisdiction along lines of a total-treatment model. Even this antithesis was lost in the vastness of the institutional horizon marked out for changes. Focus was gone and there was no system of priorities. The method was architectonic, "a painstaking effort to promote improved services for all children and youth at every level of our California economy and in every major aspect of the administration of justice in this state as it relates to minors." [40]

39. Regular Session, Sacramento, 1953, p. 196. Final Report of the Governor's Special Study Commission on Juvenile Justice, Sacramento, 1949.
40. *Ibid.*, p. 2.

This method, together with studied care to avoid catering to the special interests of particular agencies, no doubt resulted from the commission's status as a citizens' committee necessarily playing a representative and expressive role. Accordingly, it solicited and transmitted public opinion but did little to carry it down paths leading to effective social action. When the time came, recommendations got to the legislature as separate bills, each one of which was vulnerable to attack. The heavy ground swell of public opinion that had been created did little but accelerate somewhat the process of normal legislation by amendment. The alternative course of social action that impressed public opinion successfully, and led to changes in the structure of the juvenile court, is discussed in the following chapters.

4

Anomalies, Issues, and Social Action

From one vantage the juvenile court law by the late 1950's had grown disorganized. From another vantage the law had failed to evolve, in that several of its provisions reflected adaptations to problems of a past era—child labor, street trades, child abandonment, open vice, and the inability of foreign-born parents to maintain the family as an agency of control over children. Looked at in still another way, neither legislation nor judicial interpretations had differentiated the law sufficiently to control a number of juvenile court practices inconsistent with its purposes. It is these practices, whose consequences were at variance with the underlying conception of the court, that warrant the term *anomalies*.

A critical point is that the conception of the essential character of the juvenile court delimited the range of attention to the problems it generated and determined how they were defined. These were the "normal problems" of the juvenile court, the ones it legitimately dealt with. For example, as long as juvenile hall was conceived of as a "clinic" and "hospital," the length of time a youth spent there was not a special problem but rather a routine one: some cases were just more difficult to diagnose than others, or some dispositions required more time. In the same vein, as long as a judge saw his role as that of an intervening father, concerned with the total welfare of the child, the minor's lack of representation by counsel was a matter of little concern.

Anomalies appeared as facts or observations that were not

acceptably explained by logical deductions from postulates about the *parens patriae* court. To wit: if a judge was a kindly and deeply concerned father, why in juvenile court did he give so little time, often measured in minutes, to hearing cases. If detention was for purposes of clinical study, why in a disturbing number of cases was so little actual investigation carried out. If the purpose of wardship was to treat children in a therapeutic sense, why was jurisdiction assumed in cases for which there were no adequate treatment facilities. Further, if juvenile traffic offenders revealed no signs of personal pathology, why should they be processed by a treatment-oriented court. Finally, if the juvenile court protected children, why in some instances did names of wards appear in newspapers; or why was it possible for employers and the armed services to discriminate against persons with juvenile court records.

Anomalies are objective phenomena, which can be brought to light by critical research or comprehensive appreciation of all possible consequences of patterns of action. While the core idea of every institution can be shown to have its anomalies, anomalies also vary in number; they wax and wane, depending upon the changing societal context or changes in the institutional structure itself. The accumulation of anomalies is a prerequisite to crisis and social action for change, but not the determiner. It is first necessary that anomalies be converted into issues.

The emergence of issues means that anomalies are projected into the arena of group interaction in a visible way. Anomalies are no longer ignored, no longer normalized, but rather are made the focus of discussion, value conflicts, and social action. Substantial as opposed to spurious issues come up in the interaction of individuals and groups that have the power to shape public policy and initiate or forestall social change. The rise of issues is usually regarded as a prelude to social action, but it also happens that social action, once undertaken, can broaden the spectrum of issues. It can also transform issues or replace original issues with others. Since issues, when viewed distributively, have differing symbolic associations of value threat and value gain, the shifts and convergences of issues do much to account for the alignments, reinforcements, and defections of individuals and groups in the course of social action.

Although social action in the present case revolved around procedures of the juvenile courts of the state, it is incorrect to conclude that they alone were the issue, or that any one issue activated ultimate change in the law. Some of the issues were recurrent or "old hat," in that they derived from dilemmas and inconsistencies inherent in the structure and design of the juvenile court; these periodically got aired in conferences of court workers, or now and then received public attention in legislative committee reports. Some of the issues roused debate throughout the state; others engaged interests primarily of localities or regions. Whether it was the accumulation and exacerbation of issues rather than their substance that made the state situation ripe for social action to change the juvenile court law in the late 1950's is not readily determined. However, no analysis would be complete without taking into account the effects organization, leadership, and techniques of social action had on sorting out issues and assigning them priorities. Finally, it must be recognized that large public issues compete with one another, and that the prevalence of one set of issues over others within a legislative forum can be affected by intrusive events and the sequence in which they occur.

DETENTION AS AN ISSUE

One of the central issues underlying action to revise the juvenile court law in California was the excessive detention of children. Detention had become a perennial concern dating back to the first juvenile court movement, which successfully dramatized the inhumanity of incarcerating children in jails and prisons. The issue was kept alive through the years by the studies and reports of the U.S. Children's Bureau, which sought to elevate and standardize juvenile court procedures throughout the nation.

The earliest agitations over juvenile detention concerned the provision of segregated facilities and their safety, sanitation, and compliance with building specifications, no doubt reflecting the older nineteenth-century conviction that architecture had an important effect on the success of penal programs. The first legal rules for California detention homes were permissive, but by 1909 segregation was firmly stipulated, to spare juveniles from corruption by adult criminals or other undesirables.[1] The emphasis placed on adequate facilities and segregation by the board of Corrections and the Department of Welfare during their respective eras of probation supervision furthered the idea that there was nothing questionable about the detention *per se* of children by state action if done under approved circumstances.

The issue of whether detention itself was warranted and the extent to which its use was justified appeared in a very generalized way as early as 1916. At that time a study published by the Russell Sage Foundation singled out California as having the highest rate of child dependency in the nation.[2] The study took into account a number of special conditions that contributed to the magnitude of the problem in the state, but it also noted that law, policy, and administrative practice encouraged the institutionalization of children under circumstances where a parent or others could have been expected to support them.[3]

Apart from this, however, the issue of the use of detention under juvenile court auspices, in contrast to the concern over the physical surroundings in which juveniles were detained, did not come to the fore of public discussion until the 1940's. This was the decade in which the nation entered World War II, and three and a half million people migrated to California—a movement that increased its population by half. Whether the *rates* of delinquency went up in the state during this period is a moot point, but there is no doubt that family separations owing to wartime conditions were more numerous, and that absolute members of mobile and detached minors increased, capped by a highly visible problem of roaming, underage wives of service men, especially noticeable in the large metropolitan areas of the

1. Report on California Children in Detention and Shelter Care, California Committee on Temporary Child Care, Los Angeles, 1955, p. 1.

2. William Slingerman, *Child Welfare in California* (New York: Russell Sage Foundation, 1916); also State Board of Control, Children's Agents Report, Sacramento, December 1914, p. 4.

3. Slingerman, *op. cit.*

state. Delinquency, whether owing to an increase in crimes committed or to more aggressive policing, or to both, was on the rise.
Since no new state facilities for delinquents were constructed between 1924 and 1944, the increase inevitably overburdened local
agencies.[4]

The establishment of the C.Y.A. contributed to the "problem"
of detention in two ways: first, it encouraged local judges to
send youth to the C.Y.A. where otherwise they might have been
placed on probation or had their cases dismissed due to lack of
local resources. This meant interim detention for such youths.
Second, the lag in construction of C.Y.A. institutional space or
"beds" in its early years and at later periods lengthened the so-
called "dead time" committed youth had to spend in detention
waiting departure to reception centers.

Interviews and contacts C.Y.A. staff people had with committed youth, and the C.Y.A. field studies referred to in Chapter
II, soon led the director and many of his staff to the conclusion
that local detention of juveniles was excessive and in a number
of cases completely unwarranted. In 1947, nation-wide publicity
was given California's detention problem in a journalistic
exposé of juvenile correctional institutions, by Albert Deutsch.
Karl Holton, then director of the C.Y.A., was quoted in the book
as deploring detention practices within the state and "erroneous
attitudes" of judges in dispatching children to state institutions.
Deutsch added a graphic summary of his own observations:

> At both Whittier and Preston, many boys bitterly complained to
> me of lengthy jail or detention-home stays prior to admission to
> reform school. They were resentful that the time spent there was
> not deducted from their minimum stay at Preston or Whittier.[5]

Another channel through which C.Y.A. opinion on the subject
became public was the Governor's Advisory Committee on Children and Youth, which was established in 1943. There an appre-

---

4. Report on California Children, Chap. XIV; Report of the Assembly Fact-
Finding Committee on Correctional Problems to the California Legislature,
Fifty-sixth Session, 1945 (*Assembly Journal* [March 1945], pp. 1221–41).
5. *Our Rejected Children* (Boston: Little Brown, 1947), pp. 118–19.

ciation of the arbitrariness of juvenile courts in disposing cases
to the C.Y.A. was enlarged by appointments of former C.Y.A.
board members to the committee. They carried with them haunting memories of youth who adamantly clung to convictions that
they had been unfairly treated in juvenile courts of the state.
One member told me of her experiences:

> As a C.Y.A. Board member I saw cases where it appeared that
> juvenile court procedure had been summary, and the record was
> sketchy, as well as findings of fact. We talked a good deal about such
> cases but we were not in a position to do anything.

Three successive Governor's Conferences on Children and
Youth, in 1948, 1950, and 1954, passed resolutions pointing up
the problem of detention in the state and also the need for
remedial action. The report of the 1950 conference spoke unequivocally: "A cold storage conception of the function of detention . . . is definitely outmoded in California thinking. . . ." [6]

In 1952, at the instigation of the C.Y.A. director, a comprehensive study of detention and child care in the state was carried
out under the auspices of the Governor's Committee on Children and Youth, financed by a grant from the Rosenberg Foundation. According to the study's report, there was no justification for detaining 41 per cent of juvenile arrestees held in California in 1951. Further:

> This represents a high percentage of detention in the total number
> of juvenile arrests compared to police detention practices generally
> outside of California. [7]

THE SEVERAL FACES OF THE ISSUE

Holding youth in detention for long periods prior to entry into
C.Y.A. institutions was only a part of the growing controversy

6. California Midcentury Conference on Children and Youth, Sacramento,
1950, p. 189.
7. Report on California Children, p. 25.

over detention. Publicity also began to be directed to practices that had persisted from an earlier time and were now totally unacceptable to persons and agencies setting standards in the field of juvenile correctional work. Among the more common but questioned uses of detention: to insure the child's presence in court, to allow observation and "study" of the child, to impress the child with the seriousness of his conduct, to give "therapy," to allow "quieting down," and to administer punishment. The extent of these practices was indicated in the survey of the 1958 juvenile justice commission: 60 per cent of the probation officers believed detention to be justified for the purpose of case study, and 28 per cent for its "valuable therapeutic results." While judges were somewhat more conservative, nevertheless 28 per cent shared the probation officers' view; moreover, 40 per cent believed that detention was necessary to insure the child's appearance in court.[8]

Those who opposed these views argued that a child could be studied better in his home environment than in the artificial setting of juvenile hall, that detention was neither the time nor the place for therapy, and that a child's appearance in court should be sought by means other than detention, particularly when there was reason to believe that citations would work just as well.[9] Those adhering to an exclusively protective philosophy of the juvenile court could see no grounds whatsoever for making detention a means of punishment.

The issues in detention—for there were a number—tended to overlap with or become confused by others. For example, in 1951, 15 per cent of juveniles detained either were transients or from another county.[10] Furthermore, in some counties the issue was one of available rather than ideal choices, particularly

8. Report on Governor's Special Study Commission on Juvenile Justice, 1960, p. 72; for an earlier study showing how detention was used in California, see: Ruth Tolman and Ralph Wales, Report on Juvenile Detention in California, submitted to the California Advisory Committee on Detention Home Problems, Sacramento, 1945, 25.

9. Sherwood Norman, "New Goals for Detention," *Youth Authority Quarterly* 4 (summer 1951), 28; a citation system was introduced successfully in Fresno's juvenile court by Judge Wolf in 1955.

10. Report on California Children, p. 30.

where there was no camp or other facility intermediary between placing a youth on probation and sending him to the C.Y.A. As one judge explained to me:

> Yes, I believe in using our juvenile hall for punishment. Everyone does, so why not admit it. I could send boys to camp at Fresno, but if I do I lose control over them to a superintendent who has different ideas than I do. Besides that, it's too far away, the people there are different, and parents here don't like the idea at all.

JUVENILE ARREST PRACTICES

The detention issue was further clouded by the absence of clear rules or policies as to how juveniles should be apprehended and taken into custody. Moreover, police in some localities followed methods whose legality was dubious at best. Generally speaking, the locus of control over detention decisions in the state had varied among police, probation officers, and in some counties, such as Los Angeles, the probation committee. Over the years, however, the police had increasingly come to dominate detention procedures. Some claimed that the police were using detention too much for their own ends, in order to question suspects and otherwise pursue their investigations—even exaggerating charges for the purpose.[11] Others objected that the police at times held children in detention as material witnesses, while adults charged with crimes in the same cases went free on bail.

The most telling proof that the youth of California were being detained in routine or perfunctory ways lay in the 1951 detention and shelter-care study, which disclosed that of twelve large, medium, and small counties there was only one in which children detained numbered below the totals referred to respective probation departments for delinquent acts and delinquent tendencies.[12] This study also demonstrated that the police were more frequently responsible for decisions to detain than were

11. Report of Governor's Special Study Commission on Juvenile Justice (Part II), p. 95.
12. Report on California Children, p. 30.

probation officers. In only fourteen counties did the latter claim responsibility for initial detentions, i.e., until a petition was filed—this in contrast to thirty-five counties in which they allowed that responsibility rested with the police. Police, on the other hand, believed detaining power to be theirs in thirty-nine counties and conceded the prerogative to probation officers in only ten.[13]

Los Angeles, one of the largest contributors to the delinquency population of the state, experienced its own peculiar problems with detention as early as 1945.[14] Although jail detention of juveniles ended there about 1951, emergencies several years later caused its reactivation. The piling up of C.Y.A. commitments in detention between 1954 and 1956 was sufficiently grievous to spark a grand jury inquiry and report.[15] By 1956 a "detention-control" unit had been set up by the probation department in an endeavor to mitigate the problem, but confusion over the control of detention persisted. A strong indictment of the situation appeared in a widely used textbook on delinquency published in 1960:

> The Los Angeles detention quarters, in spite of a 600 capacity, is always overcrowded because the police sweep into custody anyone who violates the curfew law, and are given 48 hours leeway to obtain a court order for those they have detained. An indication of the unsoundness of the practice is that the court finds further detention unnecessary in a large proportion of the cases.[16]

Assertions like these portray the police as calloused or ruthless devotees of law enforcement. But they overlook the other side of the issue, submerged by the limited number of spokesmen for

13. *Ibid.*

14. Los Angeles *Daily Journal,* February 12, 1945; reprinted in the *Assembly Journal,* January 7, 1947, p. 85.

15. Final Report of the Los Angeles County Grand Jury, Los Angeles, 1956, pp. 30–58; Report, Subcommittee for the Implementation of Recommendations of the California Children in Detention and Shelter Care Study, San Marino, California, 1956, p. 4. Mimeo.

16. Sophia Robison, *Juvenile Delinquency* (New York: Holt, Rinehart and Winston, 1960), p. 359.

police values and their lack of a public audience. Yet thoughtful observers had this to say for the police:

> Few persons appreciate what the law enforcement officer is up against—the jail tradition, lack of immediate casework service from the probation departments, the 48-hour jurisdiction, kids who talk back, difficulty of finding parents at home, parents who will not co-operate, the irate complainant, the likelihood that the same youngster may have been involved in unsolved burglaries or that he is shielding others not yet apprehended.[17]

To this it might be added that policing in large communities that are troubled by delinquent gangs and gang warfare even under the best of conditions is likely to place strains on the laws of arrest and court procedure.

THE LEGAL RIGHTS OF JUVENILES

The question of the legal rights of juveniles can be discussed most effectively in a larger historical and nation-wide context, with specific attention directed to the various factors that molded the professional opinion of jurists, lawyers, and legally informed persons in the state. In a sense the legal issue was endemic, for it inhered in the conflicting values or ideologies on which the juvenile court rested as an institution. Appeals from orders of the juvenile court during its early years attested to these conflicts; such appeals commonly were brought on constitutional grounds, holding that due process of law had been violated, in regard to the right to trial by jury, notice and hearings, bail, findings and evidence, and, finally, access to counsel. Generally, however, appellate courts throughout the nation upheld the fulsome powers of the court, and maintained the position that proceedings in the juvenile court were not criminal in nature and consequently its orders and dispositions were not punitive. The conclusion followed *ergo*: juveniles were not being denied constitutional immunities and rights.

17. Report on California Children, p. 34.

While here and there some qualified appellate recognition was given to the legal rights of juveniles, it wasn't until the 1940's that appellate judges in Texas and Nebraska began to acknowledge explicitly that juveniles were entitled to constitutional protection. By the mid-1950's, pronouncements by the District Court in the District of Columbia and the Supreme Court in New Hampshire had broken the solid front of judicial opinion on the matter. During the same period a dissenting opinion by Justice Musmanno forcefully put the issue in Pennsylvania, whose Supreme Court up through 1954 had stood as a citadel of judicial conservatism guarding the paternalistic philosophy of the juvenile court:

> It is . . . a delusion to say that a Juvenile Court record does not handicap because it cannot be used against the minor in any court. In point of fact it will be a witness against him in the court of society where the penalties inflicted for deviation from conventional codes can be as ruinous as those imposed in any criminal court, it will be a sword of Damocles hanging over his head in any public life, it will be a weapon to hold him at bay as he seeks respectable and honorable employment.[18]

A parallel shift in legal opinion began to be reflected in the law journals of many states, which by 1950 were infused with articles critically addressed to the juvenile court and its procedures, and to the question of juveniles' right to counsel, especially in cases where they were alleged to have committed crimes. Even earlier, the constitutionality of juvenile court actions had become the concern of social scientists, whose interest was kindled by Tappan's pioneer study of the court for wayward girls in New York City.[19]

The fate of appeals from juvenile court decisions held in California both reflected and perpetuated the traditional conception held elsewhere in the nation that the juvenile court was

18. See Holmes Appeal, 379 Pa. 109 2d 253 (1954) .
19. Paul Tappan, *Delinquent Girls in Court,* (New York: Columbia University Press, 1947) ; also his "Adolescent in Court," *Journal of Criminal Law and Criminology* 37 (1946) , 216–30; and "Treatment without Trial," *Social Forces* 24 (1946) , 306–11.

a parental surrogate acting in *locus parentis*, with the nonpunitive objectives of reformation and the inculcation of "habits of industry" advanced as the paramount justification for its expansive jurisdiction and summary procedures. As brought out in Chapter II, California appellate judges consistently sustained full discretionary powers of the court, giving to the original hearing judges every benefit of the doubt, save where facts indicated such grossly arbitrary action that it could not be overlooked. One important exception was *In re Contreras* (1952), in which the appeal judges spoke pointedly to the unsought stigmatization and deprivation of liberty resulting from juvenile court adjudication without benefit of due process of law.[20] But this case had more impact outside the state than within, doing little to redirect the train of judicial thought in subsequent California cases. The state of judicial opinion on the eve of action by the juvenile justice commission conceded little beyond the right to hearings by minors and parents in juvenile court and notice of such hearings; failure to warn against self-incrimination, acceptance of the probation officer's report as evidence, denial of bail to minors, and rejection of the concept of double jeopardy were all held to be consistent with the benevolent purposes of the court.[21]

THE RIGHT TO COUNSEL

Although the right of minors and parents to counsel in juvenile court was raised a number of times on appeal in California, it remained an unsettled issue, chiefly because it was never put in such a way as to secure an unequivocal decision. As of 1960, the guiding opinions seemed to be that minors and parents had a right to be represented by counsel, but that the court had no duty to advise them of this right, to provide counsel if it was requested, or to determine if one was needed. Absence of counsel *per se* did not deprive minors of their legal right; this had to be demonstrated on appeal. A number of attorneys who had

20. *In re* Contreras, 109 Cal. App. 2d 787, 789, 241 P. 2d 631, 633 (1952).
21. California law revision commission, E-34, Sacramento, 1960.

appeared in juvenile court cases discovered that the right to engage counsel could be an empty one under the procedures they encountered. Furthermore, as many as half the judges in the state were ill-disposed to the appearance of attorneys in juvenile court.[22]

Whether the sense of futility and frustration felt by attorneys who chanced into juvenile courts and met hostile judges was shared by the rank-and-file lawyers in the state is doubtful. There may have been an increase in the number of attorneys consulted by disturbed parents after 1940, and possibly more individual attorneys became aware of the arbitrariness of juvenile judges. The statistics on youth involved in traffic offenses lends support to an interpretation of this sort. However, most attorneys in the state remained pretty much ignorant of juvenile court problems; whatever concern they showed was spotty and at most confined to a few more aggressive members of the bar.

The first definitive challenge to the existing juvenile court law by an attorney must be credited to Robert Fraser, in Orange County. In 1956 Fraser took on the case of a girl held in detention as a material witness against her father, following his arrest for child molestation. Neither the mother nor Fraser was permitted to see or talk with the child, and an order was necessary before he was allowed to see the records in the case. A writ of *habeas corpus* was finally issued, but only after being held over by the judge until the child had testified. Aroused, the attorney discovered that this particular judge customarily acted without hearings, and usually denied access to children, as well as to case records. Also, it was his wont to certify to adult courts all children who refused to admit allegations against them. For the first time Fraser read the Welfare and Institutions Code and was shocked at what he found there, namely, that children had few if any legal rights as he saw them. When other cases similar to the first came to him, he took them on appeal but with indifferent results. Finally Fraser approached the Orange County Bar Association, which, under his leadership, introduced a resolution

22. Estimate made by Karl Holton in interview with me, based on his experience as C.Y.A. director.

at the Conference of State Bar Delegates in 1958 calling for a
series of amendments to the juvenile court law. Their general
tone was conveyed by a preliminary statement:

> The Juvenile Court Law shall be interpreted in such a manner as
> to promote no fewer safeguards to the child, his parents, guardian,
> legal or usual custodian for the liberty of the child and the main-
> tenance of the normal parent-child relationship, than is afforded a
> defendant in regard to his life, liberty, or property, in a criminal
> action.

The resolution urged a full complement of procedural guarantees for juveniles and parents: the right to counsel, trial by
jury, bail, scheduled hearings, proper notice, and mandatory
criminal rules of evidence in contested hearings. The conference
approved the resolution in principle and referred it to committee
for study. Thereafter it lay in files, for the State Bar Association
took no action on the matter. However, in the meantime the
Orange County group, seeking the largest audience possible, distributed mimeographed copies of their resolution to interested
persons throughout the entire state.

In retrospect, the Orange County Bar people must be credited
with having sharply crystallized the issue of the right of minors
to counsel by stating the most extreme civil rights position compatible with continued existence of the juvenile court as an
institution.[23] While their action proved abortive in a sense, it
nevertheless awakened attorneys and probation officers in southern counties and elsewhere to instances of gross unfairness in the
treatment of juveniles in court. It must be assumed that the chief
probation officer of Orange County, who was not opposed to
having counsel appear in juvenile court, communicated the
details of the struggles between Robert Fraser and the local
juvenile court judge to other probation people of the state, not

23. Actually the Los Angeles Bar Association had recommended in 1945
that "all children involved in any proceedings in any court have legal counsel
in every stage of such proceedings." However, this was simply one of several
recommendations largely concerned with the problem of inadequate detention facilities in Los Angeles. Report of Los Angeles Bar Association Juvenile
Crime Prevention Committee, Los Angeles, February 2, 1945.

the least of whom was Karl Holton, former director of the C.Y.A.

John Pettis, an Oakland attorney, who later was to become project director for the 1958 juvenile justice commission, was well informed about the "Orange County cases." He himself had already clashed with an Alameda County judge in a juvenile case, in the course of which he was made to feel that neither he nor attorneys in general had any place in juvenile court proceedings.

Later, in 1959, after action to change the juvenile court law was under way, an attorney in Merced County, Charles Goff, became embroiled with a local judge in a juvenile case whose circumstances paralleled those met with by Fraser and Pettis in their counties. Goff, like the others, was made to feel that he had no right to be in juvenile court, a point made clear by the judge's refusal to allow the attorney to cross-examine the probation officer on his report. Goff's experience is cited here, not so much because of the appeal that followed, but because he worked in a law firm that previously had included Senator James Cobey, a man of some power in the legislature and who became directly involved in the struggle to insure the right of counsel to juveniles.

Two reactions stand out·above all others in cases where California attorneys crossed swords with juvenile court judges: their indignation over affronts to their right to be present in juvenile court, and their feeling of helplessness in the face of informal, behind-the-scenes procedures. Characteristically, attorneys were less perturbed about excessive detention of juveniles than about ways in which detention was brought about. As one attorney confided to me:

> There ought to be a uniform law for the juvenile court. As it is now a judge can decide to hold boys to punish them a little before he lets them go. I don't believe in this half-assed or backhand way of proceeding. If punishing juveniles is necessary, then put it in the law. Now there are neither informal nor formal controls. It gives a lawyer a terrible feeling to be before a judge who is operating informally.

Another attorney described the lawyer's vulnerability in juvenile court more grandiloquently:

You have to recognize the great power which judges hold. You are bleeding and they throw a spear into you. They don't get any wounds. It's the battle of Troy all over again. Judges are the natural enemy of the lawyer.

THE CALIFORNIA LAW REVISION COMMISSION

Another line of action that pointed to the issue of counsel in juvenile court was a by-product of the establishment of the California law revision commission, whose ostensible purpose was to facilitate an ongoing codification of laws of the state under the guidance of the legislative counsel. This commission was created in 1958, and among the laws given to it for study were those of the juvenile court. Two men played important parts in steering the commission to a detailed examination of the problem in its various legal aspects. One was Arthur Sherry, a professor of law and teacher in the School of Criminology at the University of California, who served as a consultant to the commission. The other was a member of the commission itself, Senator James A. Cobey. Sherry had long dwelled on the need for counsel in juvenile court, both in his class lectures and in public addresses. Senator Cobey's pertinent interests already have been indicated.

The law revision commission, after a somewhat formal study of the law, appellate rulings, and other opinions, concluded that the right of juveniles and parents to representation by counsel had never been squarely put to the appellate courts of California. In order to remove the issue from its judicial limbo, the commission recommended that the juvenile court law should be amended to require that alleged delinquent minors and their parents should be advised of their right to counsel, and also that the court should appoint counsel for those without means to employ their own.[24] The commission also inveighed against the stigmatizing effects of juvenile court wardship on nondelinquent children. In support of a recommended change designed to elim-

24. California law revision commission, E-6.

inate the designation of such children as wards, the commission cited a concurrent resolution of the 1957 legislature:

> To be made a ward of the juvenile court often operates to the detriment of a minor when in later life he is required to show that fact in job applications and other documents of vital importance to his standing in the community . . . such a stigma should not be allowed to attach to a minor who is merely a victim of circumstance and who is guilty of no wrongdoing.[25]

The action of the law revision commission was largely collateral and supplementary to that of the Juvenile Justice Commission. This later became quite clear when Senator Cobey introduced a separate bill into the Senate as a kind of stand-by measure to secure counsel for juveniles in the event that more comprehensive legislation of the Juvenile Justice Commission failed passage.

THE TRAFFIC ISSUE

Still another issue charged with legal implications centered on the diversified and anomalous methods for handling juvenile traffic offenses. The heated debates stirred by this issue in part stemmed from the desire of many people to apply more stringent controls or penalties to traffic violators, especially where accident and injuries occurred. At the same time, however, they pointed up the fundamental conflicts between the paternalistic philosophy of the juvenile court and legal rights.

After 1940 the burgeoning volume of juvenile traffic offenses everywhere in the state severely strained law enforcement and court facilities. The problem was met with a variety of police, judicial, and administrative expedients, for which the legal basis was tenuous at best. Some cases were heard and disposed by police, others by lay justices designated as referees, others in regular traffic courts, still others in juvenile courts, or by probation officers without juvenile court processing. The situation was touchy in Los Angeles, where the responsibility of handling

25. California Senate Concurrent Resolution No. 31 (Regular session, 1957).

traffic violators had been shifted from police to probation officers. The latter were far from easy about the legal sanctions for the authority that had been administratively assigned to them.

In 1945 the legislature had tried to ease the situation by allowing juvenile court judges to appoint judges, justices, recorders, and probation officers as referees, primarily to cope with traffic violations of minors. But there were those in the state who condemned this as a serious step backward in the history of the juvenile court.[26] In 1950 the Governor's Traffic Safety Conference reported on the pressing need for uniformity in handling juvenile traffic violators. A year earlier the juvenile justice commission had recommended a simple, practical method for handling juvenile traffic offenses, taking the position that in this type of case there was "no conclusive need for a complete investigation by a probation officer and a hearing under a juvenile court petition." [27] However, the bill introduced by the commission toward this end failed passage. In 1951 essentially the same bill was sponsored by the C.P.P.C.A., but again it failed, dying in the Senate. During this same year two interim committees, one in the Assembly and one in the Senate, submitted reports strongly criticizing the quality of justice in traffic courts, and recommended stronger penalties against serious offenders. Both reports called for more uniform procedures, and that of the Assembly committee stressed the need for a system of determining which traffic offenses of minors should go to juvenile courts and which to adult courts.[28]

Arguments to keep jurisdiction over juvenile traffic offenses in the juvenile court developed several themes. One was that adult traffic courts dispensed such a low and cynical order of justice that minors should not be exposed to it, or, instead, should receive some sort of driver education. A more specific objection was that youths would be unable to pay the heavy fines

26. Report of Governor's Conference on Youth Welfare, Administration of Justice, Sacramento, 1948, p. 6.
27. Final Report of the Governor's Special Study Commission on Juvenile Justice, p. 40.
28. Margaret Greenfield, *Juvenile Traffic Offenders and Court Jurisdiction*, Bureau of Public Administration (Berkeley: University of California, 1951), pp. 23, 24.

extracted in the regular traffic courts, and might, as had happened, be sentenced to jail or road camps in the company of disreputable adults. Finally, it was held that lay justices who dealt with juvenile traffic violators lacked the competence to duplicate juvenile court methods. A more positive argument came from some California judges, who ingenuously spoke of the special utility juvenile traffic jurisdiction had for bringing before them youths "in need of treatment":

> Moreover it seems to have been demonstrated that the broad powers of the juvenile court can be helpfully invoked on behalf of children whose maladjustment has been brought to light through juvenile traffic violations. A girl companion of a youthful speeder may be protected from further sex experimentation. Boys whose only amusement seems to be joyriding in family cars can be directed to other more suitable forms of entertainment before they reach the stage of "borrowing" cars when the family car is unavailable.[29]

It was, of course, the arrogance and assumption of limitless power in these judicial pronouncements that, however vaguely understood, made many people highly sensitive to the legal-rights aspects of the juvenile traffic controversy. By the same token, some California judges reacted to the issue as if it were basically ideological, and as such, a challenge to the paternalistic philosophy of the court. Commenting on legislation proposed in 1951, one judge said:

> Sound jugment would indicate that the best thing to do would be to leave our present court system alone, utilize the experience that has been gained and try to rectify the defects in the present law rather than constantly try to scrap or tear down all that has been accomplished in the past. . . .

Another judge expressed his anxiety as follows:

> I am afraid that were such legislation to be passed, it would be but the opening wedge in an effort to scuttle the present jurisdiction of the juvenile court.

A third judge spoke more bluntly:

29. *Ibid.*, p. 29.

As judge of the Juvenile Court of Solano County for the past seven
years, I am opposed to these two bills, both of which are clearly
violative of the express purpose of the Juvenile Act. . . .[30]

THE MERGING OF ISSUES

Other issues that entered into action to change the juvenile court
law were: the improvement of salaries and work facilities for
probation officers, the removal of conflicts and ambiguities in
the existing law that complicated their jobs, and the possibility
of vesting more power and authority in the probation department vis-à-vis the court itself. However, these were old and
familiar issues to probation and correctional people, and it is
doubtful that they excited strong interest in more than a minority of probation officers. According to a 1957 report of the
Special Study Commission on Correctional Facilities and Services, about 35 per cent of the state's probation officers favored
some kind of subsidy for probation services; however, only 29
per cent thought there was a need for "rationalization of the
juvenile court law." [31]

A tenable conclusion is that all the issues outlined above, when
put together, promoted a widespread desire for change in the juvenile court. But in fact social action for change emerged primarily within the context of the legal-rights issue. At least this is the
way in which many people in the state came to see it, namely,
as a kind of power move by attorneys or members of the legal
fraternity. This despite evidence that relatively few attorneys
knew the issues surrounding the juvenile court, and of those
who were informed, no more than a handful were interested
enough to become involved. Aside from this, as already indicated, scarcely more than a quarter of the probation officers in
the state believed that legal modifications were necessary for
improvement of the juvenile court. Although probation officers

30. *Ibid.*, pp. 30–32.
31. Special Study Commission on Correctional Facilities and Services, *Report
on Probation in California,* Sacramento, 1957, p. 84.

in many areas were perturbed about their role or lack of it in juvenile hearings, there were some in large probation departments who were opposed to changes of any kind, because workable solutions for this problem had already been devised, illegal though they might be.

In overview, the most to be said is that long-standing issues of the juvenile court were aggravated with passing time, others were redefined, and an entirely new one was created by the massive congestions in traffic courts. Changes or splits in legal opinion made the climate for change in the juvenile court law somewhat more favorable after 1950, but there was no large, powerful group or alignment of groups actively pushing for change. There was instead only a small number of individuals—a few exasperated attorneys, a handful of judges, some chief probation officers, a few administrators in the Department of Corrections and the C.Y.A., and a college professor or two—who agitated for the legal protection of juveniles. This "little band of men" in no sense rode a crest of public opinion demanding change but, on the contrary, were confronted with the formidable task of welding together under the banner of legal rights a variety of interests and values, some favorable to change, some not. In order to understand their success and failures, one must consider the value hierarchies of those vested with power to make decisions, the organizational instruments and strategies they employed, and the relevant processes of large and small group interaction they set in motion.

THE JUVENILE JUSTICE COMMISSION

The organizational device through which changes were sought in the juvenile court law took form when Governor Goodwin Knight appointed the Governor's Special Study Commission on Juvenile Justice late in 1957. While this was done for political reasons, it was not done for any particular political reasons. As the title indicates, it was a special type of commission, whose sponsorship and control differed significantly from those of legislative interim committees, under whose auspices a number of studies of delinquency, correctional procedures, jail conditions, and justice had been conducted in years previous.

Interim investigative and study committees in the past seldom had achieved any substantial modifications in the juvenile court law, largely because of their spurious status in the scheme of legislative action.[32] Such committees often, if not typically, were appointed to allow dissident groups and individuals to voice their dissatisfactions or otherwise to channel public opinion. Chairmen of these committees were taken seriously by other legislators only when they were personally respected or had status within the power cliques of the legislature. Until about 1959, various departments of the state government customarily worked through the committees when it was to their advantage, or cooperated when it was necessary. At the same time, departments pursued their own goals through independent contacts with legislators and standing committees. This latter practice, however, came to an end, at least formally, when Governor Edmond Brown decided after a short time in office that henceforth there would be only one administrative legislative program.

While the governor had the power to appoint special study commissions as early as 1923, by an Act of 1944, the board of Corrections could recommend the appointment of such bodies and more or less act as their housekeeper. Five commissions were appointed under Governor Warren's administrations, including the ill-fated 1949 juvenile justice commission. In 1957, at a meeting of the board of Corrections, Karl Holton, no longer C.Y.A. director but now vice-chairman of the board, proposed that a commission be established to inquire into the need for revising the juvenile court law. Heman Stark, director of the C.Y.A., and former Judge Eugene Breitenbach readily joined with him. Richard McGee, director of the Department of Corrections, forwarded the idea together with his own support to Governor Knight, who acted forthwith. On request, Governor Brown renewed the commission's appointment when he came into office in 1958.

32. For a general statement on this, see: Julius Cohen, "Hearing on a Legislative Bill," *Minnesota Law Review* 37 (1952), 34–45.

COMPOSITION OF THE COMMISSION

Appointees to the commission all could be termed political, but only purely political in the case of a Negro attorney, George Vaughn, from Oakland. Mildred Prince, who was named chairman, had been active in Republican politics, but was a qualified lawyer. Her spouse was an attorney in a prominent San Francisco law firm, and she had served on the probation committee for San Francisco county. Another appointee, Robert Kingsley, had been politically active in Los Angeles, but more so his wife, who also was on the board of Corrections. Kingsley could claim a special competence for his assignment by reason of his position as professor of criminal law and dean of the Law School at the University of Southern California. A fourth member of the commission, William Dienstein, likewise had professorial status, teaching criminology at Fresno State College. Although his background was that of a police officer, he had done research on attitudes of teachers and police toward juvenile problems and published a book critical of court procedures in criminal cases.[33] The last member of the commission was Mrs. Kenneth Spencer, president of the State Parent Teachers Association, who, as might be expected, stood for the interests of educators and parents in a broad sense.

The staff of the commission excites particular interest because of the crucial part it came to play in policy deliberations. John A. Pettis, an Oakland attorney, on recommendation of the dean of the Boalt School of Law, Berkeley, was named project director. He had done work for the American Law Institute and easily was the most deeply committed participant in the commission work, perhaps describable as an embattled parent as well as a crusading attorney. I. J. Shain served as research director; he had worked for the Department of Education, knew the "ways of Sacramento," and leaned toward a kind of doctrinaire libertarianism. A simple arithmetic consideration of the commission make-up, including its staff, leaves no doubt that persons with

33. *Are You Guilty?* (Springfield: Charles Thomas, 1954).

professional allegiance to legal values were in the majority. But the elevation of their values to a position of dominance in deliberations of the commission was by no means inevitable; rather, the translation of these values into recommendations and ultimately, with some accommodations, into carefully worded statute revisions was problematic.

THE GROWTH OF POLICY RECOMMENDATIONS

Three factors operated importantly to guide interaction within the commission sessions along the theme of legal rights. First was the explicit awareness of a time limit on the task at hand; second was the arrogation of leadership by the project director; and third was a recurrent appreciation of the importance of strategic, step-by-step movements toward commission goals.

The time limit was more or less imposed upon the commission by the executive order under which it worked, which specified that recommendations were due in one year's time. As it turned out, this was extended, but the sense of working against time and deadlines continued to be present. The personal ascendancy of Pettis, the project director, to some extent rested on recommendations he had received for the job and on the persevering support of Richard McGee, director of Corrections. The chairman of the commission, being a woman and less assertive than a man might be, left wide room for maneuver by other members of the commission. Further, since recommendations were to be based upon research, the full-time project director was in an excellent position to set down conditions under which topics could or should be pursued in discussions. Finally, due heed must be given the superior persuasive powers of Pettis, born of his skills and his conception of himself as a kind of lawyer-negotiator.

One of the first tasks of the commission was to delimit the scope of its work, made necessary by the governor's sweeping directive, namely:

> to study, evaluate, and make recommendations respecting all matters related to juvenile justice and the protection of minors together

with general problems involved and dealing with dependent children, minor offenders against the laws including their apprehensions, detention, prosecution, supervision, treatment, and rehabilitation.[34]

At first the commission sought to demarcate its areas for study by soliciting ideas from semi-official agencies in the state, following precedents set by earlier commissions. However, this effort soon became much more "inner-directed," for one reason because letters of reply to inquiries were slow to come in. Only one had been received by the time of the second meeting of the commission. Meantime the minutes revealed that the subject of legal rights already was conspicuous in the ideas voiced by its members. To some extent this tone or emphasis had been set by Heman Stark, who, in preliminary appearance before the group, reviewed the history of prior action to study and change the juvenile court law.

Early in the game the commission decided that its chief task would be that of making juvenile court statutes more effective, and in so doing, assumed that the existing structure of the juvenile court would continue. However, in the very first meeting Pettis attended, he took exception to this decision:

Mr. Pettis said he noted in the minutes of the previous meeting that the Commission should proceed on the assumption that the juvenile court structure will continue to exist as we have known it. He thought that, aside from questions of segregated detention and treatment, questions which are raised as to counsel and other rights of juveniles strike at the heart of the whole idea.[35]

The commission members offered no objections, despite their prior stand, and on the surface almost casually took on what was to eventuate in a wholesale revision of the law. The recorder states:

34. Governor's Executive Order, September 23, 1957, Executive Department, State of California.
35. Minutes of the Governor's Special Study Commission on Juvenile Justice, January 9, 1958, p. 9.

The group appeared to agree that one area for study should be: To "spell out" the complete philosophy related to the whole juvenile court situation.[36]

Both Kingsley and Pettis were in accord on the necessity for narrowing the orbit of the commission inquiry. Dienstein, though agreeable to this, wanted it made clear that the "whole field" had been considered. In the same session (number two) the chairman voiced her sense of the pressure of time and also her sensitivity to the strategic or public-relations aspects of the commission's work:

> Mrs. Prince said that after a certain stage in the work had been reached, it would probably seem necessary to have a series of public hearings to which should be invited a comparatively large number of groups to give them an opportunity to receive a progress report and also to express their own opinions. . . . She thought as a time-saving measure, it might be expedient to have individual members conduct hearings in different areas. . . . She recognized the public relations value in being able to bring to the attention of the legislature the fact that the thinking of other groups had been enlisted.[37]

After a list of six areas for study had been prepared by the staff, the project director cited the limitation of time to argue for a focus on legal rights and procedures:

> Mr. Pettis stated it was the feeling of the staff that under present limitations of time, it was unlikely that an adequate job could be done on more than one of the topics listed . . . [he] then proposed that, subject to the Commission's approval, the focus of the study be on the juvenile court.[38]

Having won on this point, the staff then submitted to the commission a list of eleven topics falling directly in the area of

36. *Ibid.*, p. 11.
37. *Ibid.*, p. 15.
38. Minutes of the Governor's Special Study Commission on Juvenile Justice, March 11, 1958, p. 8.

legal rights, jurisdiction, and procedures of the juvenile court, stating that it had been guided by five sources in arriving at the proposals: the frequency of suggestions by informed persons, the governor's executive order, recommendations of previous commissions, recent studies, and nation-wide literature. The assignment of priorities to "key issues in the administration of justice," however, was attributed to the interests of the commission, its consultants, and what had been "uppermost in the minds of members of the Board of Corrections when they requested the Governor to establish the Commission." [39]

THE ADUMBRATION OF A PARADIGM

For obvious political reasons the early deliberations of the commission did not begin with a bold explicit plan for a new-style juvenile court. Yet the inference was plain that among some of the commission members and their partisans some such paradigm already existed, as demonstrated by reference to what had been "uppermost in the minds of members of the Board of Corrections when they requested the Governor to establish the Commission." This coterie was looking at the world of juvenile justice with new and different eyes, and as a consequence they began to perceive new "key issues," which had been of little concern or awareness to those committed to the old philosophy of the court. These were soon spelled out:

1. Whether separate characterizations of court wards was not preferable to loose and generalized categories.

2. Whether facts should not be determined by court hearings instead of informally by probation officers.

3. Whether rights of juveniles should not be protected by specific means rather than left to the general concern for their welfare.

4. Whether the idea of "allowing" counsel in juvenile court should not be replaced by a positive right to counsel.

39. *Ibid.* (Appendix) , March 3, 1958, p. 1.

5. Whether the "pre-sentence clinic idea" should not be replaced with rules for restricted use of detention.

6. Whether sharply defined allocation of powers between police and probation departments should not replace the loose and variable *ad hoc* arrangements that existed.

Further evidence that there was a pre-existing focus of plan and thought among some members of the commission was disclosed by the manner in which digressive ideas were handled. In the first few sessions of the commission, some members suggested a need to study the "social concepts of the juvenile court," and Mrs. Spencer, responding to claims of her outside role, asked the commission to examine the relationship of the schools to the juvenile court. However, these ideas were more or less bypassed, in the first instance by Heman Stark's reminder that there was no need to expand the social concepts of the court, and in the second, by the expedient of "farming out" a school-court study to the Department of Education. The semblance of a more comprehensive inquiry was further achieved by delegating a bibliographic study of literature and delinquency and the juvenile court to be done by the Bureau of Public Administration, of the University of California, Berkeley.

COMMISSION PROCEDURE

Aside from carrying on intensive discussions of its own, the commission consulted with state and national authorities, organized public hearings in several cities, north and south, and created a professional advisory committee. At the same time, commission members and staff individually interviewed or talked informally with a variety of interested people, including representatives of associations throughout the state. Most of the consultants who came before the group at its scheduled sessions were "friendly," tending to reinforce rather than question the commission's emphasis on legal rights and juvenile court procedures. Public hearings were not expected to contribute useful ideas but were arranged largely with the intent of deflecting or containing public reactions to the commission's work.

Dean Kingsley . . . remarked that although public hearings are actually more therapeutic than educational, the therapeutic value is great and should not be neglected.[40]

The appointment and use of a Professional Advisory Committee, in contrast, was crucial to the commission's procedure, since it was both to provide technical advisors for working out study methods and to act as a sounding-board for recommendations. More important, this committee was to be formal and demonstrable evidence that the juvenile justice commission had fully consulted with working specialists in courts, correctional agencies, and welfare organizations of the state. Be this as it may, the commission did not intend the committee to consent as well as advise, as shown by the careful manner in which members were chosen—either known or assumed to be sympathetic to the commission's plans—and also by the special way in which they were brought into discussions.[41]

The advisory committee was first convened to criticize and comment on questionnaires devised for circulation to juvenile court personnel. Later these were mailed to 96 law enforcement officers, 57 juvenile court judges, and 54 probation officers in 58 counties. A second advisory committee was convened after the commission had formulated its preliminary recommendations and encouraged those present to give candid criticism and advice. Although many of the recommendations prepared for discussion escaped criticism, not so others. In the two-day meetings, Pettis, Kingsley, and Dienstein had to meet vigorous and pointed challenges to a number of pivotal proposals. One judge felt sufficiently disturbed to state that the basic philosophy of the juvenile court was in jeopardy:

40. *Ibid.*, May 27, 1958, p. 5. Plans for the meetings included suggested topics for discussion, invitations to speakers, time limits for speeches, and provision to submit statements in writing to the commission. See Minutes, May 10, 1958, p. 3.

41. A high-ranking C.Y.A. official explained to me: "I recommended a number of appointments to the Professional Advisory Committee. We were sure of everyone. Law enforcement was under-represented in the south but not in the north. We planned it that way."

Judge Cronin also agreed that some uniformity of handling is needed. However, he believed that many of the Commission's proposals to achieve this goal would lead to destruction of the juvenile court.[42]

One recommendation (no. 33) particularly aroused the displeasure of judges at the meeting, even those known to be cordial to the commission's general purposes. It also made some of the probation officers uneasy. The controversial proposal specified that judges should leave treatment decisions entirely to their probation departments and "in the event that the court chooses to reject the recommended treatment plan, the court be required to set forth in the court order the reason for its action." [43]

The commission had mixed reactions to its meetings with the committee, revealing an inconsistent tendency to minimize the importance of criticisms coupled with an implicit recognition of their validity, or at least of their existence:

> Their general reaction to the proposed recommendations was considered favorable, although a few of the proposals evoked criticism. However, there was no consensus among P.A.C. members on the items under consideration. Nevertheless, the Commission agreed to revise several of the tentative recommendations in the light of the Advisory Committee comments.[44]

As a matter of fact, the commission changed or reworded most of the recommendations, among them the touchy number 33, which was revised to read that judges merely had to "certify that they had read and considered the probation report prior to issuing treatment orders." The commission's plan to place jurisdiction over ordinary juvenile traffic offenses in regular traffic courts, like proposal 33, was strongly opposed, and indeed, earlier there had been differences within the commission itself on this matter. In this one instance the advisory committee actively "consented" or participated in drawing up two alternatives, one

42. Minutes of the Governor's Special Study Commission on Juvenile Justice, October 2 and 3, 1959, 8.
43. *Op. cit.*, 29.
44. *Op. cit.*, October 20, 1959, 1.

putting juvenile traffic cases under juvenile court referees, the other under regular traffic judges, leaving the way open to settle the issue at a later date, or by the legislature itself. However, by the time of the commission's report, members had swung over to acceptance of the first alternative.

The commission retreated only slightly from its explicit recommendations on the rights of juveniles and parents to counsel, by deleting no more than a provision that they had to *expressly* waive their rights. A recommended separation or "bifurcation" of jurisdictional hearings and dispositional hearings also was altered, to allow these hearings to be held on the same day.

INFORMAL CONSULTATION

The amount of informal consultation by commission members and its staff with administrative specialists and field workers was considerable and took several forms. Some members attended professional meetings, whose actions they reported. Others, such as Pettis, met with persons on the advisory committee in different localities, and also with middle-echelon C.Y.A. officials. Shain did considerable traveling about the state, interviewing probation officers and judges in conjunction with the commission's questionnaire study. Inasmuch as both men began their work with little or no direct experience with juvenile court work, consultation was for them an educational process. According to one C.Y.A. official:

> At first Pettis and Shain made their contacts through our Director [Stark] and his assistant. Later they came directly to us. Proposals were presented to us on about the same basis as to the P.A.C. Some of them were pretty naive, and we pointed out a number of things that were totally unworkable. We influenced some changes and failed to get other changes. We were at least as influential as the large probation departments.

It is quite possible that this type of informal interaction significantly influenced the commission to change and reformulate its ideas. A case in point is the dialogue between Kingsley and Shain regarding the traffic issues. The difficulties the latter pointed out in the way of Dean Kingsley's desire to see juvenile traffic violations handled in regular courts appeared to be direct reflections of outside attitudes he had absorbed in his state-wide travels.

The picture of informal, as well as formal, consultation that emerges is of a one-way flow of positive ideas from members of the commission, the staff particularly, and a counterflow of agreement or disagreement from those consulted, accompanied by their reasons and arguments. Aside from the traffic problem, there is little evidence that persons outside the commission were called on to formulate or reformulate its proposals; at most they could secure changes in ideas already stated. The recommendation, wording, and drafting of the new juvenile court statute were all closely monopolized by the commission. The draft statute, for example, was almost entirely Pettis' work, with a little assistance from the legislative counsel.

The over-all pattern of consultation followed by the commission was distorted both by inadvertent and by designed ambiguity. Quite early, commission members decided that whenever they appeared before interested organizations, they would be speaking for themselves rather than for the commission as a whole. Further, the pose consistently taken by Pettis and others in consulting was that nothing had been settled definitely by the commission, and that all of its conclusions were open to continuing criticism and amenable to change. Uncertainty about the commission's final intentions got compounded by the decision to delay issuance of its two final reports until November 1960, in order for them to have maximum impact on the legislature. Two legislative hearings already had been held on recommendations before their publication. Perhaps the delay was a move to forestall opposition, which had begun to be sensed by the commission members after the last P.A.C. conferences, on October 2 and 3, 1959. If so, it would not be inconsistent with the meticulous attention given by the commission to the strategic problems of securing the most positive reception possible for its work in legislative circles.

THE FINAL RECOMMENDATIONS

The final report of the commission contained thirty-one recommendations plus a draft statute for the new law. These advocated radical departures from the old law, specifying the right to counsel, separate jurisdictional categories for dependent, neglected, and delinquent children, restrictions on dispositions derived from these categories, bifurcated hearings to establish jurisdiction of the court before it considered dispositions, procedures for juvenile traffic hearings, recordings of hearings, special rules of evidence, elimination of "double jeopardy," requirement that "findings" be made by judges, standards for the appointment of referees, provision for detention hearings, clarification of juvenile arrest procedures, establishment of probation departments as agencies of county government, and the organization of annual conferences of juvenile court judges.

These and other recommendations were stated to rest upon eight basic principles, which heavily accented the priority of parent-child relationships and the rights of minors to fair treatment under formal guarantees of procedural law. At the same time, the commission members, by now well aware of growing opposition to their work, sought to make their stand more palatable by stating that the principles were consistent with juvenile court philosophy and also that they were "widely accepted." There was an implication of the commission's sensitivity to criticism in the italicized statements asserting that full participation and consultation had been obtained from juvenile court workers in the state:

It is significant that virtually all of California's juvenile court judges, chief probation officers, chief law enforcement officers and administrators voluntarily participated in the field study. . . .

Or, again in italics:

The recommendations presented by the Commission in this report are products of an extensive, conscientious process of review and re-evaluation in which numerous local juvenile control and judicial officials throughout the state actively participated.[45]

THE PROCESS OF CONTROL

An apt and full conception of the process by which the juvenile justice commission of 1958 maintained legal values in a position of dominance during its studies, deliberations, and consultations is not easily formed. The tenets of the commission, despite its claims that they were accepted widely as principles, closely resembled implicit, or *precarious*, values, to invoke Clark's term. Meaning: (1) that they had to be defined; (2) the position of their advocates was not fully legitimized; (3) they were, as it materialized, unacceptable to a goodly number of the "host" population.[46] To establish their base in public and legislative opinion was a formidable task likely to require unusual procedures.

The anomalous form of the commission, being more or less an *ad hoc* body lodged in the interstices of official policy-making and administrative organizations of the state, offered opportunities to wield novel or charismatic power, if not to create a new power structure. For this reason, many legislators were opposed to the perpetuation of commissions like these. The part-time status of the commission's members, the passive role of the chairman, and the emphasis on research gave a good deal of pre-emptory power to the project director. Yet his assumption of leadership over policy formation in the stead of the chairman could only provoke questions about the legitimacy of his role.[47] The director of Corrections, like other powerfully placed per-

45. Report of the Governor's Special Study Commission on Juvenile Justice (Part I) , pp. 10, 11.
46. Burton R. Clark, "Organizational Adaptation and Precarious Values," in *Complex Organizations*, ed. Amitai Etzioni (New York: Holt, Rinehart, and Winston, 1961), pp. 160–61.
47. There was a great deal of personal criticism of Pettis' role in the commission, and even some effort to impugn his motives as arising from his own unpleasant episodes with juvenile court judges. *Senate Committee on Judiciary on Juvenile Justice and Procedures on Juvenile Courts*, Los Angeles, November 24, 1960, p. 42.

sons in the state, could give Pettis continuous informal support but could not openly sanction his ideas or those of the commission.

Another factor affecting the techniques of influence and action elected by the commission, perhaps more historical than sociological, was the lingering shadow of failure of the 1949 juvenile justice commission. Those "around" who recalled that commission's difficulties attributed them in no small degree to the personal ineptitude or political shortcomings of its members. Close supporters of the 1958 commission shared a private conviction that its success or failure would hinge on political strategy and tactical approach to the legislature. Pettis was admirably chosen for the latter task, for in addition to being a clever lawyer, he was the son of a highly successful lobbyist; it was said that he learned the art "at his father's knee."

Sheer skill at lobbying, however, would be unavailing if the commission could not go to the legislature with a show of support from the groups and professional associations whose practices it was criticizing and whose ways it was trying to alter. The dilemma of leadership became one of gaining their support without making compromises that would undercut the fundamental aims of the commission.[48]

The pattern of operations followed by the leader of the commission—and here the contributions of its other members are not being discounted—fits most nearly La Piere's conception of "ascendancy through conference." This not uncommon method of social control in our present society appears where a demand for democratic participation must be reconciled with action to promote values that may be either unfamiliar to participants or unacceptable. La Piere discusses in some detail the way in which conferences can be used for ascendancy:

A group conference . . . may aid a would-be ascendant in the development or at least refinement of his program; he may profit from the pooled experiences of others and thus avoid some of the errors that are inevitable in thinking out the solution to any problem. More likely, he may learn the nature of the pride and prejudices of

48. See statement by Pettis. Minutes, *op. cit.*, February 11, 1960, p. 16.

various members which will have to be taken into account and
somehow circumvented in putting into effect any program of action
. . . it may serve as a setting for his maneuvering one or more members into accepting paternalistic responsibility for a policy that is
ultimately decided upon.[49]

Ascendancy through conference lends itself well to use by administrators and it is most effective when the conferees are part
of the same organization as the administrator, or to whom some
other structured controls can be applied. Policy unity among
groups loosely connected by common interests rather than by
formal organization is less predictably achieved by capturing
their leaders in conferences. In the present case, where leaders
were presumed to represent associations—such as those of law
enforcement and probation officers policy unity was even harder
to achieve. The possibility that conflicts and cleavages would
arise to undermine the claim of representatives to speak for such
associations could not be lightly ignored. A special difficulty was
the absence of any formal association among California judges
—besides which their extreme individuality made it doubtful
that any one judge or even panel of judges could be taken as
their spokesman.

As the commission passed from policy deliberations to talk
of ways and means of lobbying, some members began to voice
doubts about efforts to capture organizations by securing their
formal endorsements.

> Mr. Pettis . . . raised the question of employing Professional Ad-
> visory Committee members who support the Commission's program
> as a nucleus for any promotional group that may be organized. . . .
>   Mrs. Prince said . . . that one problem in attempting to get rep-
> resentatives of large groups to support the recommendations was
> that seldom is unanimous approval obtained . . . and small opposi-
> tion groups often develop. . . .
>   Dean Kingsley had some fear of attempting to get formal endorse-
> ments from large organizations.

49. Richard La Piere, *A Theory of Social Control*, McGraw-Hill, Inc., New
York, 1954, pp. 431, 432.

Dr. Dienstein believed that an attempt to get formal support from large organizations could easily lead to the development of minority opposition groups.[50]

GROUP METAMORPHOSIS

It was soon realized that the peculiar status of the commission was an obstacle in the way of carrying through as an action group to lobby for legislation on their recommendations. In the past it was the custom of the Department of Corrections director simply to forward study-commission reports to the governor without comment, and no departure from this was contemplated. Too, as already noted, Governor Brown's new rule that departments were not to act independently of his office in approaching the legislature gave the commission pause. Finally, in some quarters there was a feeling that commission members should not engage in lobbying.

> Mrs. Prince stated that Mr. Stark's suggestion evidently called for the Commission to release its report in June (1960) and then retreat from the scene. . . .
> Dean Kingsley said that there are probably a number of reasons why Mr. Stark did not favor the Commission's becoming involved in any lobbying activities. One may be that there is some question about department heads supporting issues without clearance from the Governor's office . . . another explanation might very well be that the lobbying efforts by previous Commission members were not too adroitly handled and it was feared that the present Commission might similarly become entangled.[51]

When the governor, or the legislature, did not put the juvenile justice commission's program on special call for the 1960 legislative session, the issue of lobbying by members lost its

50. Minutes, *op. cit.*, February 11, 1960, p. 16.
51. *Ibid.*, p. 11; see also Report of the Board of Corrections, November 20, 1959. According to one informant, communication between people on the 1949 juvenile justice commission and the governor's office broke down as a result of interpersonal difficulties with some of the governor's staff people.

urgency. By June 1960 the commission more or less fell into line with Stark's advice and decided to build support for its proposed revision of the law by means of promotional committees, but to leave the actual lobbying to an informal or *ad hoc* group.

There were two promotional committees, one north and one south. The northern committee was chaired by Helen McGregor, then an influential member of the Governor's Advisory Committee on Youth and Children, while Dean Kingsley and Karl Holton acted as co-chairmen for the committee below the Tehachapis. Funds for both committees were raised by Mrs. Prince in the Bay area. Their members wrote special articles for publication, circulated a variety of documents, and traveled about, making speeches to explain the commission's proposals and to counter the opposition, or, as one activist explained his assignment, "to smoke out the Indians."

Lobbying and appearances before legislative committees were carefully organized on a functional "team" basis, with the complete acceptance of Pettis as leader. The director of Corrections spelled out the line-up to Stark:

> Jack Pettis will act as quarterback so far as appearances before legislative committees and contacts with individual legislators are concerned and so forth. It is also understood that any assistance that can be given by Mr. Tregoning or yourself or other members of the Youth Authority will be available to him. The further understanding is that Walter Barkdull will be responsible for keeping track of the progress of legislation and notifying appropriate personnel when it is indicated. . . . [52]

This communication tells a great deal about the subordinate or auxiliary role the C.Y.A. came to play in the course of action by the juvenile justice commission. The highly explicit form of the memo suggests that it may actually have been an order phrased as a presumption, or a seemingly casual way of "pulling rank," by the head of the senior of the two correctional organizations. The hint of tension conveyed in the note may be explained by the peculiar position occupied by the C.Y.A. during

52. Richard McGee to Heman Stark, January 19, 1960.

the controversies over the juvenile justice commission's program. The stand taken by the C.Y.A. was an organic part of the more general opposition to the commission's ideas and plans, which sprang up in different parts of the state—a subject reserved for separate analysis in Chapter Five.

5
Resistance and Communication of the Paradigm

Discussion in this chapter concerns the ways in which the new conception of the juvenile court was communicated in social interaction and accepted by groups and persons having the power and influence to make relevant legislative decisions. As will be seen, the course of social action became a stormy one, and resistance built up to formidable proportions. Both social action and its resistance were complicated by a general societal context in which an ongoing shift from local and regional associational forms was as yet incomplete. Some professional people were relatively unaffected by this change and remained unorganized, and for others the development of associations was at a formative stage. Additionally important was the normal tendency for established associations to wax and wane and undergo transition in response to the swift pace of over-all social change. In this instance the California setting made for further complications, owing not only to its rapid growth, but also to the atypical qualities of its political life.[1]

THE PATTERN OF RESISTANCE

Resistance to the program of the juvenile justice commission, whose omnibus proposals were drafted into Senate Bill 332 and

1. Henry Eulau, William Buchanan, LeRoy Ferguson, and John Wahlke, *Legislative Behavior* (New York: John Wiley, 1962) , p. 429.

introduced in 1961, had already begun to be asserted by the middle of 1960. However, in its early form, opposition was scattered and unorganized. Generally, the more forceful resistance tended to come late rather than early, owing to lack of knowledge of the activities of the commission, and to the vagueness with which its intentions became invested. The procedures of the commission, particularly the delay in the issuance of its final report, plus the provisional nature of interim working copies that got circulated, made concerted opposition difficult. Furthermore, the numerous recommendations, touching on all of the code sections of the juvenile court, demanded considerable study in order to grasp their detailed meaning, as well as to decipher the intent of the commission. Some who learned of the commission's work and realized its "true" purposes nevertheless dismissed it as "just another citizen's committee." Still others, even better informed, remained unmoved because they were convinced that bills written from propositions as radical as the commission's could never pass the legislature.

While opposition in part was local in origin and significance, its more impressive cast lay in the way it transcut localities, functional groups, and professional aggregates with viable interests at stake. It also had a shifting, ineluctable quality difficult to comprehend and frustrating to the rationally organized partisans of the commission.

> The biggest obstacle we had to overcome was the tendency for people to herd together. We continually ran into generalizations. We countered with specific questions, but often we could not get specific replies.

Resistance was made complex, not only by its multi-based substantive quality, but also by its swings between substantive and ideological issues. I refer to the distinction between the kinds of choices to be made with regard to the proposed changes, i.e., between changing or not changing a system of rules, or acquiescing in changes in parts of the system in order to preserve the rest.[2] Put somewhat differently, resistance varied depending on

2. *Ibid.*

whether the changes sought were perceived as a revolutionary change in the conceptual design of the juvenile court. While it seems clear that the commission intended to substitute a new design for the old, this intent was never so publicized. Moreover, the new design, while likely to affect systems of rules evolved by some juvenile courts of the state, was not necessarily a basic threat to established systems in all the courts. Conflict along this dimension and the aggregation of resistance along substantive lines can best be clarified by consideration of each of the large groups whose interests variously were at stake.

PROBATION OFFICERS

The first definitive resistance to the revision of the juvenile court law came to life among probation officers, who had the opportunity to examine an early draft of the law, which was mimeographed and distributed by several of their number. Opposition began to be aired in lively discussions of regional chapters of the California Probation, Parole, and Correctional Officers Association. Anxieties of probation officers got communicated back to their respective judges, some of whom were aroused by "dangerous proposals" included in the draft materials. Judges in turn reinforced or activated these anxieties, and here and there caused some probation officers to change their announced views from favorable to unfavorable. Involvement of the judges, predictably, centered with degrees of indignation on the recommendation that probation departments be made independent departments of county government.

Probation people gave their first official indication of resistance in January 1960 by urging the governor not to place revision of the juvenile court law on the program for the 1960 legislative session. This action was taken by the board of directors of the association, following a long discussion of the commission's recommendations at a plenary meeting of the entire membership.[3]

3. Report, Board of Directors, California Probation, Parole, and Correctional Officers Association, January 21, 1960, p. 4.

By June a strong negative stance toward the law revision was well established among probation officers, at least among those who attended the meetings of the association at that time. One resolution left little doubt about the majority attitude:

> *Therefore be it Resolved* that the California Probation Parole and Correctional Officers Association opposes repeal of the present Juvenile Court Law and favors changes of the existing law through amendment thereof.[4]

The reason given for the action formalized in the resolution was that definition of the law is properly a function of appellate courts, the Attorney General, district attorneys, and county counsels, and that repeal would mean the "loss of the precedents of case law." Another section of the resolution made it clear that the proposal to remove juvenile traffic offenses from the jurisdiction of the juvenile court caused the probation officers much alarm, which may help explain why sometime between June and November 1960 the commission did an about-face in its position on the traffic issue.

The C.P.P.C.A. in recent years had grown to embrace a very large and heterogeneous membership of parole officers, custodial officers, and juvenile hall counselors, as well as probation officers. Just where the more powerful heads of probation departments stood in its midst was not readily determined. However, a questionnaire poll of chief probation officers in November 1960 disclosed that of thirty-nine who replied, twenty-three opposed and only fourteen supported the commission's proposals. Twenty-six of the chiefs thought the revisions would be of "major importance" in the functioning of their courts, twelve said not. Twenty-nine said they would seek support for their views from their legislative representative, three would not.[5]

Much if not most of the opposition tabulated in the poll concentrated among chief probation officers in the Central Valley counties.

Closer analysis of probation officer resistance reveals that in

4. Resolution No. 5, C.P.P.C.A., Long Beach, June 10, 1960.
5. Letter, files of Chief Probation Officers Association, November 21, 1960.

the beginning a good deal of it could be attributed to a feeling that their integrity had been impugned and their public image blemished by assertions of members of the commission. These aggravated a kind of symbolic wound made previously by criticism implicit in the 1958 survey of the California juvenile court.[6] Passing time, however, caused the feeling to diminish and be replaced with more specific reactions:

> Initially we all responded to the Juvenile Justice Commission recommendations as an attack on us, and we were defensive. We were already somewhat defensive because of the *Stanford Law Review* article. But we got over this and came to feel that the criticism was actually aimed at the judges. Eventually we got to a point where we thought we could live with it. Some of us also saw it as a life time opportunity to get some things we had always wanted.

To say that "we," meaning most probation officers, came to accept the recommendations before they became law overdraws the facts. More accurately, the early total opposition developed a deep fissure almost equally splitting the pros and the cons. With continued group discussion and individual reflection, the early status anxieties subsided to the point where the obvious gains for probation officers in the recommendations began to exert their undeniable appeal. It was seen that their net effect was to enhance, rather than lower, the status and power of the group, as indicated in the proposal to make them independent of judges, and in giving them decision-making precedence vis-à-vis the police in filing petitions.

But the articulation of opinion, sharpening of issues, and concern over the costs of anticipated changes also had the dialectical effect of clarifying other sources of opposition. Many of the probation officers in less populated counties believed (with good reason) that the contemplated changes were heavily, if not exclusively, weighted in favor of large urban counties. A very explicit cost aspect was attached to the provision of attorneys for juveniles, for smaller counties were confronted with the painful question of how they were to be paid. In addition, the oppor-

6. *Stanford Law Review* 10 (1958), 471–524.

tunity for independence, so attractive to a number of chief probation officers, proved an anathema to those in several "valley" counties, whose chiefs feared that control by their particular county supervisors would be far more hazardous than durance under the caprices of judicial control. Ultimately legislators came to agree with them.

A small number of probation officers saw the proposals as a direct attack on the traditional, and to them sacred, form of the juvenile court, which threatened to destroy the court's informality or replace it with a full-fledged system of adversary justice. Indeed, there continued to be a feeling of uneasiness about the "adversary features" of the proposed law even among those who made calculated decisions that its positive aspects outweighed the negative. The most extreme statement of resistance, on grounds that the essence of the juvenile court system would be abolished, came from a highly articulate chief probation officer of a Central Valley county, Robert Mowrers:

> It has been said that the proposed law represents no basic change from the present Juvenile Court Law. Actually the change is so fundamental and profound as to create an entirely new philosophy in court work with juveniles. We are to abandon a guardianship type of proceeding for an adversary proceeding without a prosecutor present. The social court is to become a junior criminal court without a conviction of crime possible.[7]

A final broad base on which the opposition of probation officers rested, and which continued to make those supporting the new legislation ambivalent, derived from a sense of illegitimacy or unfairness associated with the methods followed by the commission. These were seen as secretive, manipulatory, or denying participation to professionals legitimately entitled to jointly formulate changes in the law as sweeping as those presently envisioned:

> The primary basis for opposition may be the uncertainty commonly expressed as to exactly what the Commission is proposing. Even at

7. Statement by Robert Mowrers, files of Subcommittee of Assembly Committee on Criminal Procedure (SB 332), n. d.

this late date, two months prior to the convening of the legislature, the Commission has not made its specific recommendations known, although everyone knows that they have made a report to the Board of Corrections, as required by law. Some persons have procured copies of the proposed legislation . . . but also have been informed that "some further changes" have been made. Just what these changes are and what caused them to be made is not known. But the operation seems strange to many and gives credence to the idea that mysterious forces are operating to force through the legislature a whole new juvenile court law without subjecting it to any reasonable criticism of informed persons.[8]

The same sense of exclusion from participation in changing the juvenile court law was voiced by another probation officer, who agreed with the commission in principle:

There is no quarrel with the expressed principles of the Juvenile Justice Commission, but its proposals underwrite the principles only vaguely where they do at all . . . what the Commission says it wants . . . can be provided by changing the law in specific details, and should be done by a cooperative effort of the judges, probation officers and law enforcement officials who have the job to do after the changes are made, as well as before.[9]

While most of the chief probation officers undoubtedly shared the feeling that they had not been brought into significant decision-making preliminary to revision of the law, this feeling underwent a late-hour change. According to the president of the C.P.P.C.A., Loren Beckley, "We began to feel a sense of participation towards the end." This, he further indicated, came after a "high point in the opposition," when the board of directors of the association voted 13 to 10 to approve a resolution of support for the commission's bill:

It is recommended that the Legislative Committee be authorized to give support to Senate Bill 332, without actual appearance in the

8. Don Sansone to Mr. Cocks, Los Angeles Board of Supervisors, November 7, 1960.
9. Statement by Robert Mowrers to Senate Judiciary Committee, n. d.

Committees of the Legislature, and to continue to negotiate with the Commission and its representatives for further modification in incidental detail.[10]

In sum, the course of the probation officers' resistance began with initial total opposition motivated by symbolic resentment. There followed a period of protracted conflict and debate, in which law items got sorted out in a more studied way, which allowed possible instrumental effects of the changes to be gauged, as well as the threat they posed for systematically held values. Eventually the influential leaders of the group grew convinced that they could accommodate to the changes. Some even saw the chance to upgrade their values, especially after they found means to secure amendments in the commission's original legislative draft. Opposition was quieted, rather than eliminated.

The late entry of law enforcement people into the controversy undoubtedly did much in a tangential way to firm up support among probation officers and weaken their opposition. Police resistance was total and intransigent in its organized expression, and few probation officers wanted to be identified with their extreme position. In the end the opposition dwindled to the lone and alienated voice of one chief, Robert Mowrers. He was accused in some quarters of being a "backwoodsman" and also of "going over" to the police, but this is an oversimplified interpretation of his actions.[11]

JUDGES

Resistance of judges to the commission's proposals from first to last was a direct response to the attack seen on the philosophical foundations of the juvenile court. In contrast to the proba-

10. Report, Legislative Committee, C.P.P.C.A., February 9, 1961.
11. Actually, Mowrers had been publishing articles in the *California Police Officer* since 1957. A more charitable idea is that like a number of other probation officers, he was more law-enforcement-oriented than the great majority of those in his field.

tion officers, very few judges changed their positions from one side to the other during the conflict. Judicial opposition simply went down to defeat, a consummation owing in no small part to their special characteristics as judges.

In the survey conducted by the chief probation officers, respondents stated that seventeen of their respective judges would oppose the proposals and nine would support them. My own intensive study of the matter, based on interviews and document files, suggests that judges in twenty-six to twenty-eight counties were opposed to changing the law. Proportionately more of these judges could be found in Central Valley areas, in the so-called "class B" counties. The opposition judges are most correctly designated a plurality, inasmuch as judges holding strong pro views or those actively working for the prospective law were few in number; the majority were either apathetic on the issues, or at most, marginally interested.

Resistance ran strong among judges because the announced objectives, research findings, and public agitation of the juvenile justice commission and its action group successors cast judges in the role of devils of the piece. Like probation officers, some judges had been put on the defensive beforehand, largely the result of publicity or professional gossip about the Orange County cases. Rumors and reports of the plans of the commission, the informally circulated copies of its conclusions, and its published reports led many judges to feel that they were being condemned out of hand, and that public trust in their offices was being undermined. One judge wrote:

> The Commission seems to have fixed the idea of protecting juveniles from cruel, inhuman, irresponsible, and sometimes incompetent judges.[12]

Many judges were willing to concede that some of their people were arbitrary in general or had acted in an arbitrary manner toward attorneys who appeared in their juvenile courts. But they also felt that the majority of their colleagues were fairminded and that they were being tarnished or stigmatized for

12. Ross A. Carkeet to Senator Regan, November 21, 1960.

the misdeeds of a few. To them this was simply a part of the more general problem, long-standing, of the qualifications of judges. The real issue was one of disciplining or removing a few "bad guys" from their midst. It was a grievous mistake to drastically alter the law, which had evolved from judicial practice and interpretation over a long period. A judge recollected how he had felt at the time:

> I think that somewhere along the line the people who make the law are going to have to impose some trust in the juvenile judges. I didn't think the juvenile court law should be rewritten just because it was fifty years old, because it worked very well for fifty years and it's done a very fine job. Just because we had some rotten areas, some judges abusing rights—that situation should have been cleaned up; the judges are the ones that should have been taken to task, not the law.

As a whole, judges were less informed than probation officers about details of the contemplated revision of the juvenile court law, yet were more unified in statements of opposition. Judges were aroused to the threat of the new law changes almost single-handedly by the energetic action of Ross A. Carkeet, who presided over superior and juvenile courts in a small mountain county. He studied the changes, then sent out letters of critical analysis and statements urging other judges to act. In addition, he sent letters to probation officers, sheriffs' departments, constables, and boards of supervisors. The response was letters of protest to the Senate Judiciary Committee and to individual legislators.

In their letters addressed to legislators and legislative committees, judges singled out for strong objection a number of specific items in the law draft. However, the common theme of their complaints was that the philosophy of the juvenile court would be destroyed, informality in proceedings would disappear, and the court would be replaced by a "pint-sized" criminal court:

> I feel that you have stated . . . the main and most important issue, namely, the well-established concept of our Juvenile Court Law

in the state of California, the benevolent and protective philosophy
of the Juvenile Court in its effort to do what is best for the child.[13]

I for one would approach with distaste the handling of the average
juvenile offender in a formal manner, hedged about with technical
requirements rather than in the spirit of paternalism and helpful-
ness.[14]

I am unalterably opposed to the creation of a "Junior Criminal
Court," and many of the provisions which I note in the Committee
brochure would appear to me to do just that. I feel strongly that
the more you bring in bailiffs, court reporters, district attorneys,
and the like, the farther away we are getting from counseling youth
in trouble.[15]

Judges even more than probation officers took offense at the
manner and method in which the law revision was being made—
imputing something of lese majesty to those responsible. More
specifically, they felt that they had been either deliberately or
unaccountably disregarded by those seeking to replace the old
law with one of their making:

It seems to me that the juvenile court judges themselves are the
people who are best qualified by experience, training, and day-to-
day administration of the Juvenile Court Law to evaluate and
recommend any needed changes. . . . At no time, to the best of my
knowledge, were the juvenile court judges of this state as a group
ever given the opportunity to discuss in detail with the Commission any of its findings, recommendations or proposed changes.[16]

While protest was first articulated among probation officers,
its burden was taken up by the judges, whose opinion and
action became a middle phase of the resistance, and its high
point. Many of the probation people feared the divisive consequences of continued opposition. Those who were still disposed to carry on the battle apparently pinned their hopes on

13. Judge Elmer Heald to Judge Ross A. Carkeet, May 11, 1961.
14. Judge Samuel Finley to Judge Ross A. Carkeet, March 19, 1961.
15. Judge Quincy Brown to John Bohn, Secretary, Senate Judiciary Committee, November 18, 1960.
16. Judge Quincy Brown to Assemblyman Bruce Summer, January 24, 1961.

the superior prestige of the judiciary.[17] But the opposition judges, while united, failed to stem the tide; their tactic of getting Senate Bill 332 referred to an interim committee for further study was unavailing. Reasons for this failure will presently be given in a more general context. Meantime, the resistance was taken up by the police, who spun out its last, somewhat chaotic phase. Yet, despite the lack of concert in police opposition, in many respects it was to become the most redoubtable.

POLICE

A full understanding of police resistance to the proposed revisions requires attention to their late appearance on the scene of controversy, and their keen sensitivity to more than a decade of appellate court decisions they believed attenuated their power and impeded their efficiency. A special truculence colored police opposition, owing to its focus in the southern part of the state under the direct influence of the strong-minded Los Angeles chief, William Parker, who was a leading exponent of police organization and efficiency.[18] In marked contrast were the attitudes of many police in northern California, who had a stronger tradition of co-operation with community agencies and felt no direct threat to their vested interests.

The police in Los Angeles had long been at odds with the probation department and the county supervisors. In addition, both in Los Angeles and in Long Beach, the police had for some time become accustomed to utilizing jail detention for their purposes. Comments by Jack Pettis indicate the connection between tangible losses the police faced with change in the law and their strong reaction:

17. In a letter to Judge Carkeet, March 2, 1960, Robert Mowrers stated that he believed "judges will have to make the opposition."

18. Parker himself was involved in A.C.L.U.-promoted litigation lasting six years, a suit having to do with criminal evidence allegedly obtained illegally through the use of dictaphones. See Wirin v. Parker, 48 Cal. 2d 890 (1957). Parker and other police for some years had continued to be bothered by the inequity of the Cahan decision. See People v. Cahan, 44 Cal. 2d 434 (1953).

Most of the static came from police departments—Los Angeles in particular. This centered around their desire to continue to use jail for purposes of detention. The Georgia Street jail was used in this way. Also, Long Beach had built a new detention section in the jail, and police as well as the Probation Department there woke up and realized that they were not going to be able to use detention as they had before. All of this is related to the police's routine use of detention for punishment purposes.

The police also grew perturbed over a number of other sections in the revised law after some of their people studied the commission's draft proposals. First the forty-eight hours allotted before a detention hearing was too short for the police investigators to "make a case" when necessary. Second, the transferral of control over custody of juveniles during this interim from the police to probation officers made the situation of outlying police divisions in large counties trying or impossible. Finally, the lack of any allowance for police referrals was interpreted as a serious disruption of the policy and procedures for juvenile arrests that had been carefully devised and followed in Los Angeles.

While the police gave some marginal allegiance to the *parens patriae* philosophy of the juvenile court, their criticisms of the prospective law neither revealed nor implied a firm defense of the concept. Rather, they directed their attacks at what to them was cynicism or insincerity on the part of members of the commission. They charged that the recommended legal changes were represented as leaving the juvenile court philosophy unimpaired, when in reality they were newly instituting an adversary system. They also argued that synthesis of two systems was impossible, and that if an adversary system was brought in, the interests of the state would be sacrificed, because there was no provision for their representation in hearings. The obvious remedy was to make a role for the prosecuting attorney, yet the commission was unprepared to do this.

That status anxieties were writ large across the face of police resistance is not to be denied. More and more the police had come to look on themselves as an aggrieved group whose power was being eroded by judicial decisions and changing public attitudes. At the same time, they entertained a more expansive view of themselves as defenders and spokesmen for public morality, decency, and ethics, whose decay had reached intolerable proportions. To their way of thinking, the latter was linked to change from a "society of morality to a society of normality," to the decline in family controls, and to the growth of a treatment ideology placing foremost the fear of doing anything likely to traumatize youth. And, as they saw it, these developments could have only adverse effects on the motivation of youth to comply with the law. The official comments of several leaders of police opposition are variations on this theme:

> In retrospect, I suppose it was inevitable that the brand of legal fetishism, which in recent years has made our adult courts a mockery, would attempt invasion of our Juvenile Courts. The steady parade of decisions by Appellate Courts, which have given protection to the criminal at the expense of the community, stands as a contributor to the appalling and increasing crime rate.[19]

> This [recommendations of the Juvenile Justice Commission] appears to be an extension of the obvious trend in legislative and judicial decrees in recent years. The police are charged with the responsibility of protecting the community, and no group does more to protect the rights of individuals who compose the community than the police. However, there are those who have developed and continue to foster the theory that on one hand is the community and on the other is the law violator, and somewhere out in space is the enemy of both.[20]

A number of these leaders charged, as had probation officers and judges, that they had not been adequately consulted, or consulted too late to successfully effect the outcome of the law revision. Some contended that members of the commission "knew what they wanted before they began," thus implying that they had never sincerely tried to consult with interested parties. Finally, there were those who displayed a kind of festering resent-

19. Comments by Deputy Chief Roger Murdock, Los Angeles Police Department, before Senate Interim Judiciary Committee on Juvenile Justice, November 29, 1960. Mimeo.

20. "California's New Juvenile Court Law," Jack Collins (captain, Juvenile Division, Los Angeles Police Department), n. d.

ment that they should even have to fight such legislation, which
was an overtone of their belief that they occupied a special position as protectors of community morality, which should be
inviolate. One hard-line police representative put it this way:

> If we lie doggo, bills get passed making the situation worse. We
> shouldn't have to fight bad legislation and promote good in order to
> help us do our job. I am not personally inclined to that sort of thing,
> nor are many of the rest of us.

Police opposition was pushed on several fronts. The California
Juvenile Officers Association appointed a committee to study the
early (first draft) recommendations of the commission. The
chairman was Captain B. James Glavas, then president of the
Southern California Juvenile Officers Association. At the end of
1960 the committee reported tnat the "wholesale revision of the
Juvenile Court Act is undesirable and administratively and pro-
cedurally dangerous." Later this was passed without dissent as a
resolution of the state body.[21] Police representatives also stated
their negative views before meetings of the Senate Judiciary
Committee and of the Assembly Interim Committee on Criminal
Procedure, on television programs and public forums.

Police opposition tended to become confused in expression,
owing to the fact that subordinates, rather than Chief Parker,
authored most of the public pronouncements. Their greatest
sense of outrage was aimed at the first draft of the recommendations, which subsequently were modified. A compromise meeting of police people, probation officer representatives, and members of the commission was arranged in early January 1961
through the mediation of Chief Ray Blackmore, of San José,
who at the time was a member of the Governor's Committee on
Youth and Child Welfare. What transpired at the meeting cannot be reconstructed, but presumably it took place in a highly
charged atmosphere. Thereafter, Chief Parker's role as a focal
antagonist receded. However, Captain Glavas and some other
police carried on the fight to the end.

Opposition in the northern part of the state and Central Val-

21. Southern California Juvenile Officers Association Bulletin, December 1960.

ley never became as vehement as it did in the south. Police officers in the north were agreed that police problems in the south differed from those elsewhere. Furthermore, police systems in the north were more flexible than the highly rationalized organization of the Los Angeles Police Department, and could more easily absorb the features of the new law. Consequently, for them, the change in the law posed no problem of a new system and policy to supplant existing ones. While resistance in the south had conspicuous aspects of irrationality and "status politics," still it was anchored in "real" commitments or administrative procedures whose perpetuation was incompatible with adherence to the proposed law revision.

THE NEUTRALIZATION OF POWER

A precondition but not a determinant of success for the action groups of the juvenile justice commission was neutralization of the power of the opposition. Success came less from capturing organizational support than from divisions of opinion, splits in organizations, counteraction of action, and public discreditation of positions assumed by more extreme and ardent members of the resistance. Some of this neutralizing process was designed— a product of "divide-and-conquer tactics"—but a good deal of it simply "happened," as the result of contingency and circumstances.

The recommendations of the commission and subsequent compromises struck by its lobby group under the leadership of Jack Pettis contained some very powerful attractions to police, probation officers, and even judges. Recommendation 24, for example, permitted police to take juveniles into custody without a warrant when they had reason to believe that the juvenile's actions came within any of the three jurisdictional sections of the new code. That this new power was enticing to many police was disclosed in a statement by Inspector Harold Stallings, of the Los Angeles County Sheriff's Department, to a legislative group:

> Gentlemen, this is a high honor and a sacred trust given to law enforcement. We want to say that we will not take it lightly, that we

will increase our efforts to screen and we do appreciate this trust that has been placed.[22]

The gains accruable to probation officers from the law revision seem so bounteous in retrospect that it is hard to understand why any significant number of them continued to resist the change. Like the police, they enjoyed greater power, even though eventually the revision was amended to return probation departments to their position of dependence on the court. The clarification of procedures for handling juvenile traffic violations and the retention of their jurisdiction in juvenile court was a clear victory for probation officers. In addition, subsidies were recommended to upgrade standards of probation work.

While positive values for judges were less discernible in the proposed legislation, still there was "something for everyone," in that provision was to be made for an advisory board of judges henceforth responsible for making rules of practice and procedure for the juvenile court. In large perspective, the code revision submitted numerous, varied sections, some of which maintained or advanced certain values, weakened or destroyed others. The omnibus form of the new law more or less demanded that it be evaluated on its various perceived merits and demerits; it made categorical reactions difficult to sustain. This proved highly conducive to splitting of the opposition.

ORGANIZATIONAL CONTINGENCIES

A further explanation of the success of social action by the juvenile justice commission groups lies in organizational contingencies. Put simply, proponents of change were well organized, while opponents were not. The extra year gained by the former was well spent in perfecting their action groups and in planning strategy and tactics; indeed, there was consensus that if the commission had taken its recommendations before the legislature in 1960, it would have been defeated. But, apart from this, the

22. Senate Judiciary Committee on Juvenile Justice, Los Angeles, November 28, 1960, 325. Committee files.

political engagement in 1961 caught probation officers in a period of organizational transition; it exposed weaknesses of organized police resources for presenting their case before the legislature; and it found judges politically unorganized and compelled to rely on improvised means to defend their values.

By 1960 the C.P.P.C.A. had grown very large and unwieldy through the accumulation of a widely differentiated membership. The interests of chief probation officers had become differentiated, specialized, and cut by a widening rift between large-county and small-county chiefs. In this year the C.P.P.C.A. was reorganized and constitutionally revised and a Chief Probation Officers Association established. Against this background, internal conflict over revision of the juvenile court law rose to a magnitude that endangered the life of the association, evidenced by personal attacks made on the competency of members of the legislative committee. In a very real sense the choice for many probation officers became taking a stand on the recommendations versus preserving the association, with the latter value prevailing among most. Peace and moderation took precedence over substantive issues, symbolized by the election of Loren Beckley as President of the association and his assumption of the role of peacemaker.[23] The struggle ended with the C.P.P.C.A. board's approval of a resolution to endorse the recommendations but to act by seeking amendments only on specific items. In so doing, they effectively relinquished whatever formal power might have been theirs to exert.

Probation officers collectively had been handicapped for some time by a lack of means to do their jobs of lobbying. They had no paid representatives, and relying upon whatever free time they themselves had for the task did not work well. To make things even more difficult, county supervisors and managers in larger counties had begun to impose more control on legislative appearances of county employees. Yet, with all these political disadvantages, probation officers might still have been a potent force had their relationship to the C.Y.A. been of a different order.

23. Much of the data for this passage came from interviews with Loren Beckley and from files of the Board of Directors, C.P.P.C.A.

THE SILVER CORDS OF THE C.Y.A.

The plight of the C.Y.A. during the controversy over changing the juvenile court law is best pictured as an agency caught up in the strands of its own carefully nurtured policy of service and consultation. Being in a special position, the C.Y.A. could be neither neutral nor actively supportive. The core of the problem was the organizational commitments being met on a day-by-day basis with juvenile court judges, probation officers, and law enforcement people. C.Y.A. administrators had to honor such commitments to the Department of Corrections, ties that were made very real by the joint use of institutions administered by the older department and by the fact that youth eighteen through twenty could be sent to the C.Y.A. from the adult courts. To cap the picture, the director of the C.Y.A. was a member of the Board of Corrections, which had sought the appointment of the Special Study Commission on Juvenile Justice. Even more, the C.Y.A. had played a historical role in forming professional opinion leading up to this action.

Although Heman Stark lent his counsel and seeming approval to the early endeavors of the commission, by the end of 1958 he and others in his organization began to feel threatened and disturbed as resistance mounted among probation officers and judges. To this was added concern over the repercussions of conflict going on within the C.P.P.C.A., to which the C.Y.A. was tied in various instrumental ways. Finally, Stark vented his anxieties in an editorial, "A Time for Caution," published in the official organ of the C.Y.A. Here he unequivocally condemned the more extreme proposals of the Orange County dissidents, such as allowing bail to juveniles and trial by jury. Somewhat less positively he scouted the idea that the juvenile court law needed major revisions, and questioned the belief that a serious problem existed in respect to the protection of minors and parents by legal counsel:

> We also hear the proposal that a child or his parents or guardian should be guaranteed representation by an attorney at all stages of

a proceeding. An attorney may already appear in a juvenile court and represent a child. We believe there are ample safeguards now in the law to provide a child with legal counsel.[24]

This was as close as the C.Y.A. or its leader ever came to adopting an official position on the law revision, suggesting that it solved its dilemma by the expedient of not taking a stand. In practice this meant that higher leaders of the C.Y.A. acceded to the commission's requests for personnel and facilities to conduct their study and to consult, with a loose directive, "Give them what they want." They themselves, however, withdrew to other tasks, and later made it known that they did not plan to make any appearances before legislative committees. Heman Stark described the dilemma thus:

> Some of our people wanted me to take a stronger stand on the controversy. But I couldn't take an extreme position on i.. We have to advise the legislature—that's better than being out leading the crusade. Not all of the probation officers supported us and the Juvenile Officers were never completely sold on it. I am on their Executive Board and do a lot of things for them. The police trust us because we never release a youth without consulting them. They think we do it for them but we do it for our kids. It prevents rousting. Our function is to pull groups together. It's a consulting role.

A final comment is needed to locate Karl Holton's place in the controversy, since he had been director of the C.Y.A. in its formative years and responsible for early moves to get better legal protection for juveniles and more restraints placed on judicial discretion in dealing with them. But, like Heman Stark, he believed that the commission's ideas went too far, and in his then capacity as chief of the Los Angeles Probation Department, he had to preserve some common meeting-ground with the militant police in his turbulent metropolis. While Holton, like many other probation officers in the south, stood against any locus for juvenile traffic hearings other than the juvenile court, his strongest feelings bore down on "tough" sixteen- and seventeen-year-

24. Heman Stark, "A Time for Caution," *California Youth Authority Quarterly* 11 (1958) , 2.

old offenders with lengthy records, who committed brutal crimes. He believed that such cases should be referred to superior courts and sent forthwith to the C.Y.A. While he generally approved of counsel for minors and parents, nevertheless he held that if the older, "hard" cases were heard in juvenile courts, the prosecuting attorney should be brought into the hearings.[25]

Karl Holton shared a dilemma generically similar to Heman Stark's; he was caught by his role as member of the Board of Corrections, but was also constrained from more open resistance by his image as an early crusader for reforms in the juvenile court law.

A parenthetical question that should be raised is why the Department of Corrections, unlike the C.Y.A., was not constrained from supporting the commission, considering that many of the same judges, probation officers, and police serving the C.Y.A. also served the Adult Authority. No satisfactory answer is at hand, other than the possibility that the question was defined exclusively as a problem of the juvenile courts.

POLICE PUT FIRST THINGS FIRST

On evidence, it would seem that the police bungled an opportunity or opportunities to defeat Senate Bill 332; a more tenable conclusion, however, is that their structures of political influence and policy formation, crude and inefficient though they may have been, nevertheless fashioned a rough-hewn hierarchy of immediate interests, in which minor values were subordinated to major ones. Given limited means to ends, i.e., lack of a paid lobbyist and a shortage of funds for travel to Sacramento, the police, like other involved groups, had to make choices as to which ends would be sought and in what order. Care also was proscribed by the fact that the legislative structure in the California Peace Officers Association had never been tried or tested in a rigorous campaign in the legislature.

Agitation among officers in the Southern California Juvenile

25. Karl Holton's testimony, Senate Judiciary Committee, pp. 138–58.

Officers Association over issues in the commission's proposals, in order to get transformed into political influence, had first to move upward through its own legislative committee, thence to the legislative committee of the California Peace Officers Association, and from there to the executive committee of that organization for final disposition. The president of the Juvenile Officers Association is on the legislative committee but not the executive committee, which tends to be made up of chiefs of police.

There is no question that the conflict over the commission's program came before members of the Peace Officers Association, notably in the form of articles con and pro written by Robert Mowrers and Arthur Sherry,[26] and speeches by Mowrers and I. J. Shain at the annual conference of the association in 1960. How much this affected the policy-making elite at the top is unclear,[27] but what is known indicates that any action finally contemplated on the matter had a low priority. The Peace Officers Association was preoccupied with more pressing issues in the 1961 session of the legislature, to wit, the forceful attempt to abolish the death penalty for homicide, and efforts to strengthen penalties for narcotics offenses. Police representatives also continued to give wary attention at this time to all moves dealing with the admissibility of evidence in criminal prosecutions. That the recommendations of the commission entered into this latter issue as a special manifestation of the problem was only collateral or subsidiary in importance to the larger organization, in contrast to the Juvenile Officers Association. This was demonstrated by the space allocated to the various police interests in the *California Peace Officer* between 1958 and 1961.[28]

26. See Robert Mowrers, "What's Right about the Juvenile Court?" and Arthur Sherry, "Some Questions Answered," *California Peace Officer* 11 No. 5. (May–June 1960), p. 16f; for reference to Mowrers' and Shain's speeches, see *ibid.*, p. 38.

27. My impression from attending meetings of juvenile peace officers is that rank and file follow the practice, not unique to them, of spending their time in socializing, leaving serious matters to a small oligarchy of leaders.

28. See the "Legislative Panel," *California Peace Officer* (September, October 1961).

It can even be held that Chief William Parker's early fervent condemnation of the commission's proposals was tangential to larger legal and moral issues bothering him. His published speeches and addresses fail to show any more than routine administrative interest in juvenile delinquency. Indeed, in one instance he stated that "prevention of crime is not one of the traditional police tasks." [29]

It can be guessed that Chief Parker retreated from the notion of committing his department and its influence to an all-out fight against the juvenile law revision. He was content to leave continued public agitation to lower echelon officers or in the hands of the head of the juvenile bureau. Whether by design or not, this restraint pushed police views toward extremism. In consequence, they very likely did more to alienate than to gain support, particularly when some of the intransigent police questioned the value of civil rights in general and impugned the motives of their advocates:

> In evaluating the integrity of those who insist on extending "rights" to the few at the expense of the many, one should be reminded that this increasing emphasis is strangely concurrent with the advance of Communism throughout the world.[30]

This poorly chosen expression of police resistance was compounded by statements of one of their spokesmen, who was reported to have said that "too many civil rights are being granted." [31]

---

29. *Parker on Police,* ed. O. W. Wilson (Springfield, Ill.: Charles C. Thomas, 1957), p. 12.

30. "President's Message," Southern California Juvenile Officers Association Bulletin, December 1960.

31. The statement attributed to Captain Glavas most probably was the one made before the Assembly Interim Committee on Criminal Procedure (Los Angeles, September 27, 1960): "I think a lot of our so-called fundamental rights are created rights, and my personal view is that privilege against self-incrimination and invoking of the fifth amendment in many cases, is an unnecessary burden which this country must carry. This is probably heresy, but this is my opinion."

JUDGES AT BAY

Judges worked against the revision under several distinctive handicaps. First of all, legislators dislike having judges come before them or solicit their indulgence, because many of the former are attorneys who face the uncomfortable prospect of having to try cases before these same judges at a later time. Second, judges, because of their particular temperament and isolate tendencies, tend to be an unorganized or loosely organized professional lot. Consequently, judicial lobbying perforce was organized on an *ad hoc* basis around the personalities of one, or at most, three judges. Undoubtedly Judge Ross A. Carkeet became the pivotal person or anchor man for the whole judicial protest. He was (and is) a man of courage and integrity, who was thoroughly familiar with the Welfare and Institutions Code. Moreover, he was prepared to discuss and argue issues in fine detail, which he proceeded to do in speeches, item-by-item analysis, and statements. Their effect was to convince judges, as well as others, that he had the expertise necessary to wage their fight. However, the informal delegation of a leadership role to him by other opposition judges had a weakness because Judge Carkeet's regular work assignments kept him from attending some important legislative hearings, thereby precluding the impact his personal confrontation otherwise might have had. Another obvious flaw was that the opposition had to stand or fall with Judge Carkeet.

The tactic of the opposition judges was a familiar one: to kill the law revision by securing its referral to an interim committee for "further study." Actually there were good and defensible reasons for this attempt, in the light of the numerous and profound changes the law promised to bring about. But the tactic failed, and sometime during the course of its movement in the legislature, Judge Carkeet reached a point of resignation to the inevitability of the passage of Senate Bill 332. Certain modifications were made in the original draft of the new law, which in part at least removed one of the features most objectionable to him—namely, the phrasing of the section of rules of evidence

applicable in cases of youth alleged to have committed the
equivalent of felonies. The original draft, which specified "a
preponderance of evidence *not subject to timely objection by
competent counsel* under rules of evidence observed in the trial
of criminal cases," was altered to read, "a preponderance of
evidence under rules of evidence observed in the trial of criminal
cases."

Judge Carkeet found that he "could live with the new law"
after this and other amendments had been made. It may be that
his change of attitude derived from the part he played in securing the amendments, and his sense of participation in the law-
making process this afforded. Undoubtedly his self-consciousness
was greatly intensified by his role, which made him feel "a
little like Don Quixote at times." Presumably, there was a point
in the conflict at which passage of the new law seemed imminent, and he was forced to decide whether or not he wanted to be
identified with intransigent "bitter-enders," and run the attendant risk₁ of professional degradation or isolation. In any event,
there came a pass when he retired from the fight in good grace,
retaining the respect of his opponents, as well as of his adherents.

From the other side, the partisans of Senate Bill 332 pursued
a tactic of mutual cancellation of the influence of each opposition judge by putting forward a judge equally prestigious and
convincing in his support of the bill. This move in sum turned
out to be a stand-off, with three judges on either side, plus one,
Judge Melvyn Cronin, who changed from the con to the pro camp
during the controversy. An indication of the dead-center nature
of the counterbalance of the two groups was shown by the inability of a special committee of judges convened by the judicial
council to take any definitive action.[32] In the last analysis, judicial opposition suffered less from cancellation of their ideas or
defeat of their logic than from dramatic discreditation in the
quaint and curious person of one of their number.

32. A juvenile court committee of the Conference of California Judges
neither met nor took action on the proposals of the juvenile justice commission, although it was supposed to consider them. Its successor committee met
in 1961 but could not agree on any action. See Report of Committee on
Superior Courts, Conference of California Judges, September 26, 1960; also,
letter, Ross A. Carkeet to John Bohn, March 19, 1961.

THE DRAMATIZATION OF EVIL

To say that the play's the thing wherein was caught the conscience of the Senate Judiciary Committee is perhaps an unpardonable desecration; nevertheless, dramaturgic analysis offers the best key to comprehending the radically changed perspectives of that committee's members toward Senate Bill 332. For although a very strong case had been made to change the law, and a heavy phalanx of power marshaled to this end, the ensuring "do pass" given by the committee depended for a catalyst on the dramatic interaction of a hearing; within the hearing there was a profound "gut-level" reaction, a total reperception of extant facts together with their re-evaluation. The existential version of the juvenile court held by the commission people finally broke through the perceptual defenses or cognitive rigidities of the "powerful Judiciary Committee."

Depicting the legislative hearing as an analogue of a drama is not a proprietary conception of sociology, for political scientists have drawn the parallel in explicit terms.[33] In several important features there are marked similarities, in that such hearings are staged, actors are cast and coached in their parts, and there are scripts and performances. There may be heated acting, comic relief, and intermissions, and finally the plot moves toward resolution. The significant audience in this instance, of course, was the committee itself, and it is correct to say that resolution came during the hearing, rather than after.

Most of the judgments made by informants were that Senate Bill 332 could have "gone either way." This uncertainty to a considerable extent inhered in the weak party discipline in the California legislature, its lack of partisan emphasis, and the unpredictability of member votes.[34] The committee consisted

---

33. Bertram Gross, *The Legislative Struggle: A Study in Social Combat* (New York: McGraw Hill, 1953), Chap. XV. For sociological statements of dramaturgic analysis, see Sheldon Messinger, "Life as a Theatre," *Sociometry* 25 (1962), 89–109; Peter Berger, *Invitation to Sociology* (New York: Anchor Books, 1963), Chap. VI, pp. 122–50.

34. *Legislative Behavior*, pp. 43, 61, 230.

almost entirely of former prosecutors or deputy prosecutors, plus a former juvenile court judge from a small "we-take-care-of-our-own" county in the north. With one exception they were either unresponsive or covertly hostile to the bill.[35] The chairman, Senator Regan, and vice-chairman, Senator Christensen (the former judge), both had been well briefed on Judge Carkeet's critical analysis of the propositions in the new law. At the first committee hearing in Los Angeles, their adverse feelings were little concealed; they, as well as other committee members, quickly probed into the sore issue as to whether introducing counsel into the court would not lead to disruptive adversary proceedings. They also objected to the idea of adding this new cost to the already high costs of rehabilitating delinquents.

At the close of a subsequent hearing the committee held in Sacramento, Senator Regan revealed the depth of his disapproval of the manner in which the bill had been brought before the legislature:

> It was unfair to try to ram such a piece of legislation through on such short notice . . . any bill that took such a Commission three years to put together was worth at least a year's study by a legislative committee.[36]

Senator Christensen from the first had little respect for the commission, and described its methods (to me, no less) as "a sociologist's study with a check list." Only Senator Cobey could be safely counted as a committee member on the side of those

35. It is fair to say that the composition and chairmanship of the Senate Judiciary Committee closely followed the infra-power structure of the legislature, which before reapportionment (1966) was stated by some to be dominated not only by the Senate but beyond that by a so-called "cow-county elite" within the Senate. The full committee consisted of Senators Edwin Regan, chairman; Carl Christensen, Stanley Arnold, Richard Dolwig, Hugo Fisher, Ronald G. Cameron, Donald L. Grunsky, Fred S. Farr, John W. Holmdahl, Virgil O. Sullivan, Joseph A. Rattigan, Stanford Shaw, and James Cobey.

36. Release Farm Bureau, Merced County, April 26, 1961. In an interview with me in Weaverville in July 1964, Senator Regan stated: "The normal thing to do in a session with five thousand bills would be to refer a bill as important as SB 332 to an interim committee."

wanting the law changed. The first change of view came in Senator Cameron, after an early Los Angeles hearing by the committee:

> We were skeptical at first and had to be convinced. In Los Angeles I began to believe that there were abuses, especially in that police who couldn't get youth on criminal charges were using the juvenile court to get them sent to C.Y.A. About this time I attended a State Government Association meeting in Chicago and I learned that abuses existed in Illinois also. So I began to study the report carefully.
> However, at that time the Committee was pulled in two directions. We recognized the need for greater protection for juveniles but we didn't want youth to develop adult attitudes towards crimes, law, and "beating the rap."

The net effect of early committee hearings was to make attitudes of its members ambivalent, or better, to change a stabilized perception of the existing juvenile court in California into an ambiguous one. It remained for a hearing performance by Judge Richard B. Eaton in March 1961 to change the ambiguous perception into a fixed negative view, and to open minds to the necessity for a different design in the court. The assumptions made about judges as persons, on which the juvenile court systems had hitherto rested, were rudely shattered.

Judge Eaton presided over adult and juvenile courts in Shasta County, and in many ways was an almost unbelievable anachronism. A bachelor, with a closely regulated life, precise in manner, he sometimes startled visitors to his regular court with phrases like "Prithee, bailiff, cry the court!" or "Go ye hence, bailiff, with the costs!" Judge Eaton ran his juvenile court almost singlehandedly, showed irascibility at times, and was nearly always pre-emptory and demanding with probation officers and police witnesses. He took an immediate, personal interest in the direction of the county detention home, which he pridefully regarded as one of the chief tools by which delinquent youth were disciplined.

Judge Eaton arrived before the Senate Judiciary Committee in a black suit, carrying a furled umbrella, and with guileless candor he proceeded to reveal his methods for the character-building of youth he took under his jurisdiction. He explained first that he expected minors who came before him to admit their offenses. If they denied the allegations against them, he forthwith dispatched them to detention to stay until they were ready to make the necessary admissions. These and other revelations produced dead silence, disbelief, amazement, and a growing sense of embarrassment in the committee.

Thus was exposed Judge Eaton's conception of juvenile court law, already known to the commission members from a communication to Jack Pettis over a year earlier:

> When a youngster, on interrogation by an investigating police officer, admits criminal misconduct (as upwards of 95% do) I believe that he should be detained on the spot and not discharged until he satisfies the judge of at least his present desire to do better.[37]

Even more revealing of Judge Eaton's juvenile court philosophy was a statement made to Senator Cobey following the hearings before the Senate Judiciary Committee:

> The presumption of innocence is an entirely proper rule of evidence in a contested case; but applied administratively in an uncontested case, it produces a result as absurd as any other presumption of law contrary to fact.[38]

The full impact of Judge Eaton's disclosures on the committee is gauged by the explosiveness of the reply Senator Cameron made three years later to my low-keyed inquiry about its effect: "We talked about nothing else for four days, and still couldn't believe it!" The effects of the performance on the committee were obvious to all, so much so that a member of the commission

37. Judge Eaton to Jack Pettis, December 9, 1959, Senate Judiciary Committee files.
38. Judge Eaton to Senator Cobey, March 30, 1961. Judge Eaton's views, unacceptable though they were, were part of a definite rationale related to the well-organized use of detention for discipline, work assignments, and punishment. His methods had considerable support in his community. See Richard B. Eaton, "Detention Facilities in Non-Metropolitan Counties," *Juvenile Court Judges Journal* (January 17, 1966), pp. 9–12.

could say: "We couldn't have arranged it better if we had been Machiavellians. When Senator Grunsky's mouth dropped open we knew we had won."

THE MYTH OF POWER

In addition to the negative, neutralizing factors contributing to successful social action in the present instance were certain technical conditions, such as the fact that the recommendations to change the law were submitted in a "package," and that time limitations more or less compelled the legislature to "take it or leave it." A larger question concerns the part played by positive power in the ultimate passage of Senate Bill 332. My pursuit of this subject, however, proved to be an elusive game, a little like "button, button, who's got the button."

Informants made a good deal of the fact that "this was a governor's bill," or, among those more cynical, "something cooked up in a corner of the governor's office." But this was not literally true, for in late 1960 Governor Brown, after his own inquiry, simply adopted the recommendations of the juvenile justice commission as part of his legislative program. Very likely it was the good politician in Brown that led him to seize upon the recommendations as "good program material."

It is true that the governor indicated his support for the bill in a number of ways, as at special luncheons for supporters and in press releases, and converted them into an issue in the 1960 election campaign. But as far as could be determined, he never directly intervened in the legislative process itself. Nor did any legislator I interviewed feel that refusal to go along with the bill would bring reprisals. In this vein, the suggestion that Heman Stark "had to go along" with the action for change because his appointment as director of the C.Y.A. was up for renewal was sheer speculation.

The belief that a congeries of powerful people, headed by the governor, Pettis, McGee, and others, pushed the law revision through with "raw power" is inconsistent with the facts, particularly in California where politics haven't revolved around monolithic power since 1910. Furthermore, modern pluralistic society outmodes older proprietary, baronial power structures, such as could be found in some areas in the late nineteenth and early twentieth centuries.

Banfield, drawing upon empirical studies of social action in urban politics, concludes that stabilized power or "influence" transecting a variety of groups is largely a mythology. The absence of any inured "top leadership" he explains on these grounds: (1) the time cost of maintaining the constant communication that would be necessary between such leaders was prohibitive; (2) a leadership cohort based on this kind of power would put too many organizational obstacles in the way of protecting, maintaining, or advancing other values or extraneous commitments of the constituent members of such a group.[39]

Sociological analysis, however, goes beyond Banfield's negative criticism to propose that the myth of power is an important concomitant of group interaction, which at a crucial phase helps explain the quiescence of the opposition to social action. The myth of power may well be an esoteric expression of an accommodative pattern of American political culture colloquially known as "If you can't lick 'em, join 'em." Subjectively, it allows opposition leaders to adopt new stances reconciling past action with their present status and identity needs.

Several data are relevant to interpretation in the present case. For example, the previously noted conviction of some probation officers that "mysterious forces are operating" undoubtedly reflected attitude shifts, which, although rueful, were followed by changes in their positions. Robert Mowrers became convinced that the opposition was overpowered by something like a C.Y.A.

39. See Edward C. Banfield, *Political Influence* (New York: The Free Press of Glencoe, 1962), pp. 294–303. A good illustration of the last point is found in the decision of the Board of Directors of the California Taxpayers Association to stay out of the controversy over SB 332. In some part this judgment was affected by the fact that Mrs. Prince had been on the executive board previously, representing the Bay Area tax groups. Fear of alienating her and others, plus "having other fish to fry," probably explains why the association assumed only a minor obligation to inform taxpayers of possible costs of the new law. As the director of legislative activities said: "We have a system of priorities."

Mafia, which went up and down the state threatening reprisals and promising rewards, such as jobs or job promotions, to those who would line up with the partisans of the law change. This explanation not only made defeat more palatable; it also helped preserve his identity in a complex local political situation.[40]

Finally, it is plain that Judge Carkeet sheathed his sword and withdrew from the battle because he believed the opposition had become too powerful to overcome. In a form letter sent to judges in February 1961, he referred to the "considerable pressure being exerted for passage of the bill," and to "rather prominent names" on the rosters of the citizens' committees fighting for the bill. He also noted that the C.Y.A. was exerting pressure *sub rosa*, using the promise of a probation subsidy as bait. In May, Judge Carkeet wrote that judges were going along with the bill because of political pressure. At this time he also indicated his lack of interest in the possibility of continuing "total resistance" by a small number of groups.[41]

CONCLUSION

The success of social action in the case under study here may be attributed to: (1) the formation of a small, well-organized group of deeply committed people with a set of reasonably clear and integrated goals; (2) having access to individuals and groups in positions to make decisions supporting or opposing these goals; (3) neutralization of the power of the opposition by design or circumstance; (4) a dramatic demonstration of the evils stated to exist, which facilitated a radical shift from the traditional conception or paradigm of the juvenile court; (5) the rise of a myth of total or undefeatable power in the minds of the leaders of the opposition; (6) utilization of this myth to convert statuses and identities among the opposition leaders.

40. Mowrers worked under a judge who was almost fanatically opposed to changing the juvenile court law. Coincidental with and following the change, Mowrers, the Merced County Board of Supervisors, the probation committee, the bar association, the editor of the local newspaper, and Senator Cobey all became embroiled in a local political battle.

41. Judge Ross A. Carkeet to judges, February 27, 1961.

6
Adaptations and Normal Law

Whether legislation induces discrete and identifiable social change or whether it is an expression of social change are not easily settled questions. A plausible mid-ground is to say that both possibilities exist. Some legislation is enacted in such form that it does little more than offer symbolic satisfactions to actively interested groups, or resolve their conflicts of interest at a purely ideological level.[1] Resulting statutes often betray their spurious legislative history by an absence of definitions and specific directives necessary to activate social control. Other legislation can be distinguished by its lucidity and clarity of intent; it "has teeth" in that stipulations establish new authority or confer additional power on extant agencies of the state; it enjoins new procedures, which change the order in which values can be satisfied in particular settings; sometimes it destroys values by eliminating the means for their satisfaction.

It is not always easy to separate the two different types of legislation, because "legislative intent" must be determined, and there is not always agreement on how this can be done. However, despite this and its dubious "group-mind" overtones, intent has meaning in a short-term historical context, particularly if it is inferred from the sequence of interaction that leads up to legislation. Attention will be given, not only to the kinds of values elevated to dominance in this interaction, but also to the means

1. Vilhelm Aubert, "Law, Communication and Conformity." Files, Center for Study of Law and Society, University of California, Berkeley, pp. 7–10.

embodied in law to insure this dominance in subsequent judicial and administrative action.

Drawing the intent out of legislation in this way permits examination of the adaptations those subject to the law make to the new claims on their loyalties and to their altered situations. The central and most general question here is the degree to which values made dominant by the juvenile justice commission and the legislature subsequently were given dominance in the aggregate value patterns of juvenile courts in the state. In more detail this is an inquiry into decisions that establish new ends, treat new values as means to old ends, or treat existing values as expendable. Back of this is a query similar to that which underlay much of the controversy over passage of the law, to wit, whether systems of rules governing the conduct of juvenile courts are changed wholesale, or whether partial and segmental sacrifices suffice to preserve the stability of the systems. Here, however, the emphasis is on the law in action, rather than the law in anticipated action.[2]

Several distinctive aspects of the data must be kept in the foreground. First, the general intent of the legislation was stated with a modicum of clarity, also documented in some detail by an accompanying set of recommendations. The salient goal, which became well enough understood, was to redesign the juvenile court so as to make an official place for attorneys. Jurisdictional categories and procedural mandates put into the law gave potential impact to the attorney's role, at the same time modifying the roles and discretionary powers of police, probation officers, and judges.

Another differentiating fact about the law revision in the present instance was that its subject population consisted of functionaries whose job was to administer law, who, collectively and individually, put a high value on "compliance with law." Likewise, the nature of their work made them more sensitive to the procedural basis of justice than, for example, lay persons. This

2. The methodological problems of so-called "impact" or "evaluation" studies of law and social change are discussed in Richard Lempert, "Strategies of Research Design in the Legal Impact Study . . ." *Law and Society Review* 1 (1966), 11–32.

sensitivity was sharpened by the historical or epochal qualities the law revision took on in retrospect—"the earthquake of 1961," to borrow the colorful imagery of one judge. Finally, awareness of problems of juvenile court procedure was kept alive among judges by a crude monitoring device more or less built-in by law in their loose professional organization.

FACTORS MAKING FOR VARIABLE ADAPTATIONS

Differences in reactions to requirements of the new juvenile court law were the result of several factors mutually at work in local settings. Among these were: (1) the process by which the intent of the legislature was communicated; (2) the values perceived in the law in relation to local values and interests; (3) changes in personnel of the courts; (4) the experienced costs of adaptations.

Stating the general intent of the revised law in a comparatively straightforward manner did not guarantee that its meaning got diffused fully and uniformly in all areas to juvenile court workers. Furthermore, it remained to be seen how understandable the law would be after attempts were made to apply it on a day-to-day, case-by-case basis. Finally, communication of the intent of the law varied accordingly with the perceptions, conceptions, and motivations of those who formally interpreted its meaning.

Interpretations of the new law were disseminated in an organized manner by probation department heads, in turn influenced by programmed discussions among a small nucleus of chiefs. As early as July 6, 1961, two months before the law went into effect, a number of chief probation officers requested C.Y.A. leaders to call a meeting for the purpose. John Pettis was asked to be present and to clarify "points at issue in the new Juvenile Court Law and to provide some guidance to other Chief Probation Officers on methods of implementing the law."[3] At this

3. Minutes of Selected Representatives to Analyze Senate Bill 332, (C.Y.A.), Sacramento, July 6, 1961.

time they agreed to call regional and zone meetings of probation officers and acquaint them with the new law. Some large probation departments followed these meetings with orientation programs for their staffs lasting several months. Responsibility also fell upon probation departments to acquaint law enforcement officers, school officials, and welfare workers in their areas with new policies and procedures being adopted in juvenile court.[4] How far and how well this concentric pattern of communication served its purpose cannot be told, but impressions suggest that the influence of opinion of the new law diminished as it moved from large to small departments, where there was more dependence of probation officer on judge.

Judges, as might be expected, independently formed their ideas of the specific requirements in the new law, being only peripherally affected by informal contacts among themselves. What effect the Institute of Juvenile Court Judges and Referees (newly created by the law, as will be shown) had on their thinking was hard to say. Some organized judicial clarification came from the activities of the erstwhile leading opposition judge, Ross Carkeet, who compiled an analysis of the new law, complete with marginal summaries. Over four hundred copies were sent out on request to judges, probation officers, and law enforcement people. Judge Carkeet and his probation officer also arranged orientation discussions of the law for sheriffs and police in his county.

Apart from these sources and discussions in community coordinating councils, there seems to have been a minimum of organized dissemination to law enforcement agents of the new legal requirements for handling minors.[5] Abundant evidence that they lacked ready interpretations of the new law lay in the uncertainty, even fear, shown by many police and sheriffs' deputies toward the options offered in the law to arresting officers, i.e., release, issue a citation to appear, or deliver to a probation

---

4. *Ibid.*
5. Some organized communication took place indirectly through training institutes for chief juvenile officers set up by the C.Y.A. twice a year at Asilomar about this time. Six of fifty hours of course instruction were given to the juvenile court law.

officer.[6] Their distress in some areas was shown in phone calls to probation officers at odd hours, asking them what to do after arresting a minor. Many police reacted to what was for them an ambiguous situation by sending every apprehended youth to the probation officers; others released youths in unduly large numbers. As a result, the rate of detention of male youths during the first year after the law went into effect was measurably depressed.[7]

The problem of "educating" law enforcement workers was more aggravated in small and remote counties than in populous areas with juvenile bureaus. Difficulties in small counties stemmed, not only from the scarcity of professionalized police, but equally from deeply rooted police customs in handling juvenile cases. This is well described by a probation officer:

> In the past almost every youngster picked up was turned over to us. If there had been a good juvenile officer in the county I would judge that 25 to 30 per cent of these cases need never have had to come to us. In effect the kids were dumped in our laps, and if you released them, they all—highway patrol, sheriff's office and city police —jumped down your throat. This was not a situation peculiar to this county; it happened in all of the small counties.
>
> After the law changed we broke them of this. Little by little we have been able to educate them, to educate these fellows [the police] to the fact that when they turn kids over to us we have to make the decision as to whether they will be held or not, and whether they will go to juvenile court or be handled informally. This is a hard pill for them to swallow, and it always has been. However, I haven't had the repercussions in the past two or three years I had previously.

Narrow interests figured importantly in police reactions, tending to block the appreciation of any positive values for them in the new law. This held especially in local areas where sheriffs' deputies or town police faced more work, including much dis-

6. California Welfare and Institutions Code, Art. 6, Sec. 626, Stats. 1961, Chap. 1616; amended by Stats. 1963, Chap. 1486.
7. Report on Delinquency and Probation in California, Department of Justice, Sacramento, 1962, p. 30f.

liked paper work, to hold minors in detention or to get petitions filed. Only slowly did firm insistence by the probation officers cause the police to utilize citation procedures, already installed but little used in many areas.

> Prior to the law change police picked up kids and said, "Here he is; you work it through; do all the investigating." That was wrong, because it was a police area. Now they are citing, and it's a better procedure, because they actually have all the evidence at hand. But it was a hard thing to come by.

The rotation of judges in larger counties in and out of juvenile court and the appointment of a large number of new judges, some in smaller counties, worked for informed and sympathetic interpretations of the new law. About the time the law became operative, a number of elderly judges strongly identified with the older, paternalistic conception of the juvenile court either retired or were encouraged to retire. Most judges who replaced them either showed outright approval of the law or were open-minded. However, resistant judges continued to hold the bench in many counties.

While added work burdens slowed adaptations to new legal prescriptions, financial costs were even more tangible and immediate barriers to their acceptance, apparent in such problems as funding salaries or fees for professional and clerical personnel now needed for the court. Judges and probation officers in small counties felt this much more keenly than those in large counties. One defect in the new law that came to notice almost immediately was its failure to specify means to pay for counsel to indigent minors and parents in counties where no public defender was available.

IDEOLOGICAL STUFF AND SOME NONSENSE

While probation officers and judges in some counties quickly responded to the installation of the new law, those in other counties either were apathetic or made only reluctant overtures toward compliance. Even when organizational changes were made and procedures modified, they were colored by a residue of resentment among judges, a good deal of it still leveled at John Pettis, the former project director of the juvenile justice commission. The intensity of the feeling was such that Pettis chose not to attend the first Annual Institute of Juvenile Court Judges and Referees.

Here and there probation officers had to bear the brunt of judicial annoyance at having to accede to legal changes deemed unnecessary. Sore feelings were made worse in some courts where the chief probation officer differed with a judge before passage of the revised law:

> During 1960 I changed my position from favoring control by judges to that of control by county supervisors. Yet I couldn't come out openly because my judge disapproved of this. After 1961 this judge complied with the new law, but only grudgingly. He often made sarcastic remarks in court—as when the petition was read—"Now we will have to comply with Mr. Beckley's law." I grew so uncomfortable that I stopped coming to court.

The most extreme reaction among judges, openly stated, occurred in Merced County, where a stand analogous to that of interposition was taken. Under the caption "Judges Holding Back on New Juvenile Court Law," the local newspaper reported:

> There was every indication that Superior Court Judge G. Maushart and R. R. Sischo along with the county probation department will not fully abide by the law until challenged by the Supreme Court. Sischo stated, "We have paid attention to the new law except in felony cases. Eventually we will be challenged . . . but as far as the Judicial Council telling judges what to do, that won't go far. . . ." [8]

Such forthright defiance, however, was exceptional, and in this case if reflected more the disorganized condition of the probation department and the local political situation than it did

8. Merced *County Star*, November 11, 1961.

the insupportable rigors of the new legal environment of the juvenile court.

The tincture of time slowly healed the wounds of controversy, particularly as judges, probation officers, and others readjusted their perspectives and looked upon the exigencies of the new law in a context of everyday problems calling for practical solutions. Probation officers and others discovered that "the sky hadn't fallen in on us." The new law in close embrace was less awesome than it had been in prospect.

> Actually the whole law didn't change so much. We were bugged by the possibility of adversary proceedings and the cost to the county was a concern. But it was largely an academic argument. I sometimes feel that when an attorney gets a kid off it is a bad thing, but then I know that usually he'll be back. Actually it's no harder to operate now than it was before. The law never will cause judges to operate the same way. Now most probation officers would be hard put to remember what the old law was like.

THE PROCESS OF ADAPTATION

Excerpts like the one above conceal the extent to which adaptations were made and also minimize problems that were dealt with more easily in one county than in another. The costs of conforming with certain features of the new law, for example, were not easily discounted as an academic matter in some areas. Nor did all probation officers so facilely accommodate themselves to dismissals won by attorneys for juveniles. Important differences unfolded in the process by which probation departments and juvenile courts sought means to incorporate, accommodate, or reject ends of the new law. Three major emphases became visible: (1) administrative reorganization; (2) entreprenurial exploitation; (3) formalism.

The new law promptly generated major changes in the structure of juvenile courts, probation departments, and such adjacent agencies as police departments, sheriffs' departments, and public defenders' offices. Within the courts, new roles were added and persons assigned official positions, including private attorneys, public defenders, referees, traffic-hearing officers, bailiffs, and court reporters. The result in broad purview was that the juvenile court became more like a court and less like an administrative agency or a consulting and advisory conference. At the same time, the administrative imperatives of the court multiplied in such matters as assigning judges, setting calendars, arranging for counsel, witnesses, and probation officers to be present, as well as investigations and paper work. Judges both individually and collectively now had to pay more heed to the court as an administrative problem.

Public defenders' offices in some counties had to be created; in others, staffs were augmented and systems worked out for scheduling juvenile work and rotating assignments. Probation departments, especially in larger counties, acquired more staff and reorganized duties to allow for more frequent court appearances of officers. In short, the process of administrative growth, or bureaucratization, well under way in large counties, was accelerated. A number of the practices already in existence or "in process" in these counties had been incorporated into the new law, although only one, Fresno County, could boast of having previously developed a prototype of the kind of juvenile court projected in the new law.[9] In the more "advanced" counties the idea that the new law expressed, as well as caused, change more or less held true. Law-related changes in very large probation departments became incidents in a fast-moving administrative process. They enlarged the legal focus of decision-making and action, but they were in no sense disruptive.

In some large departments changes promoted by the revised law coincided with other changes that had been imminent, e.g., the appointment of a new judge or a new chief probation officer.

9. The extent to which a given juvenile court or probation department had already approximated the requirements of the new law is a complex matter, and comparisons are odious. Although judges like Eugene Breitenbach, and Odell in Los Angeles, had been careful to guard the legal rights of juveniles, others in that county were less so. One large "deficiency" in Los Angeles was the lack of a working citation system. The Alameda County juveniles had been advised of their right to counsel since the early 1930's; citations for juvenile traffic and certain other offenses obtained since the mid-1930's.

Change in one county came about the same time as the physical removal of the probation department and the juvenile court to a new juvenile center, which tended to submerge the legal aspects of the change in a wholesale reorganization of space and function. Some of the larger probation departments added new staff, such as intake officers and clerks, with demands of the new law in mind, but at the same time, expansion of staff was part of their normal growth pattern. Large departments here and there made the law revision an occasion to further rationalize their organization by introducing standardized forms,[10] devising workload formulas, or seeking funds for legal consultation, but then most of these moves had been pending as "next steps."

ENTREPRENURIAL EXPLOITATION

In less bureaucratized counties, but particularly in those where the probation officer or judge was "on the make," or aspiring to the bureaucratic model of the large urban courts, the new law frequently took on a high instrumental or means value; it was seen as a way of allowing the probation officer or judge to obtain accessions of staff, space, or equipment long wanted and long sought. The possibility of a "great leap forward" changed from mere hope to achievable reality. For example, in one county the new legal specifications were immediately fastened upon to solve a problem of crowded calendars in the superior court, caused by a growing load of legal commitments of patients who had been voluntarily admitted to a nearby mental hospital. The solution chosen was to delegate all juvenile hearings to a lawyer-trained referee. In other counties, probation officers were able to utilize C.Y.A. assessment studies of their departments to reinforce the leverage that revision of the law gave them to expand operations and staff and to start totally new proce-

10. An effort to standardize forms on a state-wide basis through C.Y.A. sources failed. Forms covered such matters as petitions, notices, waiver of notice, supplementary petitions, and citations. Minutes of Southern Chief Probation Officers, July 14, 1961; March 22, 1963.

dures.[11] Adaptations of this order come closest to embodying what Lester F. Ward once called "attractive legislation." [12] The limiting factors in changing the juvenile court or probation departments in these counties became the degree to which county supervisors could or would reallocate funds and reorder the claims of competing county services.

FORMALISM

It was in counties most removed from the bureaucratic model and, as Carr pointed out years ago, "have to be substandard," owing to their small population base and short resources,[13] that the revision of the juvenile court law brought up problems of "compliance." In these courts the new legal exactions got defined as problems or costly burdens, not just because judges and probation people lacked the means to meet them, but equally because they struck directly at informal and sometimes extra-legal methods long followed and for the most part believed to be satisfactory. Judges and probation officers in a number of these counties had opposed the change, and the attendant controversy left them with a sour outlook on the situations ushered in by the new law. The implication that they had been disregarding the rights of juveniles still rankled as late as 1964, when I conducted my interviews.

While no good term is at hand in the literature of social organization to describe the mode of adaptation in counties in question, Cooley's older concept for formalism is broadly applicable.[14] Compliance was partial and inconsistent, with minimal

11. One informant spoke of the "waiting game" some probation officers play with judges and county supervisors. "So you wait until the guy who believes the way you do comes into power, then put in what needs to be done."

12. Lester F. Ward, *Applied Sociology* (Boston: Gin and Co., 1896), pp. 337–39.

13. Lowell Carr, "Most Courts Have To Be Substandard!" *Federal Probation* XIII (1949), 22–3.

14. Cooley speaks of formalism simply as "too much mechanism in society." Charles E. Cooley, *Social Organization* (Glencoe, Ill.: Free Press, 1956) , p. 342f.

psychic commitment or conviction that the changes were necessary. New roles and operations were added to the court, for
which existing staff served in more or less of a supernumerary
fashion. Detention hearings, for example, were held regularly in
only twenty-two counties prior to 1961 but subsequently in all
counties. Counties with official referees most easily solved the
problem, for they could within the letter and spirit of the law
assign the task to them.

Courts in other counties, however, were pushed to such expedients as delegating detention hearings to probation officers, to
the superintendent of the juvenile hall, or even to the local
justice court official. In emergency circumstances, judges or probation officers in a few counties omitted detention hearings or
postponed them beyond the forty-eight-hour limit; in one county
the judge signed blank forms for use by the probation officer in
his absence. In retrospect, these were less acts of defiance than
calculated risks, for today there is always the possibility that
parents may protest or that an attorney may turn a jaundiced
eye on the court and make an issue of such methods.

THE COW-COUNTY IMAGE OF THE JUVENILE COURT

The adaptations made in the juvenile courts of many smaller
counties owed much to the "cow-county" image, which mediated
interaction between local residents and outsiders. Actually the
phrase connotes little prior homogeneity of court procedures in
these counties apart from a pervasive commitment to informality. Beyond this, "cow county" simply means a sense of the necessity of difference and a measure of pride in that difference.
Roughly translated, it seems to say, "We are different because we
live differently and we like it that way."

Cow-county judges and probation officers who ignored features of the new law or gave them only nominal attention did so
with a sure conviction that they were changes primarily meant
to serve the needs of large counties. To them, the changes were
self-evidently inconsistent, incompatible, or incongruous when
put in the light of the special conditions under which their own

courts had to function. While no complete inventory of these conditions can be given, their nature is conveyed by reference to such things as: a large and "free-living" Indian population; a majority of out-of-county juvenile offenders (found in resort-area counties) ; long and slow travel between outlying populations and detention centers; high visibility of the actions of judges, probation officers, and their family members; personal politics by county supervisors; and close integration of probation officers into the county social life, exemplified by one who had "married into his job" and relied on a web of kinship ties to sustain his decisions and actions. No less important in determining a formalistic response of judges and probation officers to the new law was their persistent desire to place the "good of the kids," however conceived, over legal values. The judge of a far northern county explained:

> We're very unorthodox here. We try to keep informal. We try to get under the skin of the kids. We differ from big city courts. I am gone sometimes for as much as two weeks, which means that someone else has to hold detention hearings. Also, I have to order continuances on jurisdictional and dispositional hearings. If a felony charge is involved I advise minors and parents of their right to counsel. However, I don't do this for the "mickey mouse" offenses, and I don't worry about rules of evidence in uncontested cases. Furthermore, in hearings I ask leading questions; I try to get the boy to give out a little. I try to determine if the boy needs help and guidance. Often I tell them I am not going to make specific findings. Then there are times when I make minors wards even though there is very little to go on.
>
> Appeals don't worry me in the least. If the Supreme Court wants to differ, that's OK. The opinion of the Judicial Council likewise is of no concern, except on how I administer the court. The youngster's opinion of me is important in performing my role. What parents think of me also makes a difference, and I spend a lot of time building rapport. Otherwise, I have to satisfy my own conscience.

Comments by a probation officer in another northern county follow much the same line as he tells of his methods for working with delinquent youth:

This is a cow county, let's face it. I meet parents and foster parents all over. On the street I follow a policy of letting the kids speak first. Everyone knows me here and I don't want to embarrass them. There are no hardened city type delinquents here. We try to work with them locally. We "grow them up"—get them through their problem years. We play ping pong with kids in Juvenile Hall to establish rapport. We try to talk cows or horses to ranchers before we talk about their children. It takes a long time to get an Indian family to trust you. Then you can knock it in the head with just one court appearance.

If it is clear that informal procedures in juvenile courts were preserved in the face of the new law, it is equally clear that the cost was high, and that the new law made its share of problems for court workers in these areas. Even though compliance with new procedures was nominal, it unavoidably compounded the structure of the courts. While structure may not determine action, it can and does limit the range of choices and possible actions. Some of these levied heavy tolls on the time, energy, and attention of probation officers, e.g., where an officer had to travel three times to a nearby county whose detention hall was used, first to detain a youth, second to have a detention hearing, and finally to hold a jurisdictional hearing (case then transferred to another county). An over-all effect of greater formality in procedure was the inevitable loss of close contact with minors. Indeed, this was the chief problem aspect of change in the law for all courts of the state, save those already operating at a high level of formality. It is in the ramifications of greater formality that the less desirable consequences of the law revision are to be found.

FREQUENCY OF COUNSEL'S APPEARANCE

According to estimates supplied by probation officers and validated by spot studies in four counties—Yolo, Tuolumne, Colusa, and Sacramento—the percentage of cases in juvenile courts represented by counsel more than tripled between 1961 and

1965, rising from a median of 3 per cent to 10 per cent.[15] An important factor determining whether counsel appeared more often in one county than another was the presence of a public defender's office. This was particularly true until 1963, because although assigning counsel had been made mandatory for indigents whose offenses were equivalent to felonies in adult courts, there was no provision for payment of attorneys in the 1961 law revision. Table 6.1 shows that attorney representation increased

Table 6.1. Medians of Estimates of Percentages of Juvenile Court Cases Represented by Counsel before 1961 and as of 1965 by California Counties with or without Public Defenders

Year	20 Counties with Public Defenders	26 Counties without Public Defenders	All Counties	Range (All Counties)
Before 1961	3	2	3	0–30
As of 1965	15	8	10	0–99

by five times during the intervening years in public-defender counties, compared with a fourfold increase in those without. Both the rapidity of the increase and the proportion of cases currently represented by counsel varied greatly between counties. Current use, for example (1965), ranged from zero per cent to 70 per cent in counties where private attorneys appeared or were assigned, and varied from 1 per cent to 99 per cent in counties where the court could appoint the public defender. Only small percentage increases occurred during the four-year period in extremely large counties, such as Los Angeles, San Francisco, and Orange. Alameda County, in the large-county category, showed a jump—from 5 per cent to about 17 per cent.

15. Data from probation officers were secured by a mailed questionnaire to all fifty-eight counties of the state, from which there were fifty-six returns. I tabulated data for Sacramento and Yolo counties; data on Colusa and Tuolumne counties were obtained by graduate students Richard Jobst and Tom Martinez.

WHO GETS COUNSEL

In order to ascertain the socio-economic characteristics of youth represented by counsel, the data were collected and tabulated for a two-year series of cases in a medium-large, urban, "valley" county (Sacramento). The court in question was undergoing reorganization and expansion at the time, which may have changed the distributions of cases in years following; nevertheless, in the absence of other data, the findings are indicative of the possible differences presently distinguishing those with attorneys. Notably first is the absence of any but slight differences in the appearance of counsel according to the sex of the child (males 17.9, females 16.4). Age, however, as can be seen in Table 6.2, did substantially affect the likelihood of having an

Table 6.2 Cases with Counsel by Selected Socioeconomic Attributes, Sacramento County Juvenile Court. New or Supplemental Petitions, 1962, 1963

Age of Child	%	N	Ethnicity	%	N
12 and under	13.4	626	white	16.6	1353
13–16	17.4	917	Negro	20.6	160
17	25.2	190	Mexican	20.3	197
18 and over	51.8	27	other	20.0	50
Total	17.5	1760		17.5	1760

Occupation of Father	%	N	Religion of Parents	%	N
Prof. and mgr.	34.7	141	none	17.9	324
Clerical	23.9	117	Protestant	15.6	858
Skilled	17.2	255	Catholic	19.0	462
Semi-skilled	20.4	366	Mormon	26.5	49
Unskilled	27.2	250	other	22.3	67
Unknown	6.9	631			
	17.5	1760		17.5	1760

attorney; percentages rose with the age of the child. Ethnicity had little influence on the assignment of attorneys; there was no evidence of discrimination against so-called minority groups, and, if anything, Negroes and Mexicans received somewhat more favorable treatment in this respect than whites. Little can be said about the effects of the religion of the parents other than that Mormons seemed more likely to have attorneys than those of other religions or those without religious affiliation. This may reflect the strongly organized protective services of the Mormon church itself or a tendency of members to rally to the aid of church members needing help. While data on social-class status, indicated by father's occupation, were compromised by a large number of "unknowns," they suggest a pattern in which high-status and low-status people more often received legal assistance than those in between. While the high percentage of professional- and managerial-class youth with attorneys speaks of greater economic security, it also suggests the frequency with which the parents retained family attorneys. Many of these people, as probation officers attest, "do not make a move without consulting their attorneys."

ASSIGNMENT AND ENGAGEMENT OF COUNSEL

Although hard data are lacking for proof, at least half and probably the great majority of counsel in juvenile court cases throughout the state were those assigned by the courts. As already shown, the existence of a public defender in the county or city of the court enhanced the probability of counsel's being assigned. More active factors in decisions to assign or engage counsel lay in the type of case jurisdiction and the seriousness of the problem or offense it presented. The attitudes and values of judges, probation officers, and referees, and the nature of their social interaction with youths and parents, were equally significant.

Table 6.3 shows the distribution of cases in one court by type of formal allegations in the petitions and the percentage in each category presented by counsel. Cases of so-called unfit homes and those involving law violations were most likely to have attorneys. Closer analysis of these data showed that the court more frequently assigned counsel where there were serious law violations or delinquent tendencies, whereas private attorneys more frequently appeared in unfit-home cases. In unfit-home and delinquent-tendency cases, some courts favored a rule that counsel would be assigned where there was a conflict of interests between parents and child, e.g., where a parent or relative was charged with sexual molestation. However, this was qualified by other considerations. In a second county somewhat smaller than Sacramento, figures supplied by the probation officer disclosed that 80 per cent of the dependency and unfit-home cases (600) were assigned counsel, in addition to which counsel was assigned routinely in cases with serious law violations (602). About a quarter of the youth alleged to show delinquent tendencies (601) in this county had attorneys.

Table 6.3. Cases Represented by Counsel by Type of Allegation on the Petitions, Sacramento County Juvenile Court, 1962, 1963

Allegation	%	N
600A: dependency	4.0	445
600B: neglect, unfit home	27.4	295
601: delinquent tendencies		
(truancy, incorrigibility)	16.5	212
602: law violation	21.4	808
total	17.5	1760

The 1962 cases in the Sacramento court showed that the more serious the problem, the greater the probability that counsel would be assigned or engaged. Aggressive sexual behavior stood highest, with 46.6 per cent of the cases having counsel, followed by drug offenses, 40 per cent, violence against persons, 30.3 per cent, and alcohol offenses, 30 per cent. Lowest among problems in which an attorney entered were truancy, 10 per cent, and runaways, 14.1 per cent. Burglary, vandalism, incorrigibility, and auto theft fell between the highest and lowest percentages of those involving counsel.

The nature of the allegations and their seriousness to a considerable extent are functions of the perspectives, values, and decisions of the probation officers, meaning that their pattern of deciding which kind of disposition was most desirable, then selecting or phrasing allegations accordingly, has survived the change in the juvenile court law. Such judgments have an intervening effect on the frequency of counsel's appearance and to some extent on whether counsel will be private or public. This inheres in the probation officer's discretion in alleging either an unfit home (blaming parents) or incorrigibility (blaming the child). It is also implicit in decisions to send the youth to the C.Y.A. More often than not, anticipation of such a disposition means counsel will be recommended to parents or assigned by the court.

Cases in which youth denied the allegations of the petition generally were more apt to have counsel, but it remained problematical, especially in delinquent-tendency cases and those in which the law violation was relatively minor. The associated social interaction in interviews where advice was given as to right to counsel tended to become ambiguous. Parents often subtly probed or tested for the possible effects of having an attorney on the disposition of the case, and even tried to bargain. Some chief probation officers even issued standard instructions as to how deputies should reply to the frequent question: "What do you think I should do?" At least one probation department printed cards with the exact wording to be employed in the answer.

There was little doubt that the mien and tone of a probation officer or judge could discourage the hiring of an attorney by implying that there was no need for one, or that it might pose problems or alienate the judge.[15a] This was most apt to occur

15a. Research on judges' responses to the Gault ruling that juveniles and parents must be advised of their right to counsel shows that compliance is weak or absent. This conclusion, however, came from the study of juvenile courts in three "northern urban" communities (non California). It was based on courtroom observations and does not reflect what part probation officers play in explaining the right to counsel. See Norm Lefstein, Vaughn Stapleton, and Lee Teitlebaum, "In Search of Juvenile Justice: Gault and Its Implementation," *Law and Society Review* III (1969), pp. 491–562.

in counties where judges privately were opposed to having counsel in court, or where a sharp distinction was drawn between trivial offenses and serious misdoing or "real delinquency." If the revised law were followed fully, many of the former would be dismissed at intake. Furthermore, if an attorney were present and turned them into contests or adversary hearings, many would have to be dismissed for lack of evidence.

In contrast to these tendencies, a judge in one county assigned the public defender in 90 to 95 per cent of all cases. Although neither the probation officer nor the public defender fully approved, the judge justified his high rate of assigned counsel on grounds that he was busy and had to make his decisions strictly on the basis of what was presented in court hearings. One result was to magnify role problems for the public defender, as well as for the probation officer.

ROLE CONFUSION AND ROLE CONFLICT

A great deal of uncertainty arose in California juvenile court hearings, owing to lack of clarity and structured conflict in the roles of attorneys, probation officers, and judges. Private attorneys without previous juvenile court experience were particularly at a loss as to how to proceed; one confided to me after a hearing:

> What can you do in this kind of court? Downtown [adult courts] I know what the rules are and what I can do. Here you come in, hat in hand, and hope for the best.

Apart from lacking ideas on how to exploit the court to their client's advantage, attorneys often confronted cases in which there was literally nothing that could be done. Their inactivity confirmed the skepticism of those judges who believed they had no place in the court. One judge sarcastically observed: "They sit there like bumps on logs. They take the client's money and do nothing."

Attorneys in cases like these undoubtedly feel pressure to do something for their clients, but if they become contentious in true adversary style, they slow down the proceedings. Insisting on the right to cross-examine witnesses adds greatly to the work of the probation officer. He as well as the witnesses, and even the judge, may become irritated, particularly if they regard the case as open-and-shut and the intended disposition as lenient. The situation became critical in one county shortly after the new law went into effect, where the tactics of private attorneys and the confusion over rules of evidence piled up cases and heavily overloaded the calendar. The county bar association was drawn into discussion of the problem, with the result that one law firm was given a contract to serve as public defender in all cases where counsel was assigned. Thereafter, the work of the court went forward with less delay.

Employing public defenders for assigned cases may make a more "efficient" court, but may also cause counsel to be co-opted into the organization of the court, even becoming its superficial appendage. Factors encouraging this co-optation are the low priority public defenders give to juvenile work, and the growth of interdepartmental or informal reciprocity with probation officers. Public defenders may come to justify their passive roles on the grounds that they do not want to add to the work of already overburdened probation officers; but more important is the arousal of a differential reaction toward juvenile offenders. The following statement is illustrative:

> Ordinarily I stipulate that the probation officer's report is acceptable in the jurisdictional hearings. Otherwise he would have to bring in witnesses. In many such cases, perhaps most, the evidence would not support the judgment, but I hate to see a young kid get the idea that he can get away with something. One 15 year old boy who broke into a bar and took a case of beer told me in an interview that his problem was that he got caught. I became indignant and asked him if he wasn't too young to drink. The boy said, "No, only too young to buy." I decided he needed to be jolted—maybe with a stay in detention—so I encouraged him to admit his guilt in court. No *corpus delicti* needed to be established. If it had been an adult case I would have taken the position that the D.A. could not prove his case, because the beer was never found and not even reported until a month after it disappeared.

THE EMERGENT ROLE OF THE ATTORNEY

Disregarding the gratuitous aspects of the attorney's role in the juvenile court, it appears that exigencies and a growing organizational hiatus, to an extent developed by the law change itself, push the attorney toward the role of a negotiator, mediator, or interpreter of court decisions and actions to clients. This view is supported by my court observations, interview findings, and by questionnaire responses of probation officers. In regard to the latter, Table 6.4 shows that in nearly half the replies, counsel

Table 6.4. Evaluations by Probation Officers of the Usefulness of Counsel in Juvenile Court Hearings in 56 California Counties, 1965

Usefulness	N	%
clarifies evidence	17	14.0
suggests dispositions	17	14.0
interprets court decisions to minors and parents	34	28.1
simply makes parents and minors feel better	24	19.8
is of little value	8	6.6
is in some instances disruptive and time-consuming	21	17.3
total	121	99.8

was thought to be helpful as an interpreter of the meaning of court decisions to parents and minors, and as a source of psychic support. At the same time, nearly a quarter of the probation workers took a more jaundiced view of the attorney's presence in court as of "little real value" or "disruptive." Approval by probation officers of counsel's mediator role and their disapproval of his adversary role reflect both the adaptations and the problems that have evolved with the more formalized structure in the juvenile court.

ASYMMETRY IN THE ADVERSARY SYSTEM

One of the major difficulties brought with revision of the juvenile court law, and called its most "glaring defect" by one judge, arose from complications in adversary proceedings where juveniles denied the allegations of the petition. No provision was made in the new law to present the case against minors or parents or to "represent the interests of the state." Thus a kind of asymmetry or imbalance was sorely felt by many probation officers and judges and much decried by law enforcement people, who in 1965 made a determined but unsuccessful effort to have the law amended so that the prosecuting attorney could be required to assist probation officers in contested hearings. Meantime, a variety of adaptations to the problem have evolved, the nature and distribution of which are displayed in Table 6.5. They reveal that probation officers generally have had to assume the unpleasant burden of carrying the case; either as investigators or as court officers, they have been responsible for stating and sustaining allegations of the petition in nearly three fourths of the counties in the state.

The role of the investigating officer in presenting the case against parents and juveniles can be both anomalous and stressful, for ordinarily he lacks the legal knowledge, training, temperament, or experience to play what in reality is a prosecutor's role. In adversary hearings he may be subjected to rough, embarrassing, even humiliating treatment at the hands of a defense attorney, or may be called to account sharply by the judge. Some female probation officers, for example, were reduced to tears in

Table 6.5 Official Who Presents Case or Allegations against Juveniles and Parents in Jurisdictional Hearings in 56 California Counties, 1965

Official	*Probation Officer Who Investigates Case*	*Probation Officer Alternates With Prosecutor*
%	41	21.4

their early courtroom encounters after the law was revised. But even tougher male officers grow uneasy, as revealed by the feelings of one officer during a fast interchange between judge and attorney in a murder hearing: "Suddenly I thought, 'What am I doing here!' "

A second type of role conflict for the probation officer who presents the case resides in his necessity to attack the integrity of parents and charge crimes to juveniles. This is inconsistent with his conception of himself as one who helps others, but more important, it frequently destroys whatever chance he may have had to establish rapport:

> The change in the law really affects us. We ran a very informal court before and never felt that the charge was important unless it was a crime of violence. A kid on a petty theft charge can be harder to work with than one with burglary. So we didn't feel we had to go into the legal aspects, especially since the kids usually admitted the charge.
>
> Now we have to have the deputies [sheriffs'] in there, and the victim, and put on a big show. It makes the probation officer into a prosecutor when he has to tell the boy he is a bum. It gets tough when you have to say his old man is a drunk and that his mother is shacking up. Before, we put all those things into the report; the judge knew it and we didn't have to say it like we do now. Afterwards, it's hard to get rapport. I have to take the boy from court to my office and try to be his friend. There's where it hurts.

Entrusting court officers with presenting cases is one method by which large probation departments have sought to mitigate role conflicts of probation officers otherwise at a disadvantage in court hearings, but this doesn't always work well from an administrative point of view; or, where it does, its uses are limited.

Table 6.5 Continued

Probation Officer Alternates With Court Officer	Judge	Combinations (Judge and Probation Officer, and Court Officer and Prosecutor)
14.2	12.5	10.7

The court officer has other duties to perform. For example, here he is a supervisor. He can't be fully informed on all aspects of cases which are investigated by another officer. There just isn't time to do the homework.

I became concerned about the waiting around all morning which the investigating officer had to do for a five minute court appearance. Also I had noted the discomfort the staff felt in the presence of a good criminal lawyer. I had mixed feelings, but decided to give the court officer idea a whirl. We have been satisfied because it gives the probation department a better image. We use it in recidivist cases. In very complex cases, though, the investigating officer has to come in. In serious cases like homicide we ask the District Attorney to come in.

Although adding a court officer to the probation department may "improve its image," it is a bureaucratic solution that adds impersonality to the processing of cases and may introduce errors. As greater social distance separates the probation officer from the person he ideally is supposed to help, the need for an intermediate role in the court system intensifies. Attorneys are logical candidates for the role, but they move into the vacuum not without conflicts of their own, as has been shown.

THE JUDGE

Ideally, the American judge, in contrast to the English or continental judge, has traditionally conceived his role as that of an umpire or presiding officer who decides questions of procedure and law, rather than adducing facts and evidence. In criminal cases the prosecutor is the chief interrogator. Although the new juvenile court law clearly allows criminal-type adversary hearings, the unwillingness of many prosecutors to try juvenile cases, coupled with the legal ineptitude of probation officers, means that the judge himself (see Table 6.5) frequently not only "presents the case" but also intervenes in the questioning of the "defendant" or witnesses when the probation officer falters. At the same time, because the court is charged with protecting the interests of the child, the judge, if he deems it necessary, may preempt or intervene in the role of the defense attorney.

The mixed role of the judge is not without its problems, one being that he is likely to be something less than a complete defense lawyer or total prosecutor. One judge, seeking to fulfill the spirit of the new law, actually got down on the floor of the court, robes and all, to allow a juvenile defendant to choke him in demonstrating a murder assault. He soon stopped such behavior, however, and it is probably significant that this judge retired from the juvenile court with a fundamental dislike for his assignment.

Experienced juvenile court judges in contested cases and those involving serious issues are likely to alternate between a managerial role, in which they attempt to insure that all interests will be represented, and a hearing role, in which they seek to actualize the interplay of these interests. However, it is doubtful that many judges are prepared to let hearings become full-dress, protracted, adversary contests. Such considerations shape their decisions to appoint attorneys and their control of court procedures. In unfit-home and incorrigibility cases, the judge may assign counsel to avoid an unequal contest in which it is the child's word against that of two or more parents or a set of relatives solidly aligned.[16] On the other hand, the judge may feel that he and the probation officer can properly defend the interests of the child even though the parents have engaged an attorney.

Observations suggest that in unfit-home cases judges tend to structure the situation so that their own roles become much more neutral. The underlying reason may be that declaring wardship or removing a child from his home runs contrary to the traditional conservatism of the court in such matters. These cases have a strong potential for conflict, and hearings may be used for extraneous purposes, such as custody fights. Hence the reluctance of judges to appoint attorneys for parents as well as for children.

16. Difficulties arose in one county where an attorney representing the parents and another representing the child were discovered to be in the same law firm. Pressures on the child to withdraw the charges against his parents in this kind of situation are overpowering.

RULES OF EVIDENCE

While conflict has always been implicit in the role of the juvenile court judge, it has been made explicit by the mandates of the new juvenile code. This is owing not only to the presence of counsel in court but also to the rules of evidence specified by the new law, which, in the case of youth alleged to have committed offenses equivalent to felonies, require a "preponderance of evidence legally admissible in the trial of criminal cases to support findings." Many judges and attorneys were perplexed by the provision's implication of standard criminal procedure for such cases.[17]

Conflict arose over what evidence was subject to objection and how the objections should be made and ruled on. A conspicuous contradiction emerges if the judge takes over the role of interrogator, for logically he should rule on objections to his own questions, which would weaken the case he is making. A judge speaks to the difficulty as follows:

> I start out by telling attorneys: "I don't like this any more than you, but I am sitting up here in the role of interrogator because there's no other provision in the law. You've got to object to the judge's question. And of course I am in a pretty good position to rule here, but I want you to object whenever you think the objection is good and you would have objected if this question had been asked by the District Attorney, and I'll give you a ruling on it." Well, they do some but it does put counsel obviously at a disadvantage. And it puts the judge in a very awkward and embarrassing position.

If no attorney is present at the contested hearing and the law is followed closely, the judge may find himself in the position of

17. The recommendations of the juvenile justice commission were much stronger than the change made by the legislature. Originally the statute was proposed to read: "A preponderance of evidence not subject to timely objection by competent counsel under rules of evidence observed in the trial of criminal cases. . . ." Proposed but later omitted was a statement that no findings were to be made upon uncorroborated extra-judicial admissions or confessions of minors unless they were represented by counsel. Report of Governor's Special Study Commission on Juvenile Justice, 1960, Part II, p. 73.

interrogator, yet constrained to think of possible objections to his own questions, then rule on them. The problem is accentuated because much, if not most, evidence in juvenile cases, especially in the probation report, is legally only hearsay. With passing time, most judges have adapted to these difficulties of evidentiary proof by simply "admitting everything." The law can be so interpreted as to allow this; it can also be justified by precedents for admitting hearsay evidence in other kinds of cases. When queried on the issue, some judges said that they were capable of "mental erasure," "shifting," excluding, or otherwise weighing the competence of various items.

Inasmuch as the probation report often is the only evidence presented, many judges seek to validate it by securing admissions from the youth. Questionnaire responses of probation officers reveal that judges in ten courts of the state relied on admissions of the minor alone to making findings. In twenty-two courts they used admissions of minors plus independently established evidence. In five courts they relied on evidence other than the minor's admissions. Judges in the remaining nineteen courts proceeded "according to the case," usually requiring independent corroboration of admissions of minors in more serious cases.

Although attorneys in juvenile court now have access to probation reports and theoretically can dispute evidence much as in adult criminal hearings, it is doubtful that they are completely free to do so, especially if they must enter a contest with the judge or if they suspect that he already concurs with the probation officer's recommended disposition.[18] Furthermore, if an attorney represents or expects to represent more than one case in juvenile court, his actions are likely to be modified by his direct relationship with the probation officer or what he perceives to be a policy of the probation department. If he pursues an aggressive line of action, he may alienate the probation people and do his

18. The juvenile court might be likened to a mediation system of justice in which the judge acts as interrogator, counsel, and jury. According to Schwartz and Miller, to serve as counsel in this setting is painful, as well as superfluous, and even where the formal role emerges, it tends to be ambiguous. See Richard Schwartz and James C. Miller, "Legal Evolution and Societal Complexity," *American Journal of Sociology* LXX (1964), 167.

client more harm than good. An illustrative case is summarized by a probation officer:

> The case was a return from camp for another hearing and new disposition, and the attorney really raised hell with us. He insisted on cross-examining all of the witnesses, which meant that we had to bring about ten people fifty miles in from camp. One woman, a cook, was so upset by the attorney's cross-examination, that she said she would bring in her own attorney if she had to come again. Everyone was sore, and now the people out at camp are going to get the boy dead to the right. They'll watch him like a hawk and make it so unpleasant he can't help doing something which will get him out of there.[19]

The probation officer's often ill-concealed rancor toward the attorney's single-minded pursuit of evidence according to the rules may be explained not only by his alegalistic orientation, but also by the fact that the police sometimes send him "bad cases," or pass on to him the job of investigation, and that producing a witness many times is an almost hopeless task. Frequently, perhaps typically, the case rests on the testimony of teen-age witnesses, who, as a probation officer observed, "blow hot and cold." It is not unusual for a probation officer to go into court in a contested matter not knowing whether he has a case or not:

> My feelings about the juvenile court law are mixed because it can put me in a bad position. For example: One boy steals a motorcycle and a second sells the frame. A girl friend of one of the boys finally admits she and they were in on it. They all have attorneys. But I have no eyeball witness. If they don't go on the stand I have no case. So what do I do?

SEPARATION OF JURISDICTIONAL
AND DISPOSITIONAL HEARINGS

The last item of legal change in juvenile court procedures considered here is the separation of the jurisdictional and disposi-

---

19. A relevant fact is that camp superintendents have a great deal of power, in some cases amounting to absolute veto over who can be sent to camp.

tional hearings. Presumably these hearings were designed to make juvenile procedure more nearly like adult criminal procedure, in particular to exclude possible prejudicial effects of the so-called "social report" of the probation officer on findings of fact. In theory the court or the judge must first consider jurisdictional facts only, set down in a separate report, then proceed to facts relevant to disposition in a second report, which may include impressionistic, typological judgments by teachers, psychologists, psychiatrists, camp and juvenile hall counselors, as well as the probation officers. It is doubtful that this part of the law has been approximated in practice. In their first experience with the new law, some judges tried to hear cases without first reading the dispositional report, then gave it up as a bad job and joined the majority of judges who currently read both reports to hearings. A minority of judges comply with the criminal-procedure prototype to the extent of setting aside the social report in contested cases for later reading, but this device breaks down where the contest does not become apparent until the time of the hearing. One conscientious judge under these circumstances offers the youth or parents the option of a hearing by the second judge in his court, but this alternative is absent in one-judge counties, or where otherwise available judges have full and pressing calendars. A smaller minority of judges do not receive disposition reports on any cases before adjudication.[20]

One reason why most judges do not postpone study of the social report has to do with time and convenience. Ordinarily in

20. Replies from fifty-four counties showed that thirty-three judges read the dispositional report in all or most cases before jurisdictional hearings; thirteen did not read the report before jurisdiction was determined in contested cases; and mine did not see the report prior to the jurisdictional hearing in all cases. In a few counties the dispositional report was not even brought to the court until after jurisdiction had been established.

These figures may be compared with a study of New York judges in 1957, in which 67 per cent of those surveyed at a judges' conference stated they saw the "background report" before juvenile court hearings; 8 per cent read the report during hearings; and 25 per cent made use of the report only after adjudication. Leo J. Yehle, "Some Practices and Procedures in Children's Court," *Syracuse Law Review* 9 (1957), 1–10; see also "Survey of Juvenile Courts and Probation Services, 1966," in *Task Force Report: Juvenile Delinquency and Youth Crime*, President's Commission on Law Enforcement and the Administration of Justice (Washington, 1967), pp. 77–83.

most counties the jurisdictional hearing phases right into the dispositional. If the judge has not read the report on the latter, he must hold the court in abeyance or take a recess while he reads it, or awkwardly try to digest it while the hearing proceeds, or order a continuance. None is a satisfactory use of time, energies, and personnel of the court. Furthermore, since the great majority of youth admit the allegations of the petition, the focal problem of the court is not whether an offense has been committed but rather what should be done with the youth in question.

Despite change in the law, adjudication during hearings remains a marginal or justifying function of the California juvenile court. Inasmuch as the judge reads the entire probation report, he responds to the configuration of perspectives, facts, and circumstances upon which the probation officer makes his recommendation. In most cases the judge decides his plan of action before the hearing, and simply reserves a right for others to try to change his mind. It is the conviction of many judges that the work of the juvenile court could not be done without their reading the complete social report before hearings. According to extensive discussions of inter-county transfer cases in the 1962 and 1964 Institutes for Juvenile Court Judges and Referees, many judges believed that declaring wardship by the transferring county tied the hands of the receiving county and imposed stigma which might be avoided if additional evidence in the home county was available.[21]

INTERACTION OF JUDGE AND PROBATION OFFICER

One by-product of separating the dispositional and jurisdictional hearings in juvenile court has been more definitive and less

21. Experience with bifurcated hearings or "split trials" in personal (auto) injury cases where instituted were found to increase the percentage of verdicts for defendants greatly. One writer concludes that these hearings "distort the balance of substantive rights." Maurice Rosenberg, "Court Congestion: Status, Causes, and Proposed Remedies," in *The Courts, the Public and the Law Explosion* (Englewood Cliffs: 1965), p. 48f. Applied to the juvenile court, "real" bifurcated hearings might put the court and the public at undue disadvantage.

flexible recommendations by probation officers, because now disposition has to rest upon findings. An experienced chief probation officer in a large county raised this point at a juvenile court judges' conference:

> A bifurcated report . . . prevents the probation officer from commingling fact and fiction. You [the judge] don't have to eliminate all the things that aren't fact. It has one other advantage to the judge—it avoids the oldtime distinction we used to have—that if the court finds, then so-and-so, and if the court doesn't find, do such-and-such. The court already has to find, so the probation officer has to stick his neck out and make a definite recommendation. He can't hide behind that "If the court finds. . . ." [22]

Another result of the changed form of the probation report has been a closer co-ordination or formal synthesis between the views of judges and probation officers. Speaking of the agreement between judicial dispositions and recommendations by his department, a probation officer said:

> Right now we are running somewhere between 90 and 95 per cent [agreement]. I have always felt that if we drop below 85 per cent it is time to talk with judges to see whether or not we're interpreting their philosophies and approaches the right way. One time we went down with one judge to 64 per cent and that was a rather unfortunate situation.

Probation officers must try to accomplish their goals at the same time they satisfy the values to which judges give their allegiance. Under the new law, more factual evidence must be presented in legal form to do so, yet there is no specification for evidence of such categories as "dependency," "unfit home," "delinquent tendencies," "violating an order of the court," or a law violation that "shall not be deemed the commission of a crime." The philosophy of the judge and the values he brings to the court continue to have a selective effect on the kinds of information

22. Statement by Lorenzo Buckley, Report on the Proceedings of the second annual Institute for Juvenile Court Judges and Referees, sponsored by the judicial council, Berkeley, 1963, p. 134f.

included in the probation officer's report. At no time is this more apparent than when a probation officer has to bring cases before more than one judge, or when judges are changed. Again, to quote a probation officer in a Central Valley county:

> Getting a different judge calls for a lot of readaptation by the probation officer. Judges differ greatly in the kinds of facts and information they ask for. This means that both the investigation and the manner of writing up the case are affected.

Probation officers make judgments that the community must be protected, that a boy needs some detention time to "cool off" or, conversely, protection from the community, that parents should be punished, that county welfare costs must be kept down, or that illegitimacy should be discouraged. Normally they do not separate action (value) judgments from judgments of fact. One officer stated: "I can tell in twenty minutes what type of case it is," by which he meant whether it was destined for simple probation, foster-home placement, boys' camp, or the C.Y.A. Unlike judges, probation officers are not constrained to discover an explicit rationale for their decisions and actions, hence are freer to tailor their investigations, allegations, and procedures to ends sought. Procedures required by a judge or by the presence of an attorney in contested cases simply become obstacles to overcome or circumvent. In legally weak cases, probation officers are not above "finagling," as one harassed court officer put it, or, as another explained, a "little star chambering."

A more crucial question is the extent to which juvenile judges are willing and able under the new law to accommodate the goals of probation officers or to fulfill through extra-legal means the various purposes of the juvenile court as they see them or as they sometimes unavoidably emerge. While some judges even before the law was changed carefully observed due process in the juvenile courts, the new law undeniably has made all judges more conscious of the requirements of procedure and proof.[23]

23. The law change was popularly conceived as "Civil Rights for Juveniles," or a "Little Bill of Rights for Juveniles." See the Oakland *Tribune*, September 14, October 27, November 28, November 29, 1960; April 5, April 14, and July 14, 1961.

Constraint on the part of the juvenile court judge now is operationally or situationally induced or reinforced by the required presence of a clerk and reporter, but far more so by the mere presence of counsel and the possibility that he will object, argue, or bargain on evidence or procedural points.[24] One judge, reputed for his careful attention to procedure and proof, described a case in which he found parents to have neglected their children as alleged:

> If this case had been strongly defended or if an attorney had been present I might not have been able to sustain a finding. However, the charge downtown [under the penal code] will probably be dismissed and then I would have no hold over these parents. As it is the children will be dependent for one year only, and there will be some visits by the probation officer. I don't really think that being dependent children for a year will harm them.

MEASURABLE CONSEQUENCES OF THE LAW CHANGE

Attempts at measuring the consequences of the law changes against the intent of those who recommended and legislated them meet with great difficulty. Queries as to whether juvenile detention generally has declined as a result of the revisions are complicated by confusion over the definition of arrests and by concurrently changing factors that have affected police and court action. An effort was made by the Division of Field Services of the California Youth Authority to determine what degree the new law had increased the staff of the juvenile courts but was abandoned as worthless because the effects of changing the law could not be separated from normal growth factors.[25]

As already shown, however, it is possible to make an objective

24. One judge averred that he no longer could "put on his act," as he had to watch his language with a reporter present. Occasional older practices in hearings, in which judge and probation officer played "good guy and bad guy," are unlikely to occur now.

25. There is an additional problem in that the law change was a "package" of changes, and it becomes difficult to ascertain which change produced which result.

assessment of the success of the new law in bringing counsel into the juvenile court. In addition, there are measurable indications of the effects of the presence of an attorney on the outcome of cases in juvenile court. Data for the Sacramento County Juvenile Court are shown in Table 6.6.

In examining the entries in Table 6.6, it should be kept in mind that serious cases, particularly so-called C.Y.A. cases, were most likely to have attorneys. It is immediately evident that representation by counsel more often secured a favorable outcome for the case than when there was none. Proportionately, dismissals were ordered nearly three times as frequently in attorney as in non-attorney cases. The same was true for granting informal probation. Wardships were more often declared in non-attorney cases, and the children more likely to be placed away from their homes. Suspension of commitment to the C.Y.A. was more frequent in cases with counsel. Only in the category of youths sent to the C.Y.A. did the attorney cases fare worse than those without.

Closer analysis of the data showed that private attorneys were somewhat more successful in getting cases dismissed than the public defender—17.9 per cent to 14.9 per cent. The court more often dismissed attorney cases than did the referee—18.2 per cent to 10.8 per cent; but the referee was more lenient with non-attorney cases, dismissing 7.2 per cent, as compared with .8 per cent by the court. There was no evidence that ethnicity, occupational status of father, or prior records of the youth were responsible for these differences. Negroes fared somewhat less well than whites in percentages of dismissals in both the attorney and non-attorney categories, but there were more serious cases among the Negroes. Mexicans got about the same per cent of dismissals as whites when they had no attorneys but more when they did—20.2 per cent to 16.8 per cent. When cases were tabulated by occupational status of fathers, clerical and semi-skilled jobs ranked highest in cases dismissed both with and without attorneys, followed by professional and managerial occupations, skilled and unskilled jobs, in that order.

Important though dismissals may be in estimating the gains made from the presence of counsel, they were only a small part

Table 6.6. Outcomes of Juvenile Court Cases with and without Counsel, Sacramento County, 1962, 1963. New and Supplemental Petitions.

Outcome	Attorney (N–308)	No Attorney (N–1452)	Total (N–1760)
Dismissed	16.8	6.3	8.1
Department supervision (informal probation)	6.6	2.3	3.0
Ward to parents	29.2 ⎫	31.1 ⎫	30.8
Ward placed	10.3 ⎬ 48.8	38.2 ⎬ 77.6	33.4
Ward to boys' ranch or private institution	8.0 ⎭	6.5 ⎭	6.8
Ward to mental hospital	1.3 ⎫	1.8 ⎫	1.7
CYA, suspended, home or ranch	8.7 ⎬	4.8 ⎬	5.5
CYA	12.3 ⎭	5.9 ⎭	7.1
Remanded to superior court	2.2	.6	.9
Transferred to another county	4.2	2.0	2.4
N	99.6	99.5	99.7

of the total: fifty-two of 308 cases. Furthermore, thirty of these were cases in which the home was alleged to be inadequate or the parents unfit. Hence it may be concluded that the adversary role of attorneys in juvenile court has strengthened safeguards against unwarranted intrusion into or removal of children from the home. However, this must be qualified by the knowledge that such cases are difficult to prove.

If dismissals in unfit-home cases are disregarded, it follows that attorneys are less useful to their clients in avoiding jurisdiction or control by the juvenile court than they are in scaling down or mitigating the severity of dispositions after findings have been made. Data for the main court studied, for instance, show that attorneys had little influence on decisions to detain youth and on the length of detention stays. In fact, youth without attorneys were less likely to be detained than those with counsel—49.3 per cent to 58.8 per cent, and also less likely to have extremely long stays in juvenile hall.

My observations of about 120 hearings in this one court and several dozen scattered in other courts underscore the idea that opportunities to use adversary skills in juvenile court are limited. Occasionally attorneys can get dismissals, once in a while by instructing minors and parents to refuse to make statements. More often they succeed in getting allegations reduced in number or modified to conform to legal usage, so they can then argue for a more favorable disposition. They also have some negative power to alter dispositions simply by an implied threat to contest evidence and thereby slow down the work of the court. Occasionally this is bare-faced bargaining at the hearing. Sometimes an attorney bluntly informs a probation officer at the time of referral that he has no case, which may be enough to convince him. In other instances attorneys may show up at citation hearings and persuade the probation officer to take no further action.

Attorneys in juvenile court appear at their best when they make positive contributions by bringing new evidence into the dispositional hearing and proposing alternatives to the probation officer's recommendations. They may, for example, find relatives willing to take care of the child, eliminating the need for foster-home placement, or suggest that psychiatric counseling paid for by the parents be substituted for commitment to boys' camp. Attorneys also help their clients by convincing them to accept a recommended disposition where refusal would lead to a more draconic order by the court.

Sometimes attorneys get overinvolved in juvenile court cases either as civil-rights crusaders or as attorney-turned-social-worker. In one small county an attorney became a kind of local *bête noire*, haunting the probation office and striking fear into the heart of the probation officer, who happened to be a woman. Attorneys elsewhere have requested that youths be paroled to them, but an unfortunate experience in one county, having sexual overtones, suggests that this is a spurious development of their role.

ADAPTATIONS AS LEGAL SUBCULTURES

The law is analogous to an iceberg in that often only a small portion of its significant work can be observed in the regulated interaction that takes place in court hearings or can be learned from the official record. Equally or more important are patterns of interaction, usually unrecorded, that grow up in the interstices of formal procedures and cluster about explicit rules and official roles. Taken together, these patterns become the legal subculture of the court, and while they evolve within the limits of the same formal law, they are by no means comparable from one area to another.

Informal cultures of the juvenile courts of California prior to 1961 grew up rather freely in response to patterns of values and problems confronting judges, probation officers, and law enforcement officers in local communities. Thereafter the court and the police had to give higher allegiance to a set of "extraneous" legal values, or at the very least to treat such values as means to their own ends. The need to satisfy legal values before others reordered claims on the court, created new ones, and set in motion new forms of social interaction.

The most telling changes since 1961 have occurred in the interaction of probation officers and police with minors and parents. The older covert pattern, namely talking minors into admissions of guilt and bringing them into court "for their own good," has greatly weakened, and even disappeared in some places.

> Police used to rely on a bluff. They would say to a kid, "Come on, tell me all about it." Often a youth would tell the police of crimes they knew nothing about.

> In the old days probation officers conned kids into all kinds of confessions. Not now. Attorneys advise kids not to testify and they don't.[26]

There is little doubt that these changes are traceable to sections of the law having to do with advising minors and parents of the right to counsel. Being so advised several times, by probation officers, judges, and sometimes the police, clarifies and defines interaction that otherwise tends to become ambiguous and manipulable. Furthermore, it encourages a defensive attitude in minors and parents vis-à-vis the court. Probation officers in thirty-seven counties stated that minors were more conscious of their legal rights now than they had been before revision of the law. In only eight counties did the officers say that no change had been noted. (Eleven respondents were unable to say.)

A majority of the probation officers also were agreed that they must take much more responsibility for presenting a legally couched report, as well as a case that will stand up in court against potential attacks from judges as well as defense attorneys. It has become less possible under the present law than once was true to allege one thing and mean another. Hence the difficulty of pursuing the older practice of taking jurisdiction in doubtful cases where "the child really needs help." In some courts at least, the result is also less freedom in recommending dispositions:

---

26. After the 1961 law change went into effect in Los Angeles, there was a tendency for detention hearings to become much like jurisdictional hearings, causing many youth to "cop out." Later, Judge William MacFaden changed this situation by instituting new policy. *Proceedings of the 1966 Institute for Juvenile Court Judges and Referees,* sponsored by the judicial council, Long Beach, 1966, p. 83f; Los Angeles *Metropolitan News,* October 28, 1966.

Now we have to distinguish between the boy touching the girl's pants and putting his hand inside her pants. We used to call lewd and lascivious conduct vagrancy but we can't do that now, even though it would help in placing the girl.

Where a closer tie between legal allegations and choice of dispositions has become a reality, some forms of juvenile deviant behavior must be ignored, or new ways found to handle them. For example, the so-called weekender, the curfew violator who came in on Friday night and was released Monday morning, has disappeared from detention homes in many counties. The sexually promiscuous girl is less easily "got into" the C.Y.A.; now either she is freed or new kinds of services are devised for her. Another trend in some counties has been to redefine delinquency as a psychiatric problem and make dispositions accordingly.

Despite the greater formality and legalism of the present-day juvenile court, much of its work even in large and populous counties continues to be informal. Many cases are either dismissed by probation officers after intake interviews, and after citation hearings, or placed on informal probation. Some judges still "put over" hearings or grant continuances to help reach the diverse ends sought by probation officers. While more and more of these cases are dismissed for lack of evidence, still there are many "good" cases in which the probation officer is tempering the wind to the shorn lamb, choosing leniency over severity. Here he is in a strong position to induce "co-operation" from minors or parents by the actual or implied threat to activate a petition. His tools are moral suasion and bargaining, underwritten by the ubiquitous threat, "unless you do this we will have to do this." [27]

When an attorney enters a case he may do nothing other than satisfy himself that the facts are beyond dispute and that the probation officer is offering a more lenient disposition than could be gained by negotiation or a formal hearing. Thereafter

27. Sometimes this kind of bargaining comes out in hearings, as when procedure more or less falls apart in dealings with an irrepressible older female, or one with a foreign background and limited command of English. Even judges get drawn into the melee.

he may drop out of the case or simply not appear if there is a hearing. It is in cases where a contest is possible that an attorney's presence changes the pattern of informal interaction. However, it is a distortion to say that the legal license to contest cases has prompted a significant number of attorneys to resort to adversary proceedings for juveniles.

Decisions by attorneys to negotiate or to make a contest of a juvenile case are conditioned by the size of the juvenile court, the number of judges serving it, the willingness of the district attorney to come in and present the case, the type of attorneys appearing, i.e., public or private, and the attitudes of probation officers, judges, and the attorneys themselves. The ways in which the potential for adversary procedure has begun to affect informal interaction in juvenile courts can be grasped by a closer look at adult criminal courts, which have been traditionally regarded as arenas for adversary struggles. Contrary to popular belief, the majority of convictions there (usually over 90 per cent) result not from a combative trial-by-jury or trial-by-judge process at all but from a negotiated, bargained plea of guilty. Equally instructive are the ways in which criminal lawyers develop reciprocal relationships with the courts in which they practice. They help the courts and the courts help them, weaving a theme of reciprocity predicated on claims of time, costs, convenience, and fees.[28]

The patterns of reciprocity just emerging in juvenile courts have a generic similarity to those long followed in criminal courts. They are inherent in the kinds of leverage opposed parties can apply. Attorneys can influence the court by instructing their juvenile clients to tell the probation officer nothing, or, as noted previously, by threatening to delay proceedings. If minors stay silent, the probation officer is sometimes put in an awkward position, because he has to place a bare-bones report before his judge, who may show his ire at having to make findings or a disposition with so few facts. On the other hand, the

28. Abraham S. Blumberg, "Covert Contingencies in the Right to the Assistance of Counsel." Paper read at meeting of the American Sociological Association, Miami, August 30, 1966, p. 4; *Criminal Justice* (Chicago: Quadrangle Books, 1967).

probation officer controls access to his report until it is formally filed with the clerk. His attitude toward the attorney, especially if the latter is unfamiliar with the court, can determine whether the attorney has to go into a hearing "blind," knowing very little about his case. Attorneys also may feel constrained knowing that they will have to work with probation officers in cases that are weak or where there is no defense.

Judges have some coercive power also, especially where attorneys are assigned by the court from a local panel. Here the judge's actions can speak louder than words. That court assignments are sometimes made with an eye to controlling the conduct of attorneys in hearings was confided in these words:

> You have to be careful on your appointment of an attorney because he may be energetic; he may become adversary here and you will have problems.

Cases are not unknown in which judges have summarily ordered militant attorneys to "co-operate" with the probation officer. The leverage of the court is strongest in cases of sixteen- and seventeen-year-olds: a threat can be made to remand them to adult courts, where the attorney will have to contend with a prosecutor.[29] Again, if an attorney has other types of cases—civil litigation, for example—pending before a judge, he will be unlikely to risk alienating him. Finally, interpersonal relationships between attorneys and judges may be more important than "winning" a juvenile case.

The long-run balance of power rests with the juvenile court, and attorneys are more likely to use their power circumspectly than not. Signs of an informal rule to this effect are detectable in the attitudes of many probation officers toward the "unco-operative attorney." Some even consider these attorneys "unethical," acting against the best interests of the child. Yet "unco-

---

29. Some prosecutors say they don't like to go into juvenile cases because they are set up to operate on "beyond-reasonable-doubt" criminal rules. Getting their cooperation is difficult. One judge threatens to dismiss the case "for lack of prosecution," which, if the offense is serious, can put the prosecutor in a bad position, especially in smaller communities.

operative" or "unethical" attorneys on closer scrutiny may simply be responding to a situation in which an entrenched and arbitrary judge, an impersonal or disorganized probation department, or the expectations of minors and parents makes a combative stance the most realistic means of protecting their clients' interests.

The number of attorneys who insist on immunity against self-incrimination for juveniles, and defend them without heed to consequences when allegations are denied, will remain small because, among other things, this position creates a false structure in the counsel-client relationship.[30] The preference for negotiating dispositions, rather than contesting evidence, is reinforced by the univeralistic tendency to treat a person defined as a child differently from an adult. Differential treatment of children and adults was implicit and explicit in law long before the advent of the juvenile court.[31] Hence the distaste many prosecuting attorneys have for appearing in juvenile cases, the dislike or apathy public defenders sometimes have for their roles in juvenile court, and the ambivalence attorneys may feel at encouraging young children to refuse to admit self-evident facts.[32]

Attorneys informally integrated into juvenile court social systems in which they have confidence are inclined to follow a course of action describable as "stand-by interventionism"; they actively monitor proceedings there but reserve direct action for cases in which findings or dispositions are manifestly unfair. One public defender described his role thus:

30. This issue is connected with the larger problem of admissibility of confessions made without advice of counsel. Action by the U.S. Supreme Court in Kent v. United States [383 U.S. 541, 865. Ct. 1045, 16 L. Ed. 2d 84 (1966)] was inconclusive, but indicated that the Supreme Court expected to rule on it. See Report on the Proceedings of the 1966 Institute for Juvenile Court Judges and Referees, pp. 2–8.

31. Anthony Platt, *The Child Savers* (Chicago and London: University of Chicago Press, 1969) Appendix, pp. 183–202.

32. Although John Pettis testified that an attorney had to defend a "guilty" juvenile if he insisted on it, he also stated that a good attorney would try to get help for a youth or family if needed. See hearings of the Senate Judiciary Committee on Juvenile Justice and Procedures in Juvenile Court, Los Angeles, November 1960, pp. 126, 127.

In many cases I just put the boy on the stand and let him explain his feelings. When the judge asks for comments I don't make any. But in some cases I act. My attitude is that if a minor gets more than is coming to him I step in and correct it.

In cases in which there is literally nothing an attorney can do for a client, he may have to cope with the distrust of the youth and his parents. This may account for the occasional decision of an attorney to "go all out," and vigorously fight a hopeless case. Tolerance and leeway for dramatic demonstrations in these instances may be measures of the degree of understanding and appreciation the court and the attorney have for each other's problems.

UNIFORMITY

A concluding discussion must face the question of whether greater uniformity has been achieved in the formal and informal procedures of juvenile courts by revision of the law. A conclusive answer is difficult to make, but the question need not be begged. In their main outlines, formal procedures in juvenile courts have become more similar and this happened relatively soon after the law went into effect. Citation systems are now in wide use by police and sheriffs' departments; detention hearings normally are held in all jurisdictions; jurisdictional and dispositional hearings have been distinguished, and probation reports are written and submitted accordingly. Provision is made for notice to all parties in hearings in all or most areas; hearings are now recorded and a method for appeal regularized. Rules governing supplemental petitions are generally observed, and the majority of courts comply in making some form of annual review of cases of neglected and dependent children.

A look beyond the mere facts of compliance with code provisions now operative for juvenile courts, however, discloses that the means devised for this conformity have been many. As already noted,[33] the rule that juveniles apprehended by the police must

33. California Welfare and Institutions Code, Sec. 625.

be transferred without unnecessary delay to a probation officer has ramified adaptations, among them, deputizing juvenile hall counselors as intake officers. Probation officers, justices, and referees in some counties have had to take over the judge's role in detention hearings, or "double in brass" as traffic-hearing officers. Needless to say, such dual roles differentiate informal interaction and have indirect but important effects on the ultimate disposition of cases.

Administrative changes consequent to the law change also have diversified procedures with respect to what kinds of decisions are made by which officials. The addition of referees to larger juvenile courts and the larger volumes of cases they hear has been an administrative solution to the necessity for more court hearings. Judges must decide how cases will be allocated between themselves and referees, and more important, how to retain effective control over their adjudications and dispositions of cases apart from the clumsy device of rehearings. Such a simple thing as who makes up the daily calendar may be crucial, especially if the judge has other pressing commitments or is bored with his juvenile court assignment.

Any revision of a law code as lengthy as that covering the juvenile court inevitably will contain some oversights, inconsistencies, or conflicts. More than this, efforts to carry out systematic changes in a complex code make new situations and raise new problems on which the code is silent or equivocal:

> The revised law suggests the possibility of many problems that may or may not arise in practice, depending upon the extent to which the practices of police departments, probation departments and juvenile courts have changed since 1961.[34]

Diversity, rather than uniformity of practice, may be an artifact of law where it simply converts what was formerly a complex administrative problem into a complex legal problem. This seems to have occurred in so-called transfer cases, or juveniles arrested in one county but residing in another. The new law proved a poor guide for judges and probation officers in these

---

34. Joel Goldfarb and Paul M. Little, "Effective Uniform Standards for Juvenile Court Procedure," *California Law Review* 51 (1963), 421–47.

cases. Unavoidable delays often meant that the legal grace period to complete investigations ran out too soon to complete the transfer. Sometimes the police in the county of residence didn't even want the youth returned if the property had been recovered meanwhile. The debate over which county should declare jurisdiction in these cases can scarcely be called settled.

Rules in the new statutes on dependent and neglected children covering formal notice, the reading of petitions, the content of petitions, orders for medical care, placement, segregation, and supervision have obtained no more than qualified and partial compliance. The annual review of these cases may be excellent theoretical law, but it places a heavy burden on probation officers and has been almost impossible to complete in some cases, such as locating an alcoholic mother, or catching a hospitalized psychotic mother in a lucid interval for an interview. Many probation officers disliked this feature of the law because it "stirred up" old family issues and animosities painfully settled by earlier dispositions. According to a 1965 survey, the court in eighteen of fifty-eight counties did not require new investigations or new evidence in annual reviews if probation officers reported "no change in circumstances." Even in large, well-staffed probation departments, procedures for these 600 cases were ignored in some aspects, e.g., reading petitions to infants, revealing contents of reports to children, or making sure all of a twelve-child family are present for their hearing.[35]

ORGANIZING FOR UNIFORMITY

The groups and individuals responsible for legislation are not always the same as those who interpret and apply the new statutes. In the present instance judges, probation officers, police, prosecutors, and public defenders had no more than marginal say as to the form of the statutes. However, they had to give the law its meaning and daily expression. A unique aspect of the

35. Supervision of dependent children is sometimes a co-operative arrangement with welfare departments, sometimes not, sometimes fifty-fifty.

1961 legislation was that actions of judges became the chief target of change. One thorny issue was what could be done in the case of a judge "ignoring the law," a question complicated by the county autonomy of judges and the peculiar insular character of the juvenile court. The Attorney General's opinions were no solution, for they were a dubious force among judges who spoke of him as "just another attorney in Sacramento." Appellate decisions might give somewhat more direction to judicial interpretations, but at best these directives were sporadic, and their clarifications often only partial.

The hope or intent of those who framed the revision of the juvenile court law was that judges themselves would assume responsibility for standardizing procedures. This was to be done by the judicial council, which was delegated to convene annual Institutes of Juvenile Court Judges and Referees and also appoint a committee of juvenile court judges to study and recommend changes in rules for juvenile courts.[36]

Discussions among judges at several of the annual institutes, held in 1962, 1963, and 1964, exposed a wide gamut of interpretations of many sections of the juvenile court law, as well as differences and contradictions in the practices to which they admitted. The greatest confusion centered on the kinds and amount of evidence necessary or admissible for jurisdictional findings. Two conferences diminished the judges' uncertainties on these scores, but they were not eliminated.

In the 1964 conference, when B. E. Witkin, a noted authority on California law, spoke to the judges on evidentiary problems arising under the new law, he referred almost as many questions back to the floor as he attempted to answer. This was consistent with his view that no evidentiary code existed in the law and that diversity of interpretation was inevitable:

> The revisers were disturbed by the fact that the juvenile courts operated with no uniformity—some applying evidentiary rules strictly, others loosely, and still others not applying them at all some or most of the time. They wanted a uniform system which would maintain

36. *California Welfare and Institutions Code*, Sec. 569, Stats. 1961, Chap. 1616; amended by Stats. 1965, Chap. 412.

the informal proceeding and at the same time preserve rights available in a formal proceeding . . . the result was a revolving door statute. The judge runs the conference, as in the past, in an informal manner, without . . . objections . . . debate and discussion of competence of particular items of evidence. After it is over he makes up his mind whether the minor has proved neglected, dependent, or delinquent on the basis of competent evidence, which he screens in his mind.[37]

Witkin's critical charge has a heavy tone of academic irony, but not the ring of close familiarity with the workings of juvenile courts. Also, like any purely logical analysis of law, it does not consider the possibility that a seemingly contradictory statute may nevertheless develop common meaning or stimulate uniformity at the level of informal communication. Significantly, many judges say they are not troubled by the evidentiary section in the law, or if they were once, they have since found a way to work with it. The judge's committee made nineteen recommendations for amendments to the juvenile court law in 1963, a number of which were later enacted by the legislature,[38] but no recommendation was made to change the section of the law bearing on evidence. Probably the commonsense meaning most judges have ascribed to this part of the law is that the legislature wanted them to make definite findings from evidence, be more careful about levels of proof for declaring wardship and making dispositions, and under conditions compatible with the special work of the court, allow evidence to be controverted.[39]

It is probable that judges have progressed more rapidly toward uniform conceptions of what degree of evidence justifies taking jurisdiction over a child (wardship) than they have in assigning

37. Report on the Proceedings of the third annual Institute for Juvenile Court Judges and Referees, Monterey, May 15, 1964, p. 129f.
38. Report of Committee on Juvenile Court, California Conference of Judges, Beverly Hills, June 29, 1962.
39. An idea of how judges weigh or "sift" evidence and choose dispositions is recorded from 1966 discussion of four selected cases presented to a panel. Polls of judges in the audience showed the following distributions of choices between three or four alternative dispositions of the cases: (I) 2, 25, 6, 0; (II) 10, 15, 4, 4; (III) 15, 2, 5; (IV) 10, 6, 25. See Report on Proceedings of the 1966 Institute for Juvenile Court Judges and Referees, pp. 100–39.

a child to one of the several categories of jurisdiction. A general reason is that no evidentiary code can consistently distinguish dependency, neglect, delinquent tendencies, and delinquency. However, the apparent disinterest of judges in amending the section on evidence also suggests that more precision would tie their hands too greatly in making dispositions. There are discomforting indications that the practice of adapting findings to dispositions rather than doing the reverse, as the law requires, dies hard. Heman Stark told judges at the 1966 institute of the extent to which this was being done:

> Of 6,000 first commitments to C.Y.A. last year there were over 80 where a section 600 (dependency or neglect) had been changed to a 601 or 602 without the person leaving juvenile hall. He hadn't been tried on probation and he had not been in violation of anything unless he had been acting up in juvenile hall.[40]

Whether confronting judges with their seemingly fast and loose play with jurisdictional findings will have a constraining effect is doubtful at best. More promising is the Probation Subsidy Program authorized in 1965, designed to appeal to the self-interest of judges and probation officers to develop alternatives to C.Y.A. commitments.[41]

The destiny of the annual Institutes for Juvenile Court Judges and Referees at present is somewhat clouded. Undoubtedly some participants grew cynical about reaching the ideal of uniformity after discovering the wide differences of judicial opinion that recurred at the meetings. By 1964, criticisms were heard that discussions tended to hang on the same problems from year to year, chiefly because judges new to the juvenile courts made up a large contingent of those attending. While indoctrination of these judges was a valuable function of the institutes, some ex-

---

40. *Ibid.*, p. 22.
41. This is planned so that the size of the subsidy obtainable by local probation departments is determined by the decreased rate of commitments to the C.Y.A. from a county, using a base or average rate for several selected years of that county. Subsidy money is to be used for new types of supervisory programs. See *California Welfare and Institutions Code*, Art. 7, 1820–1827; Stats. 1965, Chap. 1029.

perienced judges lost interest and others thought discussions were a waste of time. In 1964, judges succeeded in having the law amended, so that the institutes would be called from "time to time" instead of annually.[42]

The 1966 institute may have profited from omission of the one in 1965, for one juvenile judge of considerable experience said he thought at last the discussions there had begun to show some results; by this he meant that judges were showing greater uniformity in detention hearings and jurisdictional findings, although not necessarily in choice of dispositions.[43] This, of course, is consistent with the conclusions reached in this chapter.

42. *California Welfare and Institutions Code,* Stats. 1965, Chap. II, p. 569.
43. Judge Ross A. Carkeet, in Report on the Proceedings of the 1966 Institute for Juvenile Court Judges and Referees, p. 101f.

7

The Logic of Revolution by Law

The broad outlines of the changes that took place in the history of California's juvenile court law sustain the idea that legal rules develop through alternating epochs of evolution and revolution, although no particular cyclical form or periodicity can be claimed for the process. This is not to say, however, that the two forms of change are independent; the events of change in the present case indicate strongly that there is a necessary or dialectical connection between the evolution of law and its revolution. The connection, though, is neither mechanistic, inherent, nor inevitable; it has to be established, i.e., articulated in a timely way by men motivated to organize themselves and act. Revolution is a product of their action but also of the counteraction of others, in which there is a clash between generic ideas and distributive interests or values. Partisan choices in conflict are heavily conditioned by commitments to rules and routine procedures making up extant legal systems.

The proposition, derivable from Kuhn, that an accumulation of anomalies in the course of the normal evolution of law is a necessary antecedent of revolutionary change is valid if the concept of anomalies covers discrepancies between practice and legal precept. But the growth of legal anomalies is not in itself sufficient cause for radical change in the law; anomalies must be recognized and brought forward into the arena of public interaction. This can be achieved only when there is strong involvement, effective leadership, and ingenuity in creating qualitatively different ways of looking at facts.

There is little question that it takes special kinds of people to challenge established presuppositions of systems of thought and action. Kuhn, voicing a prevalent idea, emphasized the youthfulness of scientists cast in such roles, but a more generic prerequisite for the formulation of revolutionary ideas, be it in law or science, is an attenuated commitment among those educated or socialized in the normative traditions of the field. In other words, basically new ways of looking at problems and facts in a field of knowledge are most likely to come from those formally or nominally identified with it but lacking commitment to its rules of practice.

It is significant that the people immersed in the movement to change the California juvenile court law—which is to say the members of the juvenile justice commission and their immediate supporters—included quite a few whose status and backgrounds made them "unusual." Among these: probation officers educated in the law, married women attorneys, college professors with a yen for politics, an attorney who had been a Montana cowboy, and of course the project director, with unique socialization in the lore of lobbying. The sensitivity of these people to weaknesses in the law and their willingness to entertain novel ideas for its reconstitution derived less from their youth (for they were not young) than from a symbolic committal to juvenile court issues. Having none of the practical, day-to-day responsibilities for the court's functions, they were involved but not involved, situated to contemplate a legal system at comfortable psychic distance.

REVOLUTION FROM WITHIN

To continue with a thesis that legal revolutions arise "from without" would, however, misconstrue the present case. For one thing, systems of legal education and the vagaries of socialization of lawyers and other court workers always produce a share of skeptics, or deviants, those who, as in the case of lawyers, "want to make a little law." Revolution requires that they somehow be brought into the movement for change. A distinctive feature of the 1961 juvenile law change was the origin and locus of its moving force within the Department of Corrections, which was closely allied with the C.Y.A. Field studies and reports by C.Y.A. board members and committed youth raised the visibility of juvenile court practices throughout the state. C.Y.A. structure, the influence of its field division, and its board functions permitted a "view from the top," as well as from the outside. It was relatively specialized opinion articulated within the communication channels of the C.Y.A. that made the legal anomalies of the juvenile court stand out in sharp convergent relief. Inconsistencies and "injustices" of the juvenile courts lost their ephemeral, particular, and local quality, coming to be seen in relation to meaningful parameters of the court.

WAS THERE A PARADIGM?

A pivotal question confronting a revolutionary interpretation of the 1961 juvenile law change is whether the revisions were in nature qualitative, based on a new conception of the juvenile court, or quantitative, simply a large number of adaptions built on a cumulative base. The issue is clouded somewhat because the juvenile justice commissioners stated explicitly that they sought no change in the philosophy of the juvenile court. However, this appears to have been a strategic move rather than a genuine conviction. As shown in Chapter Three, Jack Pettis quite early made plain that the commission intended to strike at the core of juvenile court structure and procedure. More than two years before the commission's final report, Pettis had developed a fairly clear idea of what he hoped to make of the juvenile code.[1] Finally, despite efforts to narrow the scope of projected changes, many judges and probation officers in the state continued to see the commission's proposals as a planned effort to overturn the old philosophy of the court.

1. Pettis told me that he had discussed the need for drastic changes in the juvenile court law with various people throughout the state two years before the commission was appointed. In the first year of the commission's history he cut up the code with scissors and rearranged it to make eighteen or nineteen changes he felt were necessary. This apparently was the basis on which he acted thereafter.

Pettis stated his conception of the juvenile court most clearly at conferences, seminar talks, and in informal communications after the law was revised. When one compares these statements with reports of the discussions of commission members and their positions during the period of controversy, there is little doubt of an underlying design in their thinking. The revolutionary character of this thought vis-à-vis the traditional, *parens patriae* concept of the court is best summarized by the following postulates:

(1) Courts for children are places where justice is a prime issue.

(2) An identity between the effective interests of judges and probation officers and those of children cannot be presumed.

(3) Judges and other functionaries of the juvenile court must be made accountable for their actions.

(4) The interests of minors and parents are best served by a balance of interaction in the court, secured by narrowing of its jurisdiction, instituting special procedural rules, and structuring of roles.

Of these, the last, the notion of balanced interests, best captures the positive, innovative features of the intended new image of the court. Balance may be taken more narrowly to mean a synthesis between inquisitorial and adversary methods, with controlled shifts between the two, depending upon choices made by minors and parents independently or on advice by counsel. In a wider context, balance refers to the exclusion of interests arising from extraneous pressures on the juvenile court, and a reordering of priorities for satisfying values of law enforcement, correctional, and welfare groups. The plan for the court made explicit in the revised law was, not to exclude the ameliorative values idealized in the early "socialized" court, but to change the order in which they would be satisfied, i.e., after legal requirements had been met, or even in some cases after property and community values had been assured.[2] A schematic repre-

2. For more generalized discussions of the idea of balance between inquisitorial and adversary systems in justice, see: H. L. Packer, "Two Models of the Criminal Process," *University of Pennsylvania Law Review* 113 (1964), 1–40; Abraham Goldstein, "The State of the Accused: Balance of Advantage

sentation of the difference between the *parens patriae* paradigm and that of balanced justice in the juvenile court is suggested as follows:

Parens Patriae	Balanced Justice
Ideology	
Ameliorative values (welfare and protection) are dominant.	Justice, fairness are dominant.
Jurisdiction	
Broad, vague, variable between jurisdictions.	Narrow, explicit, separation of categories of wards. Uniform between jurisdictions.
Powers	
1. Positivistic, outreaching, preventive.	Limited, contingent on making of findings and on jurisdictional categories.
2. Detention for numerous unspecified reasons by police as well as court.	Limited detention for a few specified reasons.
Structure	
1. Diffuse location of initiating action (petitions), by police, probation officer, parents, welfare agencies.	Centralized initiation of action by probation officer only.
2. Several alternating roles occupied by judge and probation officer, representing child, parents, community agencies, correctional organizations.	Counsel represents interests of the child.

---

in Criminal Procedure," *Yale Law Journal* 69 (1960), 1149–99; Abraham Blumberg, *Criminal Justice,* Quadrangle Books (1967), Chap. VIII. The idea of equilibrium as the central fact of justice, of course, is an old one, and is inherent in early constitutional doctrine of checks and balances in government. Law, or "institutions of civil liberty," is the instrument by which the doctrine is realized. See W. G. Sumner, "Liberty and Law," *Earth Hunger and Other Essays* (New Haven: Yale University Press, 1913), pp. 165–75.

3. No accountability for court officials, or accountability through political means, community pressures.

Accountability to attorney, parents,
child, and appellate courts through
written records.

Decision-making

1. Facts decided by the probation
officer.

Facts decided by interaction in
hearings or by stipulation.

2. Mixture of legal and "diagnostic"
facts used at all stages.

Jurisdiction decided by legal facts
only.

3. Dispositions decided by judge or
judge and probation officer *in camera* or by prior consultation.

Dispositions decided by negotiation and bargaining between attorney and court.

THE NATURE OF RESISTANCE

A salient feature of the movement for change in the juvenile
court law was the intense controversy and strong resistance it
aroused. In the light of the theory favored here, resistance was
only logical, considering only procedural changes were proposed,
thereby threatening the survival of the "rules of the game" as
they were variously followed in juvenile courts throughout the
state. It is important to keep in mind that changes did not affect
all courts equally, or in the same ways. Furthermore, there were
differences in the extent and nature of the threats as they were
perceived by judges, probation officers, and police within the
same jurisdictions.

Resistance followed from an aggregation of judgments or evaluations, in which some persons and groups saw a whole system
of values jeopardized, while others were made anxious about
discrete values. The aggregate evaluations were largely products
of group interaction, in the course of which individuals sacrificed
some values to achieve or protect others, and groups exerted their
power to maintain values in competition with other groups
moving for different values. Leaving aside the purely expressive
reactions of participating individuals, the group process was
adaptive in the sense that prospective gains and losses eventually
were sorted out and a working plurality of choice was made.

An alternative interpretation of the high degree of affect generated by the movement to change the juvenile court law may be taken from Gusfield's thesis,[3] namely that it was a "symbolic crusade," similar to the American temperance movement, or contemporary controversies over fluoridation, school consolidation, and the location of freeways. Accordingly, the attendant strife should be reducible to a form of status politics expressing conflicts between the life styles of a number of groups at odds over the distribution of power in a western precinct of American society.

Granted that status politics were interwoven with the social action to change the law, it is still difficult to see this as the main impetus. While status anxieties certainly were conspicuous among those who fought the change, their expression was episodic, being more pronounced in the first phases of the conflict and less so as time went on. Probation officers, for example, began to respond less and less to status threats and more to the relative merits of recommendations.

Considering the ferment over civil rights that had been building up over several decades, police might have been expected to be the most persistently status-conscious of all those affected by action to revise the juvenile law, but this was not the case, and for several reasons. First, the police became concerned late rather than early during the conflict. Second, while police in southern California felt threatened, those in the north did not. Third, there was a cleavage between the police leaders and rank-and-file juvenile officers, which tended to be concealed by the military discipline of the police. Finally, while the new proposals may have been construed as a symbolic attack on aspects of the police way of life, they also aroused specific anxieties within the department, notably the possibility of greater costs, less efficiency, and loss of controls. This was an especially critical issue for the Los Angeles Police Department, which had a highly

3. Josept Gusfield (Symbolic Crusade: Status Politics and the American Temperance Movement, University of Illinois Press, 1965), p. 11.

rationalized system geared to the control of gangs and other special problems, reflecting a long history of difficulties with the county probation department.[4]

The resistance of the judges came closest to a pure protest against "trespass on a way of life," represented by their deep commitment to the *parens patriae* philosophy of the juvenile court. This was best seen in the reactions of opposing judges who had not studied the commission recommendations for change, or who had simply picked out a few objectionable features to justify total opposition. But the challenge to ego was sharpest among older judges nostalgically loyal to Ben Lindsey's early image of the juvenile court.[5] Feeling the same challenge were judges whose identity was strongly bound up with the juvenile court locally in some special way.

The resistance of other judges, however, may be attributed to temperamental inclinations, to the habit of sticking to decisions once made, or even to the "natural" enmity of the judge for the attorney. Undoubtedly there were some judges who had mixed feelings about the law change but, once they adopted an opposition stance, had no graceful way to retreat, especially after their stand was known locally. What bothered many thoughtful judges, as well as probation officers, was a fear that the revisions would make it extremely difficult to preserve the informality of the juvenile court. Inasmuch as the prospective law stated that the informal atmosphere of the court should be continued, the question for many was whether such a "formal-informal" court would be workable, or would it eventually put an end to the juvenile court as a distinctive entity. In this sense, then, the change may have seemed a threat to a way of life, but this view was typically a considered one, oriented to a whole system of means and not just to their surface symbols.

4. Samuel R. Blacke, "The Juvenile Court of Los Angeles County," Los Angeles Bar Bulletin 8 (1932), 150ff.; Robert Scott, "Problems of Juvenile Detention," *loc. cit.* 16 (1940), 222–30.

5. Ben B. Lindsey and Rube Borough, *The Dangerous Life* (London: Harold Shaylor, 1931), Part II.

THE MUTED MORAL PROBLEM

A marked quality of the opposition to revision of the law was the affective generality with which it was expressed, and at times its seeming incomprehensibility to commission members. Another indicative feature was the covert or "off-the-record" personal derogation of some of the commissioners. At face value these aspects testify to generalized status anxieties among opponents of the change but they also point to a more specific conviction of the critics that methods employed to change the law were illegitimate. Hostility stemmed, not from fear that areas of professional life deemed sacred or inviolable would be invaded, but from a belief that the changes were being made without full consent of those most affected, by those least qualified to make them, and by means that were ethically dubious.

An aura of illegitimacy surrounded the commission, for although it was legalized by statute, nevertheless it was an unusual device for changing law. The suspicion that the recommendations of the juvenile justice commission were more the work of the staff than of the duly appointed commission members added substance to what became a fundamental moral problem inhering in the method of change. By its nature, the moral problem could not be made public; hence the tendency to express it indirectly in diffuse criticisms puzzling to the commissioners.

A similar problem had come up about the same time (1960) in connection with the report of a U.S. Senate subcommittee on juvenile delinquency. It inspired the following comments by Senators Roman Hruska and Everett Dirksen:

> In common with reports of many investigative efforts of this type
> . . . the report shares a weakness. . . . The document is not a report
> of the Senate Judiciary Committee, nor was it made by its Sub-
> committee to Investigate Juvenile Delinquency. In reality it is a
> staff document. It would be more truly entitled a "Staff Study,"
> "Staff Analysis," or similar designation. Staff help is indispensable
> . . . but it also has its own jurisdiction in which to work and limita-
> tions which should be observed. . . . It is for the subcommittee, acting
> as such, to make final decisions as to the character and scope of its

contents. It is not enough that its members acquiesce in the work product prepared by others . . . unless this line of demarcation between respective jurisdictions of the staff and subcommittee is observed the result is not a report "made by the subcommittee." [6]

THE CONSOLIDATION OF LEGAL REVOLUTION

The action to reform juvenile justice in California in most major respects was operationally successful. Why it succeeded where the earlier (1949) movement within the state failed, as have comparable efforts to revolutionize law elsewhere, is among the more challenging questions that sociology of law must answer. If explanation is to be found in historical contingencies, the elements common to this phase of change need describing in theoretical terms. Reference to Kuhn's answers to the question help only in part. His statement that "gestalt-like shifts in paradigms occur" certainly indicates what has to be explained, but his statement that scientists come to accept new paradigms because of their testability and "esthetic qualities" is not apropos.[7] It scarcely explains why professional associations, leaders, and politically minded legislators changed their positions on revising the juvenile court code.

Reasons for shifted perspectives favorable to the law passage, particularly among members of the strategic Senate Judiciary Committee, need factoring out of the relevant processes of group interaction. Among these are the conditions that make ordinary spurious legislative hearings instrumental in making important decisions. Included in the present case were the technicality of the questions raised by the proposals, their origin from a group outside the legislature, and the brief time available to consider the lengthy package bill. With the stage thus set, it was the unplanned dramatic enactment of issues of justice that captured

6. Report of the Committee on the Judiciary United States Senate (86th Congress, 2d. Session). Made by its Subcommittee to Investigate Juvenile Delinquency, Washington, June 15, 1960, pp. 126–28.

7. Thomas S. Kuhn, "The Structure of Scientific Revolution," University of Chicago Press (1962), Chap. XII.

a place for a new paradigm of the juvenile court in the minds of key senators holding hearings on the bill.

But if legislators changed their minds about the essential nature of the juvenile court as a result of dramatic interaction, not so the opposition. Nor can it be said that successful change followed because the opposition "collapsed" or was eliminated; rather, change in this case required accommodations, if not constructive implementation, of a professional kind from among active opponents who were in a position to sabotage the outcome. Only to a small degree was the problem solved by turnover or replacements among the opposing judges and probation officers. In much larger part it was a matter of adaptations made palatable by rationalizations and altered retrospectives. The initial and most difficult accommodation, as already noted, was facilitated by the myth that the proponents of change had unlimited power, against which further resistance would be pointless if not hazardous. This myth was useful for the opposition in preserving identities in the face of potentially invidious role changes.

But there were also some very positive factors that explained the final willingness of judges, probation officers, and police to accept the new law. While they had something to lose from the change, it was equally true that they had something to gain. In part the law formalized changes already made in some parts of the state; further, the new law promised changes that would deal with the anomalies that confronted the court people and the police.

NORMAL ADAPTATIONS

Equally crucial to the theory of this study is the question of whether revision of the juvenile code caused changes sufficiently impressive to be called revolutionary. In other words, was this something more than a mere statutory revolution.

It is much easier to speak affirmatively on this point in 1969 than it was in 1962, when the study began. However, even then there were indications that an "invisible" revolution had taken place. One was the beginning of a normal evolution along lines laid down by the 1961 law. Judges, through their juvenile court judges' conference, recommended and saw passed by the legislature in 1963 a number of "noncontroversial" amendments to the 1961 law. Although no self-conscious descriptions or terms for a new kind of juvenile court crystallized within the state, nevertheless there were signs that the perception of the court had altered radically. I was told by several probation officers, for example: "We could never go back to the old way of doing things."

More convincing signs of the systematic changes in the state's juvenile courts were the kinds of problems the revised law began to present, problems for which old solutions were inadequate. The police soon realized that they would be less able than before to pressure or circumvent the juvenile court toward their own ends, and would have to devise new policies and methods. Increasing legal sophistication among teen-age delinquents and their parents was an inevitable outcome of the requirement that they be advised of their right to counsel at several or all stages of proceedings. These changes were commented on in questionnaires almost uniformly by probation officers, often with some concealed distaste, indicating their persistent need to reconsider the nature of their roles.

Undoubtedly the presence of counsel, his conception of his role in and out of court, and the impact of these on the probation officer's role have been and are centrally significant in the unfolding of a new and distinctive design in the juvenile court. Here, of course, lies the greatest potential for conflict, and the roles evolved by counsel will have much to do with how far evolution toward formality and criminal-type procedure goes. By 1967 the legislature was at last able to consider favorably amendments to allow district attorneys in certain kinds of cases to appear in court either to assist in the presentation of evidence or to directly present the case against the minor.[8]

Even with these concessions to law enforcement interests, pro-

8. California Welfare and Institutions Code, Juvenile Court Law, Chap. II, p. 681.

bation officers working in a more legalistic court will have to accommodate to the probability of "losing cases." Presumably they will move toward new ways of helping youth, less personal, less dependent upon the cultivation of rapport. Scattered portents that change lies in this direction have been gathered from discussions of probation officers, some of whom in one California county put it this way: "We are moving from a court of therapy to one of surveillance." What rules, procedures, and subcultural innovations are relative to a court of surveillance can only be a matter for speculation, but most likely its major thrust will be toward greater emphasis on intake, screening, and referral services, as well as closer attunement to the work of community and state agencies providing youth services.[9]

NATION-WIDE REVOLUTION

Inferential but nevertheless impressive evidence that changes in California's juvenile court law were revolutionary in scope comes from decisions by the U.S. Supreme Court in the Kent and Gault cases.[10] The opinions in both cases bore down directly on the need for juvenile courts to formulate rules and policies for taking jurisdiction and making dispositions. While the Kent case was somewhat marginal in that it dealt with a waiver of jurisdiction from juvenile to adult criminal court, nevertheless the decision left no doubt about the importance the high judges attached to representation by counsel and official criteria as guides for judicial action. The case was primarily a concern of the federal court system, but it foreshadowed appellate reviews of cases from within state jurisdiction, which soon followed.

The decision of the U.S. Supreme Court in the Gault case overturned the nation's conception of the juvenile court, for it reversed positions that had been taken and held against attacks in

9. This, of course, was a recommendation of the *President's Commission on Law Enforcement and the Administration of Justice*. See *The Challenge of Crime in a Free Society*, Washington, 1967, 83ff.

10. Kent v. United States, 383 U.S. 541, (1966); *in re* Gault, 387 U.S. 1 (1967) pp. 1–81.

forty state supreme courts.[11] A further gauge of its impact can be seen in the numerous seminars, conferences, and review articles it has stimulated, and also in the hurt and anxiety of many persons who have given devoted service to the juvenile courts. Only time will reveal how profound and far-reaching the effects of the Gault decision will be, but few will question that throughout the states, as well as in California, the day of the *parens patriae* juvenile court and whatever that came to mean in local jurisdictions is over.

Both the juvenile law revision and the U.S. Supreme Court decisions were part of an over-all revolutionary trend toward administrative reorganization and procedural clarification in the court systems of American society. However, it is significant that the decision in the Kent case came five years after California changed its law, and in the Gault case, six years. More to the point, it is doubtful that the Gault decision has had or will have any great effect on California juvenile courts. When the subject was put to ten chief probation officers of larger California counties in the summer of 1967, to a man they replied that they saw no reason to study the case, because they expected it to have very few repercussions within the state. As one put it: "We already have Gault, and we have had it since 1961." Hence the Supreme Court decisions in the Kent and Gault cases have been no more than incidental directives in the process of normal adaptation already at work in California juvenile courts.

A TIDE IN THE AFFAIRS OF MEN

There may be yet another reason why the Gault decision will not appreciably disturb either the formal or the living law of the California juvenile court, a reason inherent in the course of normal law. If my thesis is correct, the California juvenile court law has settled into a period of normalcy, which for the time being makes it more or less invulnerable to radical changes.

11. Monrad Paulsen, "Children's Court—Gateway or Last Resort," Case and Comment 72 (November–December, 1967), 3–9.

Assuming that the old opposition has made its adaptations to the revised law, equanimity will follow from the fact that a new generation of judges, probation officers, and police has been or is being indoctrinated with the precepts of equilibrium justice in juvenile courts. Practices have been reconstituted and normal problem-solving goes on apace within the gamut of the new paradigm. Herein lies the core of potential resistance to further change—at least within the immediate future. While the new system undoubtedly will be found to have its anomalies, as yet they have not accumulated, nor have dissidents come forth to detect and articulate them.

This favors a conclusion that social action for revolutionary change in law must of necessity be timely. It must be roughly in phase with the tide of relevant events that have been set down as necessary factors in such change. Reforms undertaken too soon after revolution seem destined to failure, but this does not discount the importance of voluntary action in effecting legal change. A conclusion that legal change moves from order to order with intervening quiescence nevertheless leaves a place for thinking man as the force that organizes the ingredients of the new order and propels it into existence.

To rest with this conclusion does not sound a retreat to old-style evolutionary theories of social change, for no stages have been postulated, nor has any periodicity been claimed for the pattern of legal change. If anything, the theory leans in the direction of nonunilinearity. Finally, no unyielding position is taken on the relative worth or merits of one order or law over and above another. The most that can be done is to discuss in a broadly appreciative way within the context of the new legal order those ideals of justice that impress thoughtful men as durable if not universalistic.

8
Postscript on Juvenile Justice

Little has been said in substance about juvenile justice, although making it a dominant value in juvenile court interaction was the broad objective of the California revisionists. Discussion of the subject is complicated by the elusive meaning of the term "justice." While "justice" can be defined in abstract terms, it is difficult to demonstrate in any positive sense, even though it may be easily recognized in the breach. Phrases like "impartial adjustment of conflicting claims," "assignment of merited rewards and punishments," and "even-handed treatment" help somewhat to fix its meaning, but they leave a residue of definitional problems, e.g., what is "impartial," or "even-handed."

Some writers contend that there is a "natural" sense of justice, or better, injustice,[1] but it is more likely that the concept obtains its full meaning from acquired values dominant in a particular cultural setting. The most general statement that can be defended empirically, namely that substantive justice is contingent upon the methods (procedures) by which it is sought, still is relative to problems created by highly differentiated, pluralistic societies. This for the reason that instrumental values are apt to hold a high position in such societies. Given these assumptions, it is possible that some procedures are more likely than others to insure just outcomes in law cases.

A question brought into prominence by differences between

1. Edmund N. Cahn, *The Sense of Injustice* (New York: New York University Press, 1949).

the majority and the concurring, partially dissenting, opinions in the Gault case is whether juvenile justice is, or indeed should be, identical with due process of law or with rights guaranteed by the Bill of Rights and the Fourteenth Amendment of the Constitution. Predictably, Justice Black in his concurring opinion took the position that rights of the accused were an essential part of cherished freedoms in our society, not to be considered instrumentally as "tools," nor conditionally granted or withheld from juveniles on grounds of public interest.

On the other hand, the majority argument drew a distinction between rules of due process of law as means and "fairness," "fair treatment," "efficient and effective procedures" in juvenile courts as ends. The absence of due process has neither guaranteed these desired results nor diminished juvenile delinquency, therefore (the majority reasoned) the main rules of due process should be applied to child as well as adult. At most there is a concession to the special needs of juvenile court procedure in the observation that the rules need not be "ruthlessly applied." [2]

Justice Harlan, whose opinion is provocative for the sociologist, both concurred and dissented, in the course of which he noted the absence of a rationale in the majority opinion and also of any criteria by which due process of law in juvenile courts might be judged. He also voiced the suspicion that discovering a lack of due process in an Arizona juvenile court might have been made an issue to propound disapproval of the juvenile court as an institution and perhaps to invite its elimination. In contrast, Justice Harlan sought to deal selectively with the perquisites of due process of law in juvenile courts consistent with the "traditions and conscience of our people." [3]

2. The Supreme Court position thus appears close to the *"quid pro quo"* conception of juvenile justice, in which it is stated that children, in return for giving up constitutional guarantees, receive special treatment, help, or leniency. See John J. Horwitz, "The Problem of Quid Pro Quo," *Buffalo Law Review* 12 (1963), 528–35; Monrad Paulsen, "Fairness to the Juvenile Offender, *Minnesota Law Review* 41 (1957), 547–76; Margaret Rosenheim, *Justice for the Child* (New York: The Free Press of Glencoe, 1962). The position seems spuriously legalistic, implying that the state has broken its contract with children. In some ways the "social-contract" overtones make this view even more conservative than Justice Black's.

3. *In re* Gault, 387 U.S. 1 (1967), 67.

Justice Black's opinion aside, the Supreme Court judges were agreed that formal or legal rules are only a part of juvenile justice, or, to rephrase sociologically, a necessary but not sufficient condition of justice. In other words, something else is involved, which, as was proposed in Chapter 1, is the "rules behind the rules." From this point of view, study and comparisons of juvenile justice must move beyond formal procedure to scrutinize the consequences of administrative practices and legal subculture. Juvenile justice at this level requires evaluation by criteria of "background fairness," in contrast to those of formal procedural fairness.[4]

THE IMPORTANCE OF ADVOCACY

The juvenile justice commission adopted the view or ideal that a greater measure of juvenile justice would follow from installing uniform procedures in juvenile courts, i.e., treating all minors and parents in the same way. However, they faced the delicate problem of how far they could go in this direction without destroying the special, "individualized" quality of juvenile justice or inviting disregard for the new law. The firmest ground on which to argue for standardized procedures was at the hearing stages of the court process, when facts were adduced and findings made allowing detention and taking of jurisdiction. It was here that the fulcrum of the court was shifted to permit adversary interaction. Mandatory advice of the right to counsel legitimized the role of the counsel; other procedural requirements, depending on the counsel's ingenuity and skill, became his levers to exert active influence over the court process.

The mere presence of a counsel in juvenile court, as has been shown, by no means insures full measure of justice, nor do procedural requirements in themselves. Rather it is advocacy conceived traditionally as the "management of a cause" that must promote a critical balance between inquisitorial and adversary

4. Brian Barry, *Political Argument* (London: Routledge and Kegan Paul, 1965), Chap. VI.

procedures combined in juvenile justice. Effective advocacy obviously depends upon the counsel's skills and knowledge, but it is also determined by his conception of his role and the court's conception. An incompetent counsel, or his co-optation by the court, defeats the purposes of a balanced procedure, a point made in strong language by the U.S. Supreme Court in the Kent case:

> The right to representation by counsel is not a formality. It is not a grudging gesture to a ritualistic requirement. It is the essence of justice.[5]

A number of considerations argue that advocacy is more, rather than less, necessary to justice in juvenile courts than is true in adult criminal courts. For one thing, children, adolescents, and parents without counsel are no match for police, probation officers, and judges in situations where there are conflicts of interest. This inequality, most pronounced in first contacts with court people, is aggravated by the complexity of issues, such as informed waiver of rights, responsibility for acts, and testing of evidentiary proof given by child witnesses. In criticism of English juvenile courts, for example, one writer has said: "Some of the most difficult points of law in criminal cases are those which are likely to come up in juvenile courts." [6]

In American juvenile courts, whose proceedings are not accusatory, the problem is more obviously a phenomenological one, in that postulates of the child's world are cross-cut by those of the adult world on crucial matters, such as the meaning of an admission or a "confession." [7] Minors and parents must cope with a strongly organized move toward moral assessment whose invidious status consequences are more implicit than explicit. The full meaning of the administrative process leading to fateful decisions is well beyond the grasp of many of the minors and parents who come into contact with the court. When they are

5. Kent v. United States, 383 U.S. 541 (1966).
6. Winifred E. Cavenagh, "Notes, A Comment on the Ingleby Report," *British Journal of Criminology* 1–2 (1960–62), 63.
7. Joel F. Handler, "The Juvenile Court and the Adversary System: Problems of Function and Form," *Wisconsin Law Review* (winter 1965), p. 27.

large-scale, bureaucratically organized juvenile courts, the possibilities are greater that spurious definitions and distorted perspectives on juvenile actions and their situational context will
prevail. Reasons why "the interests of the excluded class may be
seen with very different eyes from those of the persons directly
concerned" can be summed up as follows:

> (1) "Facts of the case" tend to get reconstructed from bits and
> pieces of information, stereotyped and incomplete records, and inter-
> views often conducted under artificial conditions.
> (2) An inquisitorial procedure in a bureaucratic setting tends to
> reach decisions at an early stage before all facts are known, reflecting
> the human tendency to "judge too swiftly that which is not fully
> known."[8]
> (3) Administrative goals and available means for disposing cases
> tend to color the perception and recording of facts.
> (4) An inquisitor, combining the functions of investigator, judge,
> and advocate, does not and cannot fully implement the advocate role.

Facts and values may be inseparable, as Jerome Frank insisted, but nevertheless advocacy is probably the most reliable
method to assure that the widest possible array of facts will be
introduced into procedure, and that evaluations of these facts
will proceed fully from the interests of the child as well as from
others making claims upon the court. Adjudication is more completely supported and made more discriminate. That this can
make the difference between taking and not taking jurisdiction
over the child has been demonstrated. But, properly conceived,
advocacy also molds the process of disposition.

THE NECESSITY FOR ADMINISTRATIVE JUSTICE

It is simple calculus that frequent or extensive use of adversary
tactics would quickly bring large juvenile courts to a grinding

8. Professional Responsibility: Report of the Joint Conference" (Lon L.
Fuller and John D. Randall co-chairmen), *American Bar Association Journal*
44 (1958), 1159–60; Lon L. Fuller, "The Adversary System," in *Talks on
American Law,* ed. Harold J. Berman (New York: Random House, 1961),
Chap. III.

slowdown or complete halt. Furthermore, "judicalizing" the juvenile court procedure may sacrifice the welfare or "real interests" of the child in a certain number of cases.[9] One way to prevent this is to manipulate administrative power to discourage advocacy, somewhat in the manner American courts have protected themselves from overload by making litigation costly.[10] But preferred alternatives are (a) to decrease the number of cases reaching juvenile courts and (b) to provide more effective justice by administrative means. Aggressive advocacy can be urged as a continuing necessity in juvenile court to reach these very ends, if for no other reason than to make it too costly and time-consuming *for the court* to deal with marginal cases. Perhaps more important, strong advocacy can serve as continuing "hard-knocks" education or monitorship to motivate court workers to dismiss doubtful applications for petitions and to make more careful and complete investigations; from this point of view, a "competent counsel" maintains the "level of affect" in the court system. In sum, this is a homeopathic or dialectical argument that adversary values strongly pushed will lead to narrowing the jurisdiction of juvenile courts and help preserve firm jurisdictional boundaries.[11]

However, aggressive advocacy alone can scarcely narrow the jurisdiction of the juvenile court so long as it continues to be conceived broadly as an agency of moral control supported by jurisdictional categories of neglect and delinquent tendencies as they are currently written and interpreted in statutes. The vagueness of allegations under neglect, incorrigibility, runaways, truancy, depravity, idleness, and immoral life means that numerous openings are left for making extraneous claims on the juvenile court. They allow many "normal" problems of everyday life to be converted into special problems demanding interventions into family life and summary controls by formal apparatus of

9. "The Juvenile Court," p. 32ff.

10. Lawrence Friedman, "Legal Rules and Process of Social Change," *Stanford Law Review* 19 (1967), 799.

11. Edwin M. Lemert, "The Juvenile Court—Quest and Realities," in *Task Force Report: Juvenile Delinquency and Youth Crime,* President's Commission on Law Enforcement and the Administration of Justice (Washington, 1967), p. 101.

the court. Too often the result is, in Maitland's phrase, to "screw up standards of ethical propriety to unreasonable heights," and expose in a glaring manner the inapplicability of legal remedies to many important problems of child-rearing and family living.

Administrative remedies in themselves are equally questionable methods for dealing directly with many problems now falling within juvenile court jurisdiction. There is, however, an important large way in which administrative action can help discover the limits of effective legal action. This is policy-making to keep the inventory of allegations against youth close hauled to the "ethical minimum" necessary to maintain the technological advances of modern society, compatible with its diversified values and life styles. Tappan put it straight out when he insisted that "only dangerous neglect and dangerous delinquencies" should be grounds for juvenile court jurisdiction.[12]

Difficulties in the way of narrowing the sphere of juvenile court action by administratively redefining delinquent tendencies immediately come to mind. One is that many depredations committed by juveniles, even though of small significance as individual acts, may nevertheless add up to large problems in a mass society, or that even "thoughtless" random acts by children may cause heavy losses—as when expensive constructive machinery is damaged. But the solution may be less in individual treatment than in what Llewellyn called legal engineering, or legal requirements whose consequences shift the burden of surveillance and control from police and juvenile courts to property owners or associations of merchants, industrial and agricultural producers.[13] Overriding this possibility, however, is the hard fact that socialization of children, and transition from youth to adulthood, have been made more difficult yearly by the exigencies of urban life and a high-energy, technology-geared soci-

12. Comparative Survey of Juvenile Delinquency (Part I), United Nations, New York, 1958, 2; Sanford H. Kadish, "The Crisis of Overcriminalization," *Annals of the American Academy of Political and Social Sciences* 374 (1967), 157–70; Alfred Blumstein, "Systems Analysis and the Criminal Justice System," *loc. cit.*, pp. 92–100; Herbert L. Packer, *The Limits of the Criminal Sanction* (Palo Alto: Stanford University Press, 1969).

13. Karl N. Llewellyn, *Jurisprudence* (Chicago: University of Chicago Press, 1962), Chap. XVIII.

ety. It may be that many losses alluded to simply have to be
absorbed as social costs, particularly if costs and consequences
of officially treating juveniles involved are less preferred or more
costly alternatives.

Insofar as police and probation officers look on themselves as
surrogates of morality or feel compelled to respond to insistent
community pressures to enforce morality by legal means, it will
be a labored task to narrow the limits of juvenile court action
by administrative means. Police carry a heavy burden of responsibility for enforcing liquor laws and preventing vice, disorderly
conduct, and public nuisances as they pertain to juveniles.
Firmer policy of probation department administrators and juvenile court judges may initially add to this burden or magnify
inter-agency conflict. At the same time, it may encourage or aid
the police in scaling down their responsibilities to a point where
they can more realistically cope with law enforcement problems
involving juveniles. While this may seem like a counsel of amor-
ality, it is actually conservative in tone, proposing an organized
return by policy means to a more permissive "muddling-
through" morality for youth, which prevailed without formal
means in simpler community life of the past.

DISPOSITIONS AND JUVENILE JUSTICE

Criticisms of the juvenile court and the vagueness of its ideology
of "individualized" treatment leave an impression that dispositions of cases in these courts are grossly inconsistent and arbitrary. As a matter of fact, a good deal of regularity or even pat-
terning can be found in dispositions, owing to the insistent
claims made on the court, its limited resources, and certain
expectations peculiar to the operation and outcomes of juvenile
justice. What amounts to a basic conservatism was attributed to
the court by Tappan:

> The frame of reference within which the court may effectively oper-
> ate is narrowly limited by public and institutional definition.[14]

14. Paul Tappan, "Treatment without Trial," *Social Forces* 24 (1946), 309.

Regardless of special rationales invoked to justify dispositions made by the juvenile court, socio-legal realism indicates that over-all they are governed by some kind of synthesis of leniency and punishment, distinguishable from straight criminal justice by the higher value assigned to leniency. Seen from the side of minors and parents, the pattern of expectation is of graded or cumulative penalties, predicated on the nature and number of prior contacts with the court.[15] The anticipated sequence of dispositions in California courts, more or less recognized by court personnel as well, pretty much follows an implicit gradient: informal probation—official probation—foster-home placement—school or camp—commitment to the C.Y.A. The issue of justice becomes stronger the farther the case moves along this continuum, roughly coinciding with the loss of liberty, the imposition of stigma, and the possession of a potentially damaging record. The most intense anxiety feelings come with cases destined for the C.Y.A., the "last resort." [16]

Injustice is likely to be perceived when out-of-phase dispositions are made by the court, i.e., when a youth is held in detention for a minor first offense, or sent to the C.Y.A. without his chance in probation, or even, as noted, sent to the C.Y.A. when the original petition was for neglect. But there is another kind of injustice, highlighted in the Gault case: minors in fact can be incarcerated for longer periods of time than adults for similar types of offenses.[17] A youth can be dispatched to the C.Y.A. for a period of two years or more simply for violating an order of the court. If this be the equivalent of contempt of court, the

15. PMW Voelcker, "Juvenile Courts: The Parents' i int of View," *British Journal of Criminology* 1 (1960), 154–66; Peter Scott, "Juvenile Courts: The Juvenile's Point of View," *British Journal of Delinquency* 59 (1959), 200–10.

16. Not all probation officers look on commitment to the C.Y.A. as a last-resort disposition. In functional terms, the ambiguity of the C.Y.A.'s image has administrative value in that it allows for expedience in cases in which counties lack facilities for other dispositions.

17. The youth in the Gault case was committed to a correctional school for a period of years for an offense (lewd phone calls) that, if committed by an adult, would get no more than a fifty-dollar fine or two months in jail. *In re* Gault, *op. cit.* It is also true, of course, that minors can be punished for acts that are not crimes if committed by adults.

inequity is obvious, for adults receive only fines or jail sentences when found guilty on this charge.

Note too that juvenile courts can make new and more drastic orders at any time by filing new petitions to change the jurisdiction under which the child is held, i.e., from neglect (600) to delinquent tendencies (601), or from the latter to a felony equivalent (602). While many of these changes are the direct result of new offenses brought to the attention of the court, it is also true that they sometimes originate internally from administrative contingencies, or the lack of resources and facilities.

In very general terms, one can doubt the justice of committing youths for the "delinquent tendencies" of running away and incorrigibility to a bureaucratic organization that, for all its plans and programs, remains correctionally oriented. Such doubt is deepened by the awareness that often in these cases the family, school, or community values have been asserted over the youth's—a fact at times recognized by C.Y.A. officials themselves. It is even more difficult to reconcile these cases with an ideal of justice when they involve children as young as eight.

California has gone farther than any other state in delegating these ultimate dispositions, the analogue of sentencing powers, to an administrative agency. This fact alone deserves far more critical study and evaluation than it has received.[18] Meantime, there is good reason to believe that imbalance in the system of juvenile justice persists insofar as attorneys and court officers regard the disposition of juvenile court cases beyond the scope of legal protections.[19] The anomaly is striking to a person familiar with English juvenile courts, where dispositions available to the judges are narrowly hedged, and certain of them routinely subject to review as well as quick appeal. An English judge speaks to the issue:

> The California solution is criticized in that with the best intentions, it involves throwing over protections afforded by criminal jurisdiction at the very point where, it might be argued, the defendant

18. The one substantial study: Ola Nyquist, *Juvenile Justice, A Comparative Study* (New York: Macmillan, 1960).
19. "The Juvenile Court," p. 34.

needs them most, i.e., at the sentencing stage. Thus the offender may be handed over to a treatment board under an indeterminate sentence of rehabilitation, its actual length depending on the decision of at least two of six members of the Youth Authority taken at their own time and neither in public nor published.[20]

While the remedy for overextension of administrative powers at the terminal, institutional phase of juvenile justice probably is legislative, it is highly desirable, if not imperative, that advocacy in juvenile courts be dispositions-oriented. First, attorneys should intervene, preferably in a negotiator role, at the earliest possible stages in the proceedings to influence positively the inquiries and decisions of probation officers. Second, attorneys should, where necessary and without deference challenge those specialized testimonies and reports of psychologists, psychiatrists, educators, and social workers that are made the basis for dispositions. Where indicated, attorneys should present an alternative plan to the probation officer's. This is the essence of advice given to prospective counsel in juvenile matters by a committee of the Los Angeles Bar Association:

It is strongly recommended that the attorney retained in connection with a Juvenile Court proceeding obtain the name of the Probation Officer assigned to the case as soon as possible and establish contact with [him]. The attorney can frequently be of great assistance to the Juvenile Court and to the minor by suggesting facts which should be considered by the Probation Officer or matters which should be investigated by him before the report is formulated. Moreover, the attorney may find it desirable to discuss with the Probation Officer the basic problems which appear to be presented by the minor's case and to suggest a plan for the rehabilitation of the minor. If the attorney does not agree with the plan which the Probation Officer intends to recommend, he should formulate and present his own plan to the court.[21]

20. Winifred E. Cavenagh, "What Kind of Court or Committee?" *British Journal of Criminology* 6 (1966), 124.
21. "The Attorney and the Juvenile Court," Los Angeles Bar Bulletin 30 (1955), pp. 333–35.

THE RESTORATION OF AFFECT TO COURT PROCEDURE

Reference has already been made to the function of advocacy in maintaining the level of affect in juvenile court. A further aspect of advocacy, unrelated to the discovery of factual "truth," to the mitigation of dispositions, to their severity, or to the administrative necessities of the juvenile court, has to do with the expression of individual feelings and the dramatization of issues in court hearings. While emotionalism and theatricality are antithetical to the judicial ideal of rationality and the contemporary stress on efficiency in court administration, they are nonetheless important concomitants of human meaning and integral parts of "truth" in a larger sense.

One impression left by the observation of procedures in high-volume, bureaucratized courts is their frequent meaninglessness to participants, or the wide gulf of meaning between officials and clients.[22] The impression gains from comparisons between procedures in large and small county courts, and to a lesser extent from historical inferences about the nature of the juvenile court interaction in an earlier day. The distinctive difference comes to light among a portion of judges who have seen juvenile court hearings as means to encourage minors and parents to express their problems, to interpret court action, as well as to further compromises and accommodations in face-to-face confrontation. Judges in the past sometimes "put on an act," or the judge and probation officer acted out a struggle between the forces of good and evil. Crude and corny as these acts may have been, they speak of the sensitivity of human beings to each other and the need, when harsh measures are contemplated, to externalize a range of sentiments—especially antagonisms and resentments—if the purposes of the court are to be fulfilled.[23] The tentative address of the court was symbolized by the use of

22. This observation also has been made about English juvenile courts. See M. J. Power, "Families Before the Courts," annual review of the Residential Child Care Association, 1966, pp. 1–12.
23. Morris B. Abram, "The Challenge of the Courtroom: Reflections on the Adversary System," *University of Chicago Law Review* 11 (1967), 1–7.

the continuance (anathema to the modern court administrator) as a kind of disposition, to allow the last measure of freedom for problems to work themselves out or normalize.

Much of the dramatic interaction of juvenile courts has either vanished or become mere manipulation.[24] Some would say good riddance, but obviously there was a need for this kind of inter-action; possibly it was one method whereby juvenile judges and probation officers could play self-contradictory roles more sharply defining the interests of minors and parents, and better reconcile morality with law. The trouble may have been that judges and probation officers were miscast in roles that were properly counsels'.

In any event, it can be concluded that the dramatization of issues emerges best in "natural" adversary interaction, and that it has an important place in background fairness of juvenile justice, even though at times it includes outrageous conduct and flamboyant courtroom behavior by counsel. The purpose of dramatic courtroom interaction transcends mere support for the interests of minors and parents; it is the symbolizing of com-munity values, whose protagonist on occasion will have to be a district attorney or his equivalent.[25]

CONTINUING SOCIAL ACTION

Given a new departure in the form of the juvenile court, subse-quent normal evolution results from further legislation, appel-late rulings, administrative policy formulation, and the cumula-tive, day-by-day actions of court workers themselves. On the whole, appellate decisions have been ineffective means for direct-

24. Blumberg argues that the "individualization of justice" in reality de-personalizes the individual and renders him more tractable and amenable to the organizational designs of the court. Abraham Blumberg, *Criminal Justice* (Quadrangle Books, 1967) p. 170.

25. Holmes stated: "The first requirement of a sound body of law is that it should correspond with the actual feelings and demands of the community whether right or wrong." He was arguing that law must face up to the craving for retribution and liability in criminal offenses. However, he recognized that not all crimes raise these issues. Oliver Wendell Holmes, *The Common Law* (Cambridge: Harvard University Press, 1963) .

ing the course of juvenile court evolution, at least in California. Likewise legislation, which normally tends to be a form of tinkering that often complicates, rather than systematically adapts, court procedures to new needs. Early efforts at controlling court growth by the Department of Social Welfare were hardly more impressive, although subsequently the supervisory control of probation functions under the C.Y.A. regime produced more workable innovations. Yet these were limited by the structure of the C.Y.A. and the necessity to reach its goals almost entirely by co-operative methods.

The revised law of 1961 formally assigned responsibility for overseeing the administration of juvenile courts to an annual Conference of Juvenile Court Judges and Referees, to be convened by the judicial council. The council was empowered to make rules of procedure for the juvenile court, presumably reflecting the sense of the deliberations of the conference. However, such rules had to be "consistent with law"; judges had no greater power to initiate changes in the relevant law than any other group.

In some ways this was a loss rather than a gain, inasmuch as prior to 1961, C.Y.A. administrators had from time to time sponsored productive conferences of judges dealing with specific kinds of problems emerging from the "interfacing" of juvenile courts with the C.Y.A. In the absence of this kind of problem focus, early programs of the annual conferences have run to didactic, law-school-style presentations and moot-like exercises, plus a spontaneous pooling of complaints, uncertainties, and dissatisfactions of individual judges, most pronounced among those newly occupying the bench. Whatever the value of these conferences, it is doubtful that they are adequate means for directing the evolution of the juvenile courts.

It is not at all clear that attaching responsibility for the administrative surveillance of juvenile courts to a judicial council working through committees or conferences is any more desirable than fixing it to a Department of Corrections or a Department of Welfare. The reason: in situations where conflicting choices have to be made, the values of these organizations will necessarily be served before those of the juvenile court. Granted that the juvenile court is a court, nevertheless it is a very special kind of organization, responsible for the preservation of youth and family values, whose special importance in an aggregate of societal values cannot and should not be denied.

An alternative model for greater administrative control over juvenile courts is a separate agency having the authority to act, as well as to provide service. Utah has such an organ, an administrative office for juvenile courts. Significantly, competence in public administration, rather than law, is specified for the administrator in charge. Utah was specially suited for development of this kind, mainly because it already had a centralized state juvenile probation system. It is too soon to properly evaluate the effectiveness of this innovation, but its progressiveness is suggested by the fact that in 1967 Utah was one of the few states seriously considering adoption of modern electronic data-processing for its juvenile court records.

THE RATIONALIZATION OF JUVENILE JUSTICE

All things weighed, it is the interaction within the juvenile court and between the court and the community that is the most important area for studying processes by which the court changes and for devising programs of control. The court is and will remain essentially a local or at most a regional agency, responding selectively, rather than being dominated by external controls. This poses formidable problems, for, according to best analysis, the juvenile court is not an efficient organization, even on its own terms. Ordinarily it has a case-processing technology inadequate to the volume and complexity of contemporary court operations. Moreover, the court does not constrain decisions and action within the limits of uniform policy, regulations, and decision criteria. These defects have been attributed to poorly conceived means for information storage and retrieval, the absence of techniques to monitor court operations, and the lack of methods for forecasting developmental trends.[26]

26. Robert D. Vinter, "The Juvenile Court as an Institution," *Task Force Report*, pp. 84–90.

The startling innovations in automatic data-processing and computerized communications make their application to the rationalization of juvenile court operations a considered possibility. However, thus far in California, officials in only one county have seriously contemplated inclusion of their probation department records in an automated information system shared with medical and welfare agencies. But, at the same time, studies elsewhere are under way to see how and to what extent automated information systems can be utilized at the state level by Corrections and Law Enforcement; furthermore, operating law-enforcement systems already exist in several jurisdictions.[27]

Whatever may be done in separate jurisdictions, the mounting costs of juvenile courts and correctional institutions, their constantly growing volume of cases to process, the "paper-moving problem," and the proliferation of inter-agency networks in which the courts work will compel greater aggregate reliance on automatic information services. Individual juvenile courts that do not follow this course may be forced to greater rationalization of procedures, owing to the more accurate accounting of costs and the consequences of their actions for interfacing agencies that do automate. What this seems to say is that technology, rather than administration *per se,* may be the most important contemporary force for greater accountability in juvenile justice.

How far accountability and efficiency of juvenile court procedures can be pushed by technological means is difficult to predict. Attempts to reduce great masses of legal information to indexes or to "machine language" immediately useful to lawyers have not been marked with great success.[28] Probably efforts to code the less exact terminology and explicate the unspoken values that enter into decisions of juvenile court workers will be even less successful. Whatever the case, the nature and extent of resistance to automation in this area remains to be seen. Finally, it must be recognized that a degree of irrationality and inefficiency inheres in the juvenile court as an institution.

27. Edwin M. Lemert, "Records in Juvenile Court," in Stanton Wheeler (ed.) *On Record:* Files and Dossiers in American Life (New York: Russell Sage Foundation, 1969), Chapter 12.

Name Index

Abram, Morris B., 234
Adams, Stuart, 62-63
Arnold, Stanley, 152
Aubert, Vilhelm, 158

Ball, Harry, 12, 16
Banfield, Edward C., 156
Barkdull, Walter, 124
Barret, Edward, 3
Barry, Brian, 225
Barton, Allen, 22
Bary, Valeska, 32-34, 46
Beckley, Loren, 132, 143
Belden, Evelina, 27
Bendix, Reinhard, 16
Bentham, Jeremy, 5
Berger, Peter, 151
Bergler, Edmund, 22
Berman, Harold J., 227
Bernard, L. L., 12
Biscaluz, E. W., 68
Black, Hugo L., 224-225
Blacke, Samuel R., 215
Blackmore, Ray, 140
Blumberg, Abraham S., 198, 212, 235

Blumstein, Alfred, 229
Bohn, John, 136, 150
Bordua, David, 65
Bornet, Vaughn D., 46
Borough, Rube, 26, 215
Breed, Warren, 14
Breitenbach, Eugene, 108, 166
Briar, Scott, 65
Brown, Edmond, 108, 123, 155
Brown, Quincy, 136
Buchanan, William, 126-127
Buckley, Lorenzo, 189
Burgess, J. Stewart, 11
Burkhart, Walter R., 67

Cahn, Edmund, N., 22, 223
Cahn, Frances, 32-34, 46
Cameron, Ronald G., 152-154
Carkeet, Ross A., 134-137, 149-150, 152, 157, 161, 207
Carr, Lowell, 169
Cavenagh, Winifred E., 226, 233
Chorley, Lord, 6
Christensen, Carl, 152
Cicourel, Aaron, 65
Clark, Burton R., 120

239

Subject Index

243